The Historian, Television and Television History

The Historian, Television and Television History

A collection edited by Graham Roberts and Philip M. Taylor in honour of Nicholas Pronay

UNIVERSITY OF LUTON

press

British Library Cataloguing in Publication Data

A catalogue record for this book is available from the British Library

ISBN: 1 86020 586 0

In memory of Ann Heward
(1929-2001)
with special thanks to Sue Heward
and Isobel Rich

Published by
University of Luton Press
University of Luton
75 Castle Street
Luton
Bedfordshire LU1 3AJ
United Kingdom

Tel: +44 (0)1582 743297; Fax: +44 (0)1582 743298
e-mail: ulp@luton.ac.uk
website: www.ulp.org.uk

Cover Design Gary Gravatt, Gravatt Design Consultancy
Typeset in Van Dijck MT
Printed in United Kingdom by Thanet Press, Margate, Kent UK

Contents

Contributors

Stephen BADSEY is a Senior Lecturer in the Department of War Studies at the Royal Military Academy Sandhurst, and a Senior Research Fellow of the Institute for the Study of War and Society, De Montfort University

Sheri Chinen BIESEN is Lecturer in American Studies at the University of Leicester

Ian BREMNER has been working as a producer on *Simon Schama's History of Britain* since the inception of the project. He is also closely involved in the websites and online/interactive projects linked to the series.

Valeria CAMPORESI teaches film and television history at the Art History Department of the Universidad Autonoma of Madrid. Her recent works include a cultural history of Spanish cinema and a study on the image of television in Spanish films.

James CHAPMAN is Lecturer in Film and Television History at The Open University. He is author of *The British at War: Cinema, State and Propaganda, 1939-1945* (1998) and *Licence To Thrill: A Cultural History of the James Bond Films* (1999) and is co-editor, with Anthony Aldgate and Arthur Marwick, of *Windows on the Sixties: Exploring Key Texts of Media and Culture* (2000). He has also published articles in the *Historical Journal of Film, Radio and Television* and the *Journal of Popular British Cinema*. His next book is *Saints and Avengers: British Television Adventure Series of the 1960s* (due for publication in the autumn of 2001).

Luisa CIGOGNETTI is responsible for the Audio-Visual Department of the Insituto Ferruccio Parri of Bologna. She has directed several films about social and economic history. She has also published papers on the use of the audio-visual media in the study of History. In 1999 she edited, with Lorenza Servetti and Pierre Sorlin *Historians and Television Archives*.

Nicholas J. CULL is Professor of American Studies at the University of Leicester. He has published widely on propaganda and popular culture in Britain and the United States. He is also cultural advisor to the National Space Science Centre, Leicester.

Gerda HENDRIKS is a producer/director for NPS (Dutch Public Television). His work on Dutch newsreels and their coverage of the war in Indonesia became a documentary broadcast on Dutch public TV. Since then he has worked on television as a reporter and director including many programmes on historical topics.

André LANGE is Professor of History at the Free University of Brussels and director of the 'History and Television' website (www.histv.net).

David E. MORRISON is Professor of Communications Research at the Institute of Communications Studies, University of Leeds and Director of Research at the Institute. His primary interest is in the field of audience research. His publications include *Television and the Gulf War*, (John Libbey, 1992) *The Search for a Method: Focus Groups and the Development of Mass Communication Research* (University of Luton Press, 1998) and *Defining Violence: The Search for Understanding* (University of Luton Press, 1999).

Graham ROBERTS is Senior Lecturer in Communications Arts at the ICS, Leeds. His first monograph *Forward Soviet: History and Soviet Non-fiction Film* was published by I.B. Tauris in 1999. His book on Dziga Vertov's *The Man with the Movie Camera* was published by Tauris in 2000. As well as critical biographies of Nicolas Roeg and Martin Scorsese, he is currently working on a history of European cinema in the age of television.

Pierre SORLIN is Professor of Cinema Studies at L'Université de la Sorbonne Nouvelle, Paris and a past President of IAMHIST. His many publications include *European Cinemas, European Societies* (Routledge, 1991) and *Italian National Cinema* (Routledge, 1996)

Philip M. TAYLOR is Professor of International Communications and Director of the Institute of Communications, Leeds. He is chairman of the Inter-University History Film

Consortium and associate editor of the *Historical Journal of Film Radio and Television*. His many publications include: *Munitions of the Mind: A History of Propaganda from the Ancient World to the Present Day* (Manchester U.P., 1995), *Global Communications, International Affairs and the News Media since 1945* (Routledge, 1997) and *British Propaganda in the Twentieth Century: Selling Democracy* (Edinburgh U.P., 1999)

Isabel VEYRAT-MASSON   is a researcher at Centre National de la Recherche Scientifique, Paris.

Christine WHITTAKER   joined the BBC to work on programmes to be broadcast to French speaking Canada. However, a job as a researcher on a history programme led to a new career specialising in archive based historical documentaries. Her credits include *All Our Working Lives, Now the War is Over, Out of the Dolls House, An Ocean Apart, Nippon, Pandora's Box*. She was the Archive Producer on the 26 part series *People's Century*. She left the BBC in 1999 and now works as an Archive Consultant. She is currently President of IAMHIST.

Adrian WOOD   has worked as a film researcher for, amongst others, BBC and Thames TV. His work has allowed viewer to see previously unavailable material in many series including *Stalin, The Nazis: A Warning from History* and *World War II in Colour*.

The Historian and Television: A methodological survey

Graham Roberts

The aim of this book is to do for the academic historical study of television what *The Historian and Film* (CUP, 1975) did for film ie legitimising the field of study and formulating the terms of debate within the field. As Smith put it in the preface to that volume: 'The amount of work now being done by historians on and with film and the absence of a substantial survey of the field in English have together made the moment ripe for the production of this book.'[1] This comment is at least as relevant to the historian and *television* now. The 1999 conference of the International Association of Media and History (IAMHIST) held in Leeds brought together academics and programme makers involved in 'History and Television.' This volume springs directly from that conference and the dialogue that developed there. These collected essays will also serve as a tribute to the work of Professor Nicholas Pronay who continues to be such an important figure in the campaign to legitimise the study of the moving image in a historical context.

Most people in the field are fully aware of Nicholas' contribution. After working for two years as a researcher at Scottish Television for John Grierson's series, *This Wonderful World*, Nicholas joined the School of History at the University of Leeds as an Assistant Lecturer in 1964. Initially a medievalist, he began to consolidate his interests in the media by becoming one of the first historians in Britain to research and teach what was then considered to somewhat tangential to mainstream history.

He was a founding member of the Inter-University History Film Consortium in 1968 (which he chaired between 1975-8 and again in 1981-84) and of the International Association for Audio-Visual Media in Historical Research and Education (for which he served as Vice President, 1985-9 and as President, 1991-5). He was Director for Film and Television for the Historical Association for 10 years and was Chair of its Developmental Committee for its Youth Historian scheme in the 1980s. This service to the promotion of academic acceptance of historical film and television was consolidated in the three television series he wrote for the BBC, *Propaganda with Facts* (1976) *Illusions of Reality* (1978) and *Visions of Change* (1984). His academic articles on 'British Newsreels in the 1930s' remain seminal works, as do many of his 30 other published journal articles and book chapters. His relevant book contributions to the field are *British Official Films in the Second World War* (1980, with Frances Thorpe) and *Propaganda, Politics and Film, 1918-45* (1982, with Derek Spring).

In the very same period in which television was securing near total social penetration in western countries, the work of such British historians as Arthur Marwick, John Grenville and Nicholas Pronay was gradually securing academic credibility for the study of film. With the support of senior historians like D. Cameron Watt, John Ramsden and Asa Briggs, and the courage of then more junior historians like Anthony Aldgate, Ken Ward, Jeffrey Richards, Richard and Philip Taylor to 'risk' their academic careers, the teaching of film and history courses flourished from the mid 1970s onwards in the 'old' universities. Meanwhile, in the new universities, different approaches were also flourishing, ranging from textual analysis, semiotics and what we would now call 'cultural studies'.

We are still left with the surprising reluctance – on the whole – of historians to engage with film as *film* as opposed to simply another (and rather faulty) primary source. It is perhaps even more surprising that historians have been wary of television. Actually the reasons are similar to those that led to the reluctance to engage in film: methodological difficulties, academic snobbery, the fear of the new and/or transient. Much as film lost its monopoly hold on popular culture in the 1950s and '60s we are now faced with a multimedia culture that threatens the hegemony of television. It would be as ridiculous to seek to ignore the powerful and vital influence of the small screen on the popular culture of the 21st century. It would be as ridiculous as to suggest that the iconography and visual language of mainstream cinema has lost its grip on the popular imagination, or at least the imagination of the talents who continue to influence our visual culture. However we are experiencing a period of rapid change and exponential growth of many media. The changes in institutional frameworks and patterns of consumption as well as technological change are all grist to the historian's mill. All are explored in the following chapters.

Perhaps as 'the age of television' itself ends the time is ripe for us to study the medium in a serious historical manner. As Professor Taylor writes in the end piece to our volume: 'Whatever can be said for the future of television, its past has not been served well by historians. Despite being the prevalent medium for information and entertainment in most advanced countries since the 1960s, there remain remarkably few serious works of history that embrace television as a primary source of information for those years.'

This volume aims to contribute to the building of a movement towards the serious multi-disciplinary historical study of television. This serious study must involve a multidisciplinary and multi-methodological approach. We are also strongly committed to a belief that this study must begin with a dialogue between practitioners and theorists and indeed should involve theorists who are practitioners and vice versa. We have also sought a deliberate juxtaposition of different approaches and different opinions. Few readers will find comfort in every piece. Some may be annoyed by the methodology (even academic apparatus) utilised by practitioners from other fields. The editors firmly believe that in so vital and fast-changing field as the historical study of mass media we must all learn new tricks. Where better to do so than from those who have been studying or working in our field of interest long before us. If they made 'mistakes' so much the better for those of us who enter the fray in the wake of their pioneering.

This introduction – 'a methodological survey' – discusses the need for a fundamental investigation into what television can offer the historian – and just possibly what the historian might still be able to offer television. The title also points to the whole volume's concern to confront the methodological challenges of the study of TV and prefaces the various viewpoints put forward by the contributors to this wide-ranging volume.

David Morrison sets the tome for this volume by his careful and persuasive analysis of methodological developments and their imperatives. It is entirely in keeping with the spirit of our collection of scholars, and indeed the only hope for historians of TV, that we take cognisance of so noted a researcher in the social sciences when he discusses 'the rules of how we engage with the world.' Morrison ends (perhaps chillingly) with a warning: 'academic research, if it is not careful, will become a footnote in terms of social influence. The way forward, is to go back. We must become relevant, and relevancy here means to be tackling those questions that the industry itself is tackling.'

All of the pieces in this volume are focussed on the need to make our researches relevant to both understanding and influencing the (at present) most ubiquitous of global media. Our attempts to get programme makers to talk to academics and vice versa has proved, as IAMHIST has done since its inception, to be much more fruitful than a 'dialogue of the deaf.'

Pierre Sorlin warns that the content of television is in itself problematic to the historian: 'All I want to stress is that, for historians, oral testimonies and films based mostly on individual statements are highly problematic.' Professor Sorlin alerts us to the tendency of testimonies to blur the notion of context. His piece can also be read as a warning against the more unthinking and valueless excesses of postmodernism. Sorlin, like all of the more cautious contributors to this volume, does not council despair. He concludes: 'So what we historians have to do is to contrive an original understanding of the past which will combine a permanent attention to the small, the particular, the individual, and a full awareness of the importance of evolution. Let us recognise that this is not going to be an easy task.'

Luisa Cicognetti relates how and why dealing with televised material is a much more difficult and complicated than dealing with printed material, or even movies. Again there is a practical solution offered. The chapter relates how the Institute Ferruccio Parri is trying to build up a base of usable information. 'Information is power' and thus we are grateful to André Lange for his intervention which, while offering an insight into the archaeology of television, seeks to embrace the opportunities that the new media offer as a tool for research, learning and teaching.

The first piece by a programme maker (Adrian Wood's *The Colour of War*) also deals with archiving questions. Wood adds a very personal insight into the making and marketing the product of intensive study. Wood also gives us a valuable insight into the motivations that underlay the programme-maker's activities. This piece acts as bridge between the academic collection and utilisation of material and the world of media institutions and (to pay due service to Morrison's warning) the audience.

Gerda Hendricks continues our engagement with programme-makers. However, in contrast to almost all the other contributors to this collection, Hendricks approaches programme making from the position of *not* using archives. It is noteworthy that from apparently opposing methodologies Wood and Hendricks are in total agreement about their programme's needs and integrity: 'what laws apply: those of film, ie there should be a dramatic narrative, or those of scholarship, ie facts should be correct and verifiable? In my opinion, the two can be combined... Good research is a necessity, but in itself does not make a good programme. What is also needed is imagination.' Hendricks' position will certainly remind the reader of Grierson's views of the documentary. They may also find echoes of the views of notable writers on historiography such as Arthur Marwick (or even E.H. Carr).

Hendricks' historical programme making without the traditional source materials of 'history' is taken further by Ian Bremner who presents the inside story of creating entertaining but also informative television history, without a frame of archive footage in sight. As well as a fascinating insight into the dynamics of current programme production, Bremner raises important issues of ideology and of institutional pressures and parameters that certainly reach the high standard of Nicholas Pronay (as reported by Morrison) that we 'must become relevant.' Bremner also highlights an issue that runs through this book: whose history are the broadcasters promulgating?' Much as Pierre Sorlin argues that history is about historians, all of the programme-makers involved in this volume are making a clear case that television history is about television programme-makers. The interface between these two positions is fascinating, as are the questions surrounding how and where does the audience (for history, television and historical television) position itself. Wood, Hendricks and Bremner give the historian of television valuable insights into contemporary factual programme making. They also ask us challenging questions about the integrity of source material and by extension the uses to which the materials shown and indeed the programmes themselves can be put in academic study.

In the central section of this volume three historians (Biesen, Cull and Badsey) from different backgrounds and with different interests bring different historical approaches to particular television entertainment series. Whilst Biesen utilises a theoretical framework – Hamid Naficy's study of exile and the ideological dimension of an 'imaginary geography' – Cull begins with careful utilisation of the institutional archive. Both are able to use their source material to illuminate a much wider context. Badsey on the other hand begins with a historical controversy and uses his programme to explore that controversy. These chapters serve as a comparative historiographical case study. They also serve to remind us how far and wide the historical study of television can take us.

Sheri Beisen has conducted extensive primary historical research on US television series in the Jack Lord Collection at The University of Southern California Special Collections Cinema-Television Library. Her chapter examines the global narrative 'reimagining' of local identity, ethnicity, and unique exoticized 'exile' culture of Hawaii in the American television series *Hawaii Five-0*. Thus she brings much that is good about cultural studies into a historical discipline.

Biesen's research highlights the richness and complexity of television as a social text. She is particularly clear on the medium's potential as a conduit for ideology. Nicholas Cull looks at a British television programme produced by a British institution which itself became an institution. His account of the rise and fall of *Dr Who* is an exemplary piece of institutional history based upon careful archival research. What is noteworthy is how this ostensibly traditional piece of analysis allows Professor Cull to explore many of the cultural issues that are central to not only Biesen's piece but also the ideological and institutional questions raised by Bremner.

Stephen Badsey performs a correct historian's job of measuring the cultural artefact against the historical record: 'It is hard to imagine such a divergence between the known facts and the popular image in any other aspect of 20th Century British history than that of the Western Front; and it is trying to understand this image and its origins that has led historians to *Blackadder Goes Forth*.' But his historical rectitude does not allow him to dismiss the due weight of the series as 'a television cultural artefact.' Badsey explores the mechanisms by which popular television becomes popular history. He also explains how this 'problem', rather than leading to despair, can stimulate further historical research.

In contrast to the 'non-traditional' material of the preceding chapters, James Chapman turns a historian's eye to a 'traditional' historical series: *The World at War*. By examining the topic in three parts – 'television', 'documentary' and 'history – Chapman is able to explore 'both a contextual framework for analysing the series and a nexus of concepts and ideas which inform and even to some extent determine the form and nature of a series like *The World at War*.' A piece on this series is most welcome in this project for, as Chapman notes, 'In its own right, *The World at War* can be seen as a part of the "film and history" movement.'

Chapman's piece is a careful re-evaluation of the 'official' history of the series which suggests that 'the series was made when it was for technical and ... psychological, moral and political reasons'. Chapman even questions how and why *The World at War* ended up on ITV. This chapter leads us into the realms of a revisionist history of our history of TV – surely the clearest sign of a healthy, relevant area of study.

Whittaker – an 'insider' herself for many years – explores an institution's self-image: 'The importance and significance of BBC values and BBC standards continue to be stressed over the decades as the anniversary programmes kept appearing. The word celebration is often to be found in the billings.'

Veryat-Masson offers us a history less celebratory. She also expresses a chilling concern about what television might (or perhaps has) done to history: 'Are we witnessing an important trend in our culture, the decrease of the traditional interest of French (and possibly all European) people towards the past and if it is the case, are the mass media and especially television, their way of imposing a new relation to time?'

The editors of this volume felt that something vital was missing unless we included a piece which dealt with that other great audio-visual medium – film. Fortunately Valeria Camporesi offers us a chance to explore the relationship between film *and* TV. In so doing she also produces a detailed exposition of yet another methodological approach to enrich the study of television. Identifying an 'incessantly mobile scenario' Camporesi hopes that 'the intertextual game between cinema and television might produce a clear set of images'.

In Philip M. Taylor's piece we are invited to be cautious about the exiting new media world where: 'even the concept of 'broadcasting' has to be rethought.' This has led Professor Taylor to caution: 'It is a depressing prospect for the empirical sociologist and future historian alike'. whilst seizing its opportunities and challenges. Nonetheless, as with the other contributions, this chapter is a call to seize the opportunities and challenges. We are reminded that historians can still be very precious about their discipline. They do regard themselves as custodians of a past which does, as the programme-makers writing in this collection remind us, belong to everyone.

The author of this introduction was moved to become a film historian after reading (amongst other things) Smith's *Historian and Film*. I felt both exited by the possibilities and reassured that other historians (a) wanted to study film (b) had thought clearly about how to do so and (c) had begun to seriously consider the methodological challenges of such study. We, the editors of and contributors to this volume, can only hope that our collected efforts will help and inspire the historians of the 21st century.

As Professor Taylor puts it: 'For all the methodological problems, difficulties of access and cost for researching surviving broadcast output, it is surely no longer feasible for any historian of the late 20th century to either ignore or simply dismiss as a trivial side-show the role of television in society, first on a largely national basis and, latterly, internationally.'

The crux of the worries expressed by historians in this volume is a function of the sheer amount of material 'out there.' What analysts are left with is simply 'more' – and that presents them with considerable quantitative problems. A number of the contributors to this volume – including Morrison from a quantative perspective and Biesen and Camporesi from the urge to build a theoretical structure – have offered approaches that could allow us to develop strategies to develop an understanding of such vast amounts of material. In any event it would seem rather churlish for historians as a profession so long in thrall to the relative lack of primary sources to enter the 21st century bemoaning the existence of too much material. To quote Gerda Hendricks again: 'What is also needed is imagination.'

Graham Roberts
February 2001

Note

1   P. Smith *The Historian and Film* (Cambridge, 1975) p vii.

The Historical Development of Empirical Social Research:
The institutionalisation of knowledge and its relationship to the media industry, and benefits to history

David E. Morrison

It is the rules of how we engage with the world, of how we make sense of the world through rules, that I wish to address, and how certain forms for understanding the world have developed. I wish also to address how those rules structure conversations with, and about, the world. In doing so I wish to consider whether or not the conversations that sociologists have with the world might be of use to historians. In talking about rules I am talking about methods, or the language of research. I am going to suggest that perhaps historians too readily over-look the value of opinion polling.

Paul Lazarsfeld, one of the founding fathers of modern mass communications research, in his 1950 paper, 'The Obligation of the 1950 Pollster to the 1984 Historian' (1972a), poses the question: 'Don't we over-look the fact that, in a way, the pollster writes contemporary history?' Might not the 1984 historian reproach us for not having given enough thought to what we will want to know about 1950'? To illustrate his point he uses Machiavelli's 15th century work, *The Prince*, and how for several centuries afterwards 'Machiavellian' stood for everything evil in public affairs. As Macauley pointed out in 1837, though, Machiavelli was radically misunderstood by those who sought to appeal to different cultural values – that north of the Alps courage to repel hostile forces was highly valued, whereas south of the Alps in the Italian cities, ingenuity was highly valued.

Macauley illustrated what he meant through Shakespeare's characterisations of Othello and Iago in terms of how their actions would have been differently understood north and south of the Alps. His conclusion was that in the 15th century Othello would have been esteemed North of the Alps, but south of the

Alps held in contempt, the reverse holding true of Iago. Lazarsfeld comments: 'It is clear what Macaulay is striving for. He wishes someone had conducted attitude studies in Florence and London of the 15th century' (Lazarsfeld 1972a:281). Lazarsfeld then goes on to construct questions for placement on a survey that would give the desired data. He suggests, however, that no mention be made in the questionnaire that Othello was black. Why? To introduce skin colour raises the problem of not knowing what one was measuring – is it responses to the values exhibited by Othello's act of murder, or is one taking a measure of racism, or a joint mixture of the two – confounded as they say in statistical circles.

The historian must, therefore, be careful in using sociological data. I would add something else. Do not simply accept sociological interpretation of data – do that for oneself. First, ask what has been measured and then, if satisfied that the survey has measured what it is proposed has been measured, accept only the raw data and not the analysis – what it means.

Let me give you an example of the danger of accepting sociological procedures by reference to Robert Putnam's (1995) celebrated work on the decline of bowling in America as indicating a loss of community, or social solidarity, within American society.

Our modern world is predicated upon dynamic change – it is built into the system of modern life. Thus, judging the meaning of an activity as an index of something else is very difficult. For Putnam, bowling was taken as a (if not, the) quintessential measure of the health of American culture. Bowling represented sociability along with a set of values that reflected what it was to be an American. For Putnam, the decline of bowling as a leisure activity represented a loss of community in its widest sense. The mistake he makes, however, is to take an index for the measurement of something when that which is being measured cannot be fixed upon by a single activity when that activity itself is open to change. To equate X with Y when it is Y that one is interested in, and in doing so transform X into Y, results in any change in X invariably involving a change in Y. If social solidarity is expressed as Y, and X taken as its measurable index, it is essential to ensure that X is an inseparable and fundamental feature of Y without which Y would not exist.

Bowling was not an essential feature of social solidarity, but a feature of it at a particular point in history and, thus, the changed nature of leisure in America cannot be read as a change to, or indexical breakdown, of social solidarity.

Because a study looks rigorous, and often it looks rigorous because it has statistical data, does not necessarily mean that it is rigorous. Having said that – and I will not make an attack on the value of oral history – historians themselves are sufficiently given, and better qualified than me, to savage their own, but it is worth stressing that the plural of anecdote is not data. Thus, I agree with Lazarsfeld: that the systematic collection of public opinion on issues of the day can represent a valuable source of data for the future historian. Allow me, however, to go beyond Lazarsfeld, and show how survey returns can have a value greater than their use as mere top line data – how many people thought what, and who thought what. Historians should interrogate the data to fully reveal public thinking on issues. Interrogation is essential to get at that which underpins the manifestation of thinking as represented by the expressed opinion to any given single question. The historian, furthermore, has the advantage over the sociologist of being in a position to return the data to the context of historical formation of the issues asked about.

I realise that you might say, but historians are not trained in statistical interrogation of data. Fine. Learn – it is just another research language in the way one might have to learn German.

Further Lessons for History: Marienthal

Let me return, therefore, directly to the language of social research. The study I am going to examine, undertaken in the early part of the 1930s in Austria by Lazarsfeld, is *Die Arbeitslosen von Marienthal* – the unemployed of Marienthal (Jahoda, Lazarsfeld & Zeisel, 1933). I hope to show that a statistical analysis of the data collected, had it been in quantifiable format, would have been most useful to historians.

Marienthal was a small town outside Vienna, entirely dependent for its livelihood on a single woollen mill – a one company town. Its closure devastated the community. Let me set the scene.

Lazarsfeld was an Austro-Marxist – Austro-Marxism was a hybrid collection of positions, managing to combine revolutionary Marxism with reformist trade unionism. Vienna was Red, but surrounded on all sides by a hostile conservative country-side. A key issue for the Austrian Social Democratic Party, to which Lazarsfeld belonged, was the effect prolonged unemployment has on the development of a socialist consciousness. Do workers accept the conditions of their own misery? *Die Arbeitslosen von Marienthal* settled the matter. The methods he employed included participation in town life, asking inhabitants to keep diaries, interviewing the unemployed and town officials, examining children's lunch boxes, money spent at the butcher, the tavern and so on, along with engagement in hobbies, reading habits and so on.

Prior to the closure of the mill, social life in Marienthal was vibrant. All kinds of clubs existed. There was even a socialist rabbit club. Newspaper reading was high – local and world events were the subject of heated debate. As poverty bit deeper – well you can imagine what happened to the rabbits to cause closure of such clubs – newspaper reading declined as interest in the outside world shrunk, as people's horizons were reduced to no more than the pressing conditions of their immediate existence. The fall in newspaper readership – which could be read for free at the local library – was an index of apathy in social issues/political issues. The individual no longer took an interest in outside events, but withdrew in on the self. The study made for depressing reading for the SDP, but it at least clarified the consequences of unemployment on political consciousness.

My own feeling is that one might have drawn some further lessons from the study. Could such communities have been open to the type of psuedo *gemeinschaften* – false communities – appeal of the National Socialists. To establish this, however, would have required a study of the same individuals or community at a further point in time to plot change.

Had this been done, and data entered in quantifiable form, it would have offered itself as a classic case where the historian could use data collected by the social scientist to make limited causal connections between variables. Let me explain. Such data could not alone account for the rise of Hitler and the popularity of National Socialist ideology, but might have shown how effects work, and under what conditions they worked. It could have done so in a very precise micro fashion. It could absolve the need for theory/history in terms of explaining social process. I know this is an outrageous suggestion, but hold fire for the moment.

If, at a particular point in time, one had data on a whole range of attitudes, beliefs, experiences, and then similar data for a later period, which was then overlaid with a content analysis of messages, we have an interesting game at play. What we could do is examine who accepted what, and what shifts in beliefs had taken place, then through the statistical manipulation of variables, discover the saliency of some features over others in accounting for receptivity to messages. This is what I meant by my statement, absolving the need for theory/history.

Before I am accused of mindless empiricism, or whatever the equivalent term for sin is in the discipline of history, let me say that what one does, how one goes about examining the world, depends very much on the types of accounts one wishes to give, or will be satisfied by. In the above case one would still require theory/history to give account to happenings to explain the territory upon which events occurred and, thus, make full sense of them. But, through the proposed method – the statistical manipulation of variables – one would be in possession of a close and controlled understanding of what was working and how; in a way not possible by putting together varied information in the manner of a jigsaw puzzle – one would have, as we say, single source data. One would have the mechanics of the bits of the parts that the theory, or general history, explains. How variables configurate or come together is the advantage of the statistical method – the results of which, at least, provide the starting point for wider enquiry.

In this sense, therefore, moving beyond the limits of Lazarsfeld's study might have great potential for historians. I now wish to talk about the institutional organisation of knowledge, and the historical changes that have occurred.

History of educational innovation

Between leaving the history department here in Leeds and establishing the Institute as such, Nicholas Pronay made a fairly extensive tour of communications departments in the United States. The lesson he brought back was that research and instruction should never be separated if long term stability was to be achieved. Whether this Humboldtian view of the University as a unity of teaching and research can continue into the 21st century only time will tell.

In looking at the organisation of knowledge historically, one sees, almost in a Kuhnian sense, break-outs from the past. The history of innovation in higher learning over the past 500 years is instructive on this point. We see that each century gave rise to some fairly distinct points of change. In the 16th century it was the integration of humanistic studies, the new learning, into the University. The most characteristic institutional event was the establishment of the College of France. The 17th century saw the emergence of the natural sciences – the ascendancy of Baconism was carried by the academics of which the Royal Society in London was both the leader and the symbol. The 18th century is institutionally somewhat different. It was the age of enlightenment in which the French Revolution prepared, but did not firmly establish a major pattern of university innovation. It was the nineteenth century that saw the modern integrated pattern of university development for which the University of Berlin, founded in 1810 and called the 'Mother of All Modern Universities', set the main pattern.

But what of the 20th century? It was Lazarsfeld's view, as a remarkable educational innovator himself, that 'one can probably state that the rapid expansion of empirical work in the social sciences and the institutional forms this takes will remain one of the outstanding features of the twentieth century' (Lazarsfeld 196 1: I)

His reference to institutional forms is to the research bureau, the research centre, the research institute. These units go by a variety of names, but share similar characteristics. They involve teams of researchers with relatively clearly defined roles, where work is broken down into its parts under the over-all charge of a director. Money must be raised and new contracts constantly sought. This new research setting saw the emergence of a new academic role and figure – earlier times or entrepreneurial scholar. The work is often of an applied nature undertaken for some commercial client or government agency – money from research councils is, of course, also attracted. To a degree unknown in earlier times – and this is not withstanding the need to attract students – staff must pay for themselves. If Marx was right about one thing, he was right about this: labour must reproduce its value.

Market research: Late Twentieth century innovation

A Marxian perspective of *Wissensoziologie* is a good one to adopt in looking at development of such institutions – that new forms of knowledge demand new institutional forms for their management. Yet, I am somewhat in disagreement with Lazarsfeld in terms of the 'the outstanding features of the 20th century' being that of the research bureau. Lazarsfeld was observing developments in knowledge from only half way through the century. I have the advantage of observing from the completion of the century. If the production of knowledge was rationalised within the research bureau then this process has gone the furthest within market research companies, where one can rightly say that knowledge has been industrialised, put on a factory footing. By comparison, opinion research in universities is a cottage industry, but one overlaid by a bureaucracy that turns each scholar into a functionary for the administration. But, forcing the conformity of the bureau on its scribes, in the way of some Weberian story, is not my source of alarm in viewing the modern university – although it may make them more dull places to work than in the past. My concern, rather, is that industrialisation and the efficiency in the production of knowledge by market research companies has forced, or is forcing, the university as a definer of knowledge to the side-lines of influence.

Nicholas knew that unless we made ourselves relevant, both in instruction and in research, then there was no hope of survival. And we are not just about survival, we are about influence, that is, in having a say in how we want our cultural world to be ordered and the standards by which we want it to perform. I have no axiom to grind here, but I take it that knowledge must be for something, and part of that something is to have some say in the performance of the media, or if that is over-fanciful, at least to enter in the thinking of how the media is thought about.

The cultural influence in terms of problem solving and policy making that has fallen to the market research industry is one of the over-looked social phenomena of the late 20th century. Should you think, let the market researchers get on with it, it has nothing to do with us because we are scholars, then my answer would be that all cultural production is a political struggle in the control of meaning. To leave that field of struggle is an abrogation of duty at the best, and at the worst to give to the technicians of the market research world an increased say in what is increasingly becoming a technical world.

One of the marks of our age, and one of the reasons that market research companies have performed so well, is that they have not been cultured in a bell-jar, but in the real world. What research we have is very much dependent on what system we have, my point being that increasingly it is market research that exercises influence in shaping the cultural system. In terms of the sociology of knowledge, the success of market research companies as organisations is that their rhythm of production fits with the rhythm of the industries that they serve. There is an inexorable logic to the type of knowledge demanded and the development of the structures to provide that knowledge. Research as science has, in a sense, come to take the place of decision making as craft – the scientisation of decision making. I am aware that a whole tract of the history of Western European thought could be written here, but I will resist it, and merely point to the fact that an instrumental rationality demands instrumental knowledge. Values have not been abandoned in the decision-making process, but research is increasingly relied upon to do what reflective policy making should do itself: make judgements based on values, rather than make judgements based on numbers.

I will now look back to how the administrative settings of research enterprises and the forms of knowledge they produce are so intimately related.

Quantification in Europe and America

It is said of German professors at the end of the 17th century that they wrote all their papers in Latin, and that when they wished to be very condescending, they wrote in French. Indeed, Lazarsfeld had to rebuke Theodor Adorno, of the exiled Frankfurt School, while working with him on the Rockefeller-funded Princeton Radio Research Project, which forms the beginning of modern mass communication research, for his use of Latin. In an undated letter, from 1938 or 1939, Lazarsfeld wrote to Adorno, in somewhat ironic vein given Adorno's Marxist critical theory and his reliance on the notion of fetish: 'Don't you think it is a perfect fetishism the way you use Latin words all through your texts There is no doubt that the words "necessary condition" express everything which the corresponding Latin words can express, but you evidently feel magically more secure if you use words which symbolise your education" (Lazarsfeld letter, Lazarsfeld's papers).

I agree with C. Wright Mills that facts should act to discipline the imagination. For Adorno, facts merely got in the way. Where some fact supported his reasoning it was accepted, without ever bothering to look for other facts that might contradict it, and I do not mean contradiction here in the Hegelian sense. It seems that Adorno never knew how to put an empirical check upon a hypothetical assumption.

In looking at changes to knowledge, it should not be imagined that quantification is an exclusively American story. Its origins lay in early modern Europe, indeed, may be dated as far back as the 17th century, but it failed to develop as a regular branch of professional sociology. Sampling methods, for example, derived as a sequence to Booth's survey of life and labour in London; factor analysis was invented by the Englishman Spearman; family research with special emphasis on quantification developed under LePlay, the French mineralogist; and Gabriel Tarde advocated attitude measurement and communications research. The notion of applying mathematical models to voting was carefully worked out by Condorcet during the French Revolution. His contemporaries, Laplace and Lavoiser, undertook social surveys for the Revolutionary Government, and their student, the Belgian Quetelet, 'finally and firmly established empirical social research under the title physique sociale' – much to Auguste Comte's annoyance who then had to give his work the more ugly title, sociology, a name unfortunately that has stuck (Lazarsfeld 1972b:328). In Germany Max Weber was at times enthusiastic about quantification and making computations himself, and Ferdinand Tonnies invented a correlation coefficient of his own. It is the case, however, that nowhere in Europe before 1933 did empirical research acquire prestige, a home in universities to form what might be termed a critical mass. Quantification in mainland Europe is rightly to be associated with America, but as a re-export often carried by the return of exiles after the war imparting their experiences in America. Thus, Franz Neumann, the political scientist, reflecting on his own exile to the United States could rightly note in the absence of a critical mass to support empirical research: 'On the whole, the German exile, bred in the veneration of theory and history and a contempt for empiricism and pragmatism, entered a diametrically opposed intellectual climate: optimistic, empirically orientated, a-historical, but also self-righteous' (Neumann 1953.17). This was not the case, however, with the Austrian, Paul Lazarsfeld.

It should not be assumed that the Austrian tradition of research in the social sciences was that much different from Germany, although a mistake is often made in this context because of the work of Lazarsfeld. The fact is, however, that Lazarsfeld developed his empirical social research outside the main university system.

Lazarsfeld — *Forschungsstelle*

Lazarsfeld was born into a Jewish middle class Viennese family in 1901. Entry into University for someone of his background was a matter of course. Gaining employment was another matter. Vienna was the most anti-Semitic university in Austria. Even Sigmund Freud had difficult, making professor ordinaries, or full professor, and was in the lowly post of *Privatdozent* for the exceptionally long time of twelve years. Such was the anti-Semitism that the academic senate of the university attempted to pass a resolution putting a quota on the entry of Jewish students to the University in the model of Hungary and Poland.

What we see in Lazarsfeld is creativity in marginality, and marginality at several levels. There was the institutional block on his university career through rabid anti-Semitism, but even without this empirical social research would have been almost impossible.

Sociology itself was under-developed at the Univeristy of Vienna. The economist/social philosopher Othmar Spann dominated the social sciences. Spann, with his notion of organic universalism with its emphasis on *stande* – given layers of society – was the key intellectual figure in Austria in development of the idea of the corporate state. He was, not surprisingly, an implacable opponent of empirical research. There could not, therefore, have been any place for Lazarsfeld, either socially or intellectually, within the university. Even without such blocks, extensive and expensive empirical research could not have gone on at the university – it was bankrupt, as was the Austrian state. There was no money. Indeed, there was hardly enough money to pay the reduced salaries of the professoriat.

One further factor requires introduction in understanding Lazarsfeld's move into social research. His ambition of high office with the Austrian Social Democratic Party was also blocked. I cannot go into this in any detail but the fear among the leaders of the SDP, who were almost entirely Jewish, towards another leading Jewish figure was strong. Again, therefore, we see Lazarsfeld forced into the position of the outsider – the marginal figure (Morrison 1998). This marginality, combined with the ambivalent position of Austrian socialism, suspended between success and failure, deeply affected Lazarsfeld as it did his circle of intellectual friends. The attraction of social reseach was, as Lazarsfeld informed me, that it enabled 'this whole defeated socialist group' to transfer 'to a new activity which was close enough to social reality and had some academic glamour' (Lazarsfeld 25:5:73).

But to do empirical research of any scale requires an organisation, and funding. Lazarsfeld's response was to establish the *Osterreichische Wirtschaftspychologische Forschungsstelle* – Austrian Economic and Psychological Research Centre – outside the university, but to tenuously link it through the Psychology Institute, where he held the post of assistant under the patronage of the Institute's head, Karl Buhler. Established in 1925 this was the first research centre of its kind in the world. The *Forschungsstelle* consisted of leading academics and business figures – the President of Ballie was even a member – with Karl Buhler as its chairman.

The most political study undertaken by the *Forschungsstelle* was *Die Arbeitslosen von Mariethal*, but that was unusual. Most of the studies we would see as market research – how people came to choose one brand of product rather than another. But this fed one of Lazarsfeld's interests, the empirical study of action; how people came to act at the point of decision making was of great methodological interest to him. This interest has direct links to his voting studies, such as *The People's Choice* (Lazarsfeld *et al*, 1944), that he undertook in the United States – for Lazarsfeld the decision to vote and the decision to buy a soap powder come together methodologically. The central idea of the *Forschungsstelle*, however, was that the money from the market research accounts would subsidise the more academic work – a kind of academic Robin-Hooding. It never worked out that way. Lazarsfeld was a great manager, but a terrible administrator – the books never added up, money for one study paid the debts of the last and so on – actually, pretty much the same as when he later ran the Bureau of Applied Social Research.

Rise of Columbia sociology

Indeed, the model for research that he developed in Vienna was very much a straightforward transplant upon exile to America, and later became the model for other research centres that were to spring up across American universities. Despite Lazarsfeld's rather messy administration the Bureau at Columbia University came to dominate not just mass communications research, but American sociology in general, or at least the rising tide of its empirical wing. The Bureau trained a generation of scholars some of whom went on to establish sub-centres of the Bureau. Its organisation, especially the training it gave – a drill ground as Edward Shils (1970) called it – gave it enormous impact on American sociology. It was Lazarsfeld's opinion that one of the reasons that Chicago sociology during its prime in the 1920s, under the direction of such notable figures as Park, Burgess, Small, Thomas and Ogburn, declined so quickly in the face of intellectual competition from other graduate faculties was that it lacked the necessary formal organisation to extend the influence of the early great leaders (Lazarsfeld, 1972b:331).

Lazarsfeld is probably right to concentrate on the role of organisation in giving support to ideas. However, when examining for intellectual influence one must also examine what the organisation is organised around. In the case of Chicago sociology, a contributory factor to its decline was that there was a reduction of interest in the type of problem that Chicago had made itself famous for; namely, studying the difficulties associated with immigration, the disordered nature of urban life, and the marginalisation of groups within the city. By the 1940s, although not absent, these questions were no longer at the forefront of social concern. New developments were taking place on the eastern seaboard that required attention - they were national, rather than local issues.

It is at this point that I wish to weave in the biographical with the structural in the history of research in communications.

The beginnings of modern mass communication research are not hard to detect. In 1937 The Rockefeller Foundation gave a grant of $67,000 for two years — extended for a further two years to Hadley Cantril of Princeton University — to examine, as the grant release states, 'The Value of Radio to Listeners'. It was known as the Princeton Radio Research Project, run by the Office of Radio Research. Cantril's heart was not in the project, so the Directorship was offered to Frank Stanton, then a young researcher at CBS. He refused the position and it was then offered to the emigre Lazarsfeld, who accepted, with Cantril and Stanton becoming co-directors. The Foundation official in charge of the project was John Marshall, whom as far I can determine actually coined the phrase, 'mass communications research' to describe this new area. Indeed it was during a series of seminars in 1941, organised by Marshall, in an attempt to have Lazarsfeld clarify what he was doing, that one of the participants, Harold Laswell, developed his famous model of the communications process — who says what, to whom, through what channel, with what effect (Morrison, 1998).

Lazarsfeld never spent a single night at Princeton. He ran the project out of Newark, where he had a small research centre, then transferred the Office to Columbia University on the renewal of the grant in 1939. In 1944 it was renamed The Bureau of Applied Social Research. The manner in which he ran the Bureau, as stated, was very much along the same lines as the *Forschungsstelle* in Vienna. Lazarsfeld was never substantively interested in communications research, as a methodologist any area would have suited his purposes, but what it did offer, was the possibility of building his own research center. Let me explain. The reason for the decline of Chicago sociology, was in part the reason for the rise of Columbia sociology.

New York had become the main centre of the emerging communications and advertising industries, and the home of national marketing companies. As Everett Rogers comments: 'Instead of studying local community problems like the adaptation of European immigrants in Chicago and marginal or deviant subculture that ensued, Lazarsfeld and the Columbian Scholars replaced Park and Chicagoans on centre stage of American sociology and emphasised national-level research problems like the effects of mass media communications' (Rogers 1994:195). Lazarsfeld helped pioneer survey research using sampling, which allows one to have conversations with representatives of millions of people – it opens the whole world to conversation. Of course it was the development of the computer that allowed the processing of such conversations in a way not possible through prior accountancy systems – most of Lazarsfeld's major works depended on the precursor of the computer, the Hollerith machine.

Critical versus administrative research

Lazarsfeld's location in New York at the centre of the communications industry gave him ready advantage to exploit the opportunities of this new situation. Yet, Lazarsfeld's association with commerce brought its critics. Rather than go into detail, I will capture this through an interview with Bernard Berelson, a former head of the Bureau and one of the early leading figures in communications research. He recalled an attack that C.Wright Mills made on Lazarsfeld.

> I can still hear Wright Mills saying, 'Why Paul Lazarsfeld works for *True Story Magazine*, as though no self-respecting academic of any persuasion would do that. Paul always felt, 'I don't understand what Wright is complaining about. These people are generous with the research funds, they allow me to raise questions ... we have the opportunity to do the Decatur Study. (Berelson 12.7.73)

The Decatur study refers to Katz and Lazarsfeld's seminal work, *Personal Influences*, (1955) from which the two step-flow model of the communications process developed. Mills actually worked on that study, but it was foundering until Elihu Katz, I believe, helped rescue it. Evidently, the Decatur study was showing that the media had no influence on opinion – not something that a magazine client welcomed. Thus, effort had to be doubled to find an influence, which, as we now know, was found not to be from the media direct, but by personal influences through opinion leaders in the celebrated two step flow fashion. This is a classic case of how work for the industry, setting problems that it wished to find answers to, can then feed back to become basic knowledge.

In terms of the politics of the organisation of knowledge, without doubt Lazarsfeld's enmeshment with commerce, and the media industry, delayed the Bureau's full incorporation into the university. Even Robert Lynd, the key figure in the sociology department and one of Lazarsfeld's main supporters, was suspicious of what went on at the Bureau, not really understanding its operations, although he felt important work was being done. The clash of cultures between scholarship as basic knowledge and administrative or contract research that characterised the founding of mass communications research by Lazarsfeld, is given stark relief by the employment of Adorno on the music side of the Princeton Radio Research Project.

On joining the team, Adorno, visiting the offices of the project, housed in an unoccupied brewery – I think in New York's then infamous Hells Kitchen – confessed in his memoir his 'astonishment at a practically orientated kind of science so entirely unknown to me' (Adorno 1969:340). Although Adorno spoke better English than Lazarsfeld, he did not know what a research project was – research project now translated in German by the word *Forschungsvorhaben*.

There are some interesting lessons in the Frankfurt School in terms of organisation, finance and research. The Frankfurt School, even in exile, was initially extremely privileged, having escaped from Germany with its funds intact. Yet, following a downturn in its fortunes Max Horkheimer complained to Leo Lowenthal that it had now become a *Betrieb* – a business – having to attract funds to survive (Jay, 1973:342). The School had made some poor real estate investment in up-state New York - Marxist economic understanding of capitalism clearly did not stretch to intervention in the market. But forced from their privileged position, and having to pursue external funding, this period saw the most productive period of the school's empirical work – the studies in prejudice. *The Authoritarian Personality* which was part of the programme of research became a classic of the social sciences almost immediately upon publication.

Adorno's period with Lazarsfeld was not the success that Lazarsfeld had hoped for. Whether one could ever have married Marxist critical theory with administrative research working with the media industry, is open to severe doubt. But Adorno's abrasive personality, and disconcerting 'uncompromising intellectuality', (Jay 1973:23) did not make him the man for the job. The Foundation Officials, and the media figures acting as advisers to the Princeton Project, were mystified by what Adorno had to say. His inability to offer 'solutions' also bothered them. John Marshall, the Foundation official in charge of the project, noted in a memo in early 1940 that Adorno '... seems psychologically engaged at the moment by his ability to recognise deficiencies in broadcasting of music to an extent that makes questionable his own drive to find ways of remedying them'. (Marshall memo 5:1:40. Rockefeller Foundation Archives)

The idea of solution is extremely undialectical, but I think we are talking problems here beyond the 'critical spirit'. Although later, while at Berkeley working on the studies in prejudice, his stress on grasping the objective spirit rather than measuring reactions to it had diminished, the scaling techniques used in the Authoritarian Personality Studies came to serve as a bench mark in personality measurement. It would seem, therefore, that while working with Lazarsfeld in New York culture could not be measured, while working at Berkeley bias could be (see Jay 1973:224). Given the opportunity to measure culture, he vehemently objected to what he saw as American empirical sociology – really Lazarsfeldian sociology. Adorno writes in his Memoir that he was:

> ... particularly disturbed by the danger of a methodological circle: that in order to grasp the phenomenon of cultural reification according to

prevalent norms of empirical sociology one would have to use reified methods as they stood so threatingly before my eyes in the form of that machine, the programme analyser (Adorno 1969:347).

As far as Adorno was concerned, the statistical average of respondent's opinions about the stimulus remained, despite the seeming objectivity of the data, at the level of subjectivity. The solution is, therefore, that through the musical text in the hands of a noted musicologist such as himself, and armed with an understanding of the 'objective' movement of history, he will pronounce on the responses. It is certainly one way to understand the world, but I can think of others. While I would not claim to take peoples' responses as the prime source of sociological data, as he supposed Lazarsfeld did, one needs to know responses and credit them with some meaning as given by those who are doing the responding – and that is what the Lazarsfeld-Stanton programme analyser – a kind of crude polygraph linking responses to specific messages by the pressing of buttons – allowed. 'That machine', as Adorno called it, at the hands of Robert Merton, by focusing responses on the message, developed the technique of focus group research. A standard technique now, it was used extensively by the Columbia school just prior to the War, and during the War, to understand responses to morale raising radio broadcasts, appeals to war bond drives, and soldiers responses to training films – Sammuel Stouffer, as Director of the professional staff at the Research Branch, Information and Education Division, of the War Department, channelled work of the War Department through the Bureau (Morrison, 1998).

What we see during this period is a close enmeshing on Lazarsfeld's part, not just with commerce but with government agencies, to give communications research a significant profile. It laid down what has been termed, the dominant paradigm of communications research, namely, effects research. I do not wish to engage in counterfactuals but without this involvement of Lazarsfeld's with both commerce and government, it might have looked very different. The questions being set were not questions that emanated from the academy.

Mass communications and the media industry

From the very beginning mass communications research not only depended on the co-operation and funding of the media industry (as Lazarsfeld once informed me, 'everything depended on that') but, in terms of addressing its problems, academic communications also sustained the industry. It should not be imagined, however, that the industry were enthusiasts for search in the furtherance of some general understanding. It is probably better to see it, at least in the very early days, as John Marshall commented to me, as acting 'out of unenlightened self interest'. (Interview Marshall 6.7:73) In some ways, they had to be forced to undertake research, and the Foundation made repeated attempts to get them to support more basic research, but without success.

What the Rockefeller Foundation was interested in was the qualitative improvement of radio broadcasting, and the development of a radio network servicing the nation. What especially bothered the Foundation was the closely interlocked interests of the radio and advertising industries. The Foundation's concern can be gauged from the following abstract of a memorandum, probably the summary of a conversation between Marshall and Stanton, who in those days, long before he became President of CBS, was in the Research Division of CBS.

More important still in this respect is the relation which has grown up between the industry and the advertising agencies and the buyers of time on the other hand. It is a fact that one of the national chains felt obliged to curtail its research to maintain good relations with the advertising agencies who acted as intermediaries of sponsors in the purchase of time. Data which the chain was collecting proved contrary to some of the contentions on which agencies were selling time. To maintain its profitable relations with the agencies, the chain's only choice was to give up the research (Memo, May 1937 – Rockefeller Archives).

The early attitude of the industry to research is a sorry tale. For example, the pollster George Gallup wrote to the Foundation in spring of 1937:

> Most of the research in the field of radio has been concerned with the measurement of the size of the audience listening to various programmes. We know virtually nothing about the influence of radio on listeners, the reasons why persons listen to certain programmes and not others. The organisations that are now engaged in radio research are not in a position to do research of this character largely because procedures are required. (Gallup 19:5:37 – Rockefeller Archives)

For procedures, here read methods. It was Gallup's conclusion that support for examining the role of radio in people's lives would not be forthcoming from the industry, 'because the results have no immediate commercial value'. Marshall noted the industry's reluctance to support in-depth research due to commercial considerations. He provided the example:

> Advertisers have come to believe that the tastes of one socioeconomic group are much the same as the next: this leads the industry to feel that it cannot afford to support research which might threaten existing concepts of mass appeal. Or again, studies of when listening takes place involve a similar threat to the existing rate structure. (Marshall, 21:5:37 – Rockefeller Archives)

A final note on the industry's attitude to research is perfectly captured by an undated note Cantril sent the Foundation, probably late 1936 or early 1937:

> A further instance of the lack of the industries' interest in detailed listener research is revealed in their attitude towards securing data on what the listener does while he listens. While this is important in an understanding of listener behaviour, the broadcasters in most cases at least, are not interested in the findings because they cannot afford to

indicate that people do anything but listen while the radio is in use. Finally, business is so 'good' in broadcasting that the industry is not inclined to spend money for research until they are forced to do so, not only because of the embarrassment such data might cause, but because business does not demand it. Ultimately the industry will have to go deeper, in a research sense, in order to maintain its position. (Cantril, late 1936 or early 1937 – Rockefeller Archives)

Using that most exact of sciences, hindsight, that is indeed what has happened. But at that time not only did the industry restrict itself to very primitive research, and thus cannot be held to have promoted communications research as such in any sophisticated fashion, but data that was collected failed to be exploited. For example, Lazarsfeld wrote to Marshall in 1940:

> I thought you might be interested in a cute example of the relationship of academic research and commercial research. When I started surveying the field in 1937, I realised that the programme ratings which were used only for gauging the size of the audience could also be used for the study of social stratification. We obtained the permission of the Co-operative Analysis of Broadcasting to analyse their material and our publication 'The Social Stratification of the Radio Audience' came about. Then Public Opinion Quarterly published a summary of our findings. Now CAB has put out a summary in pamphlet form and is sending out many thousand of copies for their own promotion. It took them all this roundabout travelling to find out what they had at hand. Incidentally, you will find the typical inventor's tragedy; we have only been given no more credit than a footnote at the end of the forward (Lazarsfeld 6:9.4 – Lazarsfeld's Papers).

I think this letter from Lazarsfeld offering, as he says, 'a cute example of the relationship of academic research and commercial research' is pertinent to much that I have been saying, especially his comment concerning the academic researcher having 'been given no more credit than a footnote at the end of the forward'.

I think, as we look forward to the 21st century, academic research, if it is not careful, will become a footnote in terms of social influence. The way forward, is to go back. We must become relevant, and relevancy here means to be tackling those questions that the industry itself is tackling. This is not to argue that academia should slavishly become the research arm of the industry, but it is to argue for an involvement with those who are directly responsible for changes in the communications landscape.

I could, of course, be wrong. If so, then I am with Maynard Keynes. Once criticised for holding a position contrary to that which he had held some time before, he turned on his accuser and said: 'Well, when I find I am wrong, I usually change my mind – what do you do?'

Bibliography

Adorno, T., 'Scientific Experiences of a European Scholar in America', in Fleming, D. & Bailyn, B.,1969.

Crawford, W. (Ed), *The Cultural Migration; The European Scholar in America*, University of Pennsylvania Press, 1953.

Fleming, D. & Bailyn, B., *The Intellectual Migration*, Harvard University Press, 1969.

Jahoda, M., Lazarsfeld, P. F. & Zeisel, H., *Die Arbeitslosen von Marienthal: Ein Soziographischer*, Leipzig: Hirzl, 1933.

Jay, M.,*The Dialectical Imagination: A History of the Frankfurt School & the Institute of Social Research 1923-50*, Heinemann, London, 1973.

Katz, E. & Lazarsfeld, P. F., *Personal Influences: The Part Played by People in the Flow of Mass Communication*, Free Press, Glencoe, 1955.

Lazarsfeld, P. F., 'Notes on the History of Quantification in Sociology: Trends, Sources & Problems', *ISIS*, vol. 52, part 2, June 277-333, 1961.

Lazarsfeld, P. F., 'The Obligation of the 1950 Pollster to the 1984 Historian', in Lazarsfeld, P. F., *Qualitative Analysis: Historical & Critical Essays*, Chapter 14, Allyn & Bacon Inc., Boston 1972a (Reprint from POQ, 1950).

Lazarsfeld, P. F. *et al*, *The Peoples Choice: How the Voter Makes Up His Mind in a Presidential Campaign*, Columbia University Press, 1944.

Lazarsfeld, P. F.,'The Sociology of Empirical Social Research', Chapt. 16 in Lazarsfeld, 1972b (Reprint ASR, 27:6:1962).

Morrison, D. E., *The Search for a Method: Focus Groups and the Development of Mass Communication Research*, University of Luton Press, 1998.

Neumann, F. L., 'The Social Sciences', in Crawford, W. (Ed), 1953.

Putnam, R. D., 'Bowling Alone: America's Declining Social Capital', *Journal of Democracy*, Jan 1995.

Rogers, E. M., *A History of Communication Study: A Biographical Approach*, The Free Press, New York, 1994.

Shils, E., 'Tradition, Ecology and Institutions in the History of Socology', *Daedalus*, vol. 99, no. 4, 1970.

Historians at the Crossroads: Cinema, Television... and after?

Pierre Sorlin

What is history? Philosophers have written thick books to clarify the issue but, leaving aside the theoretical debate, I should say that it is the public activities of historians, their polemics, their conversations and publications that decide whether a given way of dealing with the past is history or not and, therefore, that draw the boundaries around their discipline. Up to the 16th century the exploration of the past was a mere appendix of theology aimed at explaining how what was happening on earth derived from God's project. Then emerged, during the modern era, a new form of history that did not want to explain the past with reference to God's plan, but tried to understand how the world came to be the way it is. Historians then had to establish the boundaries between history and theology. They did it by emphasizing the empirical aspect of their work, its exclusive reliance on documents and its independence from religious dogmatism. This empiricism that, initially, was a necessity, became outmoded when historians began to think that the past could not be studied in and for itself because it is part of a long-lasting process. The history that we have been used to practising can be considered a social science in as much as it takes into account the complexity of human relationships along time and aims at valuating the conflicts, or contradictions, which counteract the tendency of any system to maintain itself.

It is my contention that, today, we are engaged in a new boundary dispute and have to face something extremely menacing: the blurring of any hierarchy of facts that impinges on the status of historical explanation. Different factors account for this shift of emphasis. There is first, at least in western countries, the weakening of a national consciousness that was closely linked to the telling of national histories. That is not to say that people, in our days, no longer care for the past. On the contrary, museums aimed at maintaining the memory of far away periods, small-town historical societies, websites dealing with genealogy, research of ancestors and roots, local archaeology and history are blossoming. The gigantic website 'History 2000' opened by the BBC is typical in this respect: we shall be able to find the most infinitesimal data about any moment, date or name but there will be no synthesis of the evolution of British islands. And this is perfectly consonant with the demands of the general public which is less and less interested in all-inclusive discourses about the fate and deeds of national countries, while there are claims for a truly human history centred on individuals, families, private names, small communities, in other words for a knowledge of the past more akin to quiz programmes than to speculations about human destiny.

Television is a second factor that plays a crucial part in this modification since it is, at one and the same time, a mirror that reflects the new tendencies and an agent that accentuates them. It is often said that, on average, television sets are on four hours a day. I do not know whether that is true and I assume that, quite often, people do not look at the screen. But the very presence of television is what matters: words and images have become a major source of information, more important than books or papers. A third factor, possibly linked to the previous ones, is the decline of written information vis-à-vis visual information and, interestingly enough, it is something that can be observed even in historical research. The traditional scholarly view was long that, provided they were critical enough, historians could rely on written documents. Today many scholars are in some doubt about the historicity of texts which are literary creations, concocted for some political purpose, for instance to tell in metaphor the origins and accession to power of a royal family. Other, more 'concrete' sources like archaeology, coins, seals, medals, clothes, furniture give a picture of a very different world from that described in books. Such evidences do not aim at telling a fanciful story; in fact, they do not tell any story. They merely indicate a state of affairs and do not allow us to reconstruct an evolution throughout times.

However widening one's horizon is never a bad thing. In this respect, the admission of cinema to the dignity of historical document, in recent decades, was surely a progress. Since the 1930s cinema has not only been the most important form of entertainment, it has also been a source of knowledge assuming, in many areas, the attitude-forming role previously fulfilled by the popular press. Movies transcended people's daily reality, while maintaining a close connection with their ordinary concerns. They told them about regions or customs which did not belong to their immediate surroundings and satisfied their longing for visual information. More importantly, films helped to spread the attitudes and values of other societies, above all those of the Americans. There is little doubt about the impact of cinema in the middle of the century. The medium's influence over its viewers was considerable. But now, at the start of the 21st century, cinema is dying. More precisely the cinema that was typical of the mid 20th century has vanished, having been swallowed by television. The difference is not merely the dimension of the screen. Television is another world. To begin with, there is no immunity against it. Even people who have no television set are surrounded by its messages. In order to go to the pictures you had to make up your mind and decide that you would not stay at home. You did not spend more than two or three hours in the theatre. With television the universe intrudes into our living room and even if we are distant, absent-minded listeners, we cannot ignore it. Unlike cinema or the press, television is not only an important means of information or a form of entertainment. Nor is it simply a precious source available to the analysis of societies; it is the background of everybody's life, our common fellow traveller.

It is needless to expand on this. Few people would question the importance of television in our life. So, common sense will have it, what is the matter?: let us look at the silver screen up to the 1960s and afterwards at the small screen. Today, most historians are well aware of the importance of television, understand that it is the most influential source of information throughout the world, that it reveals instantly events that are taking place at various points around the globe and also that, in some cases, it causes these events by prompting politicians towards a decision whose motivation lies in seeing it shown on the box. A good many researchers have begun to work in television archives, excellent books have explored the role played by television during the American war in Vietnam, or the impact of Western televisions on the former socialist countries as well as the role they played in preparing the crisis of the Soviet empire. However these works still consider television as one of the many sources available to document our times.

My assumption is that what is at stake is fairly different. Television is not another version of cinema but to a large extent, the opposite of cinema. Every news bulletin brings us its share of casualties, accidents, and massacres on the road, extensively filmed in colours by a jerky, hand-held camera. It is extremely difficult to figure out that a murder, in the 1930s, was not fairly different from a contemporary manslaughter and that the contrast between what people saw then and what we see now merely results from another conception of photography. There is, however, much more than that. Television, because it is bound to broadcasting a permanent flow of images, has no time for selection. It lingers on ordinary aspects of life and collects facts likely to illuminate people's daily activities. The greater part of our life is spent in humdrum, nondescript moments and it is impossible to remember each of them. Only exceptional circumstances are accompanied by strong emotion which further ensures the endurance of the memory and prompts us to vividly record and describe them. The aim of history, what distinguishes it from chronicles, is to take these events into account and introduce them into a continuous narration. But television, surfing the world for news of the now, catches us in a perpetual present.

I shall exemplify what I am saying with two minutes of television news from the Nine o'clock news. Since historians like references I state precisely that this item was broadcast the second of October 1992 and is related to the conflict between Croatia and Serbia, but you had better forget the date because the images are timeless and could 'illustrate' events that took part in 1994 or 1997 or in any other period. The newsreader, who has only got vague details about the real situation, soon gets lost in nebulous generalities. On radio, this would require no more than 20 seconds but television is obliged to linger on the case, first because listening and viewing simultaneously requires a greater effort but, more importantly, because the screen of the television set must always be filled with images, however irrelevant they are. The talk is backed by a series of pictures which do not illustrate the words and it is even obvious that, during the last thirty seconds, a sequence of images taken at random in some archive bear no relation whatsoever to the discourse. All through the 1990s similar pictures and the same narration have been put on the air, day after day, by all television networks.

My aim is not to make fun of broadcast news for the very good reason that television is what it is and that criticising it would be useless. What strikes me is the disappearance of both the events and the attempt at explaining how events are related to each other. But who would dare maintain that a rational account of what happened is always possible? There may be no explanation for the wars in the Blakans and "the truth" might indeed well be what we see on television: lorries carrying soldiers who know neither where they are going not what they are fighting for.

I would also like to discuss another 'document', the initial minute of 'The Battle of Trafalgar Square' from a magazine programme broadcast on Channel Four, on 31st March 1990. I assume that many people remember this film that told how the police dealt with a Poll Tax demonstration. You may have forgotten its beginning. The editors had chosen to line up, chronologically, the accounts of the demonstration given by the different British authorities. What they wanted to prove is the obvious fact that these accounts were all politically biased but this is not as impressing as the fact that the commentaries are built around the pictures: the newsreaders are content with describing what can be seen on the screen; for instance police brutality is ignored when it is not illustrated but is signalled when it can be observed on the screen. This is hardly surprising; announcers have to improvise an explanation at the last minute, when the pictures arrive. They cannot but relate, in a superior tone, what they are seeing.

Well, there is no need to worry about this. Historians have other sources than television to study the Balkan crisis and the Poll Tax demonstration. Right – but that is not the point. What worries me is not the inaccuracy of television news but its impact on viewers. People who are fed, every day, with flimsy information, deprived of any background, delivered without any interpretation, will conceive of history as a collection of timeless and unrelated events. Television, for sure, does not ignore the past; it could even be argued that it takes it to be its own property. It is true that it seldom expands on foregone centuries and zoom in mostly onto the dictatorships, wars and crisis of the 20th century, but it uses extensively its archive, necessarily oriented toward past periods, or the memories of the people it interviews. However, everything, all details are told without any hint of criticism. While historians attempt at synthesizing the data they have collected and offer possible explanations, television is content with stating mere facts and illustrating them. What it displays is not so much the development of a new theoretical approach to the past as the unspoken assertion that things speak for themselves and do not need to be replaced in context. Compared to such a seemingly spontaneous, genuine vision of events, historians' history looks abstract and excessively sophisticated.

When Stephen Peet began his famous series, *Yesterday's Witness*, in 1969, spectators were enthralled. Eventually, it was the real thing, people's experience and deep feelings instead of anonymous portraits, a profile of the average factory worker or rank and file. Stephen Peet's programme lasted more than 12 years. It was imitated by countless filmmakers. Life stories have become the main source of television history, all the more so that they are easy to produce and almost costless.

My last 'document' is a short extract from *The Factory*, a film by Bob Watson broadcast on Channel Four in January1984. A worker talks about the attitude of the management and stresses its total ignorance of the workers. In face of such a programme, my reaction is twofold. On the one hand I find the testimony moving and impressive. It is obvious that this is the first time this lady has a chance to express openly and publicly her complaints and we guess that there is, at the root of her talk, a long-lasting bitterness. I cannot help thinking of one of the best books on the industrial proletariat, E.P. Thompson's *The Making of the English Working Class*: here is a very intelligent, sensitive, penetrating volume about the life, hopes, daily problems, misery and sufferings of factory workers. Still, Thompson is unable to convey as vividly as Watson's film the anger and resentment of a lady who has wasted 20 yeas of her life without ever getting a nod of approval from the management. However, from an historical point of view, there is little to be learnt from this statement; everybody knows there is a gap between executives and wage earners and that the former do not care about the opinion of the latter.This was true in the Ancient world, the Medieval Ages the modern times and will probably be still true in the centuries to come. What is more, given the fact that there is little information in this discourse, the filmmaker, however sympathetic he was to the lady, has found it necessary to 'decorate' the words by introducing first a fancy picture of the worker, filmed behind her machine, and then a useless allusion to the offices in which the clerks seem to be protected against any contact with the workers. Spectators' attention is diverted by the pictures that prevent them from fully perceiving the exasperation of the lady. Television film-makers contend that all events, however insignificant they look, may be of importance and that there is always something to be learnt from personal memories. This is a very attractive assumption. It is not my job, here, to criticize either oral history or the television programmes based on testimonies. All I want to stress is that, for historians, oral testimonies and films based mostly on individual statements are highly problematic.

A first problem is the variety of questions tackled on television. The man or the woman in the street are permanently interviewed and give their opinion about everything. I write 'they' but I had better say 'we' since, potentially, we are all the actors/interviewees of the small screen. We are twice here, while we are watching television, personally and through our proxy, the person there on the box who is potentially ourselves. As they are continuously questioned, just like us, 'the others' no longer appear so remote; the distance between us and them has been reduced to very little. A film such as *The Factory* introduces us, alternately, to the management and to the workers, we listen to them, approvingly or disapprovingly, and we tend to forget what separates us from them, the factory which is their world, not ours. What testimonies tend to blur is the notion of context. They are also likely to fade out the limit between reportage and fiction since, when tuning in, we often have problems in deciding whether what we are offered is a documentary, a reality show or a serial. Here are a few people, locked up in one room; the camera moves slowly from left to right, trying to catch the face of those who are speaking, the dialogue sounds familiar, it turns on practicalities, just like our talk with a neighbour we have met on our way home. People talk about themselves and about their concerns so that what lingers on the box is endlessly reflexive of the humdrum of daily life. It has to be admitted that, sometimes, the interviewees have taken part in important events but they seldom attempt at giving an accurate, rational account of what has happened; their autobiographical memories are rather reconstructions based on affective and impassioned factors. Contaminated with information from similar events, recollections change over the years as people encounter new experiences.

What we remember about an event depends on when and for what purpose we are remembering. It reflects our beliefs about ourselves and the world at present. There is also a tendency to dramatize and elaborate in order to evoke the emotion people wish their listeners to feel. In particular, the desire to belong can drive people to recount their stories to meet the expectations of the group. The two features of television I have mentioned, the flattening of a time which seems to have no more density, which never changes, and the preponderance of individual memories over general problems can easily be referred to what has been labelled 'post-modernism', a philosophical attitude whose most decisive characteristics are the rejection of large-scale, comprehensive social theories and the conviction that no discourse can be favoured over another because all kinds of explanations are always liable to detailed rebuttal. Being born from the crisis of grand, all-encompassing theories, post-modernism postulates that it is the task of historians neither to 'interpret' the past nor to explain how and why events occurred. Post-modernism is not a theory, which could be easily discussed and the validity of which could be tested; it is a state of mind widely diffused among people who do not even know that they are post-modern. The post-modern approach starts from the fragmented, from disconnected objects, from disjointed words, from the very simple acts performed daily by people. It is preoccupied with potential social signifiers, looks for symbols, or representations which take place in the head of individuals but which, while being private thoughts or images, could also be common to many people.

Post-modernism is, to a certain extent, a mere fashion. But what matters, for us, is that it is also a conception of history or rather that it encompasses a vision of how history should be told. The everlasting speeches typical of television, in which uttering words is more important than communicating a meaning, are an aspect of the contemporary relationship to the world (therefore of the history of this world). There is on television something new, strange but also interesting, which is the representation, the staging of duration. Viewers who meet the same questions, the same scenery, every night experience a kind of long-lasting connection with others, with society and with the passing of time which is fairly different from the short-lived liaison they would form with a character or a group described in a book or a film. Television opens a window on latent history, on what human beings endure without knowing that their pain, their efforts and their rest are history. The understanding of the past that our contemporaries have already encountered on their small screen, and that they will soon ask us to introduce into our books, is a less literary, less theoretical, less explanatory but more vivid and human one.

How shall we meet that demand? I am not aiming at offering a solution. I want to suggest that historians have to face an unprecedented situation and that, maybe, they are no longer in a position to decree what is or is not history. A great many amateurs, who watch television daily and are used to surfing on the Web, are accumulating a tremendous quantity of data; they tend therefore to consider that they know what the study of the past consists of and they ask historians to provide them with many more 'facts.' At the same time television, far from being simply another means of information, contributes to create an original way of being immersed in the world, of participating in the present without caring for the meaning of what is happening and of forgetting that the passing of time is a major historical factor. Absence of hierarchy between the details that seem all of equal importance and flattening of chronology are the core of this vision of the past. History, on the other hand, attempts at making sense of foregone events by ordering them and referring them to their relative position along the years: there is a wide gap between this approach and the conception of former times built on the basis of television and the Web. So what we historians have to do is to contrive an original understanding of the past that will combine a permanent attention to the small, the particular, the individual, and a full awareness of the importance of evolution. Let us recognize that this is not going to be an easy task.

Historians and TV Archives

Luisa Cigognetti

The Regional Institute Ferruccio Parri is part of a national network of institutes which were established after the second world war with the aim of conserving all the documentary materials regarding the resistance movements against nazi-fascism and to promote research activities on that period in European contemporary history.

Today, however, the Istituto Parri and the others throughout Italy have undergone a transformation and have become centers for the study of contemporary history in a larger sense, more inclusive and less specific. The Istituto Parri, in particular, today is characterized by two kinds of activities: one deals with historical research, that is, projects that are organized within the Institute itself or commissioned by other state or private agencies, finalized in publications, films, conferences and exhibitions. The other deals with the conservation and diffusion of its archives containing books, paper documents, photos and audio-visual materials that pertain to the period from the beginning of the 20th century to the 1970s.

There is surely no need any longer to insist on the importance of television for historians in contemporary society. For most people the small screen is the most important source of information about the world. It puts its viewers in contact with far off countries. It reveals, instantly, events that are taking place at various points around the globe and, in some cases, television is the cause of these events. Television, more than newspapers, is a documentary source and an historical agent. An historian of the 20th century cannot ignore it. But dealing with televised material is much more difficult and complicated than dealing with printed material, or even films.

The first difficulty arises when we have to know *where* the material has been stored. In some cases the networks have their own archives, but sometimes they have given a part or the whole footage to archives which can be public or private. The International Federation of Television Archives (FIAT) has accomplished an enormous undertaking in locating existing sources, but their results are not completely available to historians. Since 1994 the European Community has sponsored the Map-TV Memory Archives Programme. This Programme is intended to make a census of the existing audio-visual collections in European countries. The project has resulted in a guide, published in 1995 with the British Universities Film and Video Council (BUFVC), which represents a very useful instrument for historians, even if it does not meet all the historians needs. The Map-TV programme was not intended initially to help researchers, but to encourage the making of European programmes, by establishing contacts between archive holders and producers and informing the latter about resources available for their films.

Getting information about the location of materials is only the first step. Next we need to know if and how it has been catalogued. The issue of inventories is problematic and extremely complex. Generally, the cataloguing operation has been carried out with the end purpose of a further television broadcast. Thus the archivists have noted content that can be re-used. Their logic seldom tallies with the questions that historians are used to asking.

I want to discuss an example, borrowed from the Italian public television archive. It is part of a news programme broadcast on 8 August 1980. The introduction talks about a bomb, exploded at the Bologna rail station, which killed 80 people. What we see is the speaker talking about the explosion, the casualties, the aftermath of the event, and so on. At one point he explains that the members of an extreme right-wing group, and in particulary a man called Marco Affatigato, already a suspect in murder cases, are under suspicion and that police are working on this assumption.

How had this document been catalogued in the Italian archive? The archivist noted the title of the news programme, *Telegiornale 2*, and used the key-words: 'Italy-Police' and 'Italy-Journalists'. Obviously, if in the time to come, somebody wants to find images of policemen or journalists out of the context of the Bologna slaughter, they will easily find it. A historian interested in the event will not be able to identify the first news broadcast after the explosion. Indeed many generations of archivists have been involved in the description/cataloguing of television programmes, each one having their own way of working. Historians therefore need to be informed of the way in which catalogues have been created. The existence of a catalogue does not necessarily mean that it is accessible. Moreover, because the equipment used in production has changed dramatically over the last half century, some visual material exists on the shelves but cannot be viewed, because the video players for, say, the two inches tapes do not exist anymore. Historical researchers have therefore to accept another condition: a pre-selection stipulated only by the practical availability of footage.

A further factor to be considered is the enormous quantity of material. In Italy, in Great Britain, in France, and in other countries the total amount of news broadcast every day comes to more than twenty four hours, so that an historian who would like to see all the news broadcast in 1997 for example would have to spend more than a year, full time, in front of his videoscreen. Historians and all those involved in television thus have no choice but to start considering new ways of carrying out a legitimate and accurate selection of the available material.

Viewing alone is not enough. The moving image and its soundtrack cannot be quoted as if it were a piece of text: it must be shown. Here the problem of quotation arises and involves, in particular, the entangled topic of rights. Today every television archive – public or private – grants images only at very high prices that are often prohibitive for historians. If they do not want to lose the opportunity to study the 20th century – and the centuries to come – historians have to begin to tackle the problems that television presents.

In December 1998 the Institute organised, with Pierre Sorlin, a seminar between people directly involved in the use of televised material. We invited four archivists, from various European countries, to explain to us how television archiving works in their countries together with a group of historians who have already had experience in using television archives for their research.

Before the meeting we sent either the archivists or the historians a questionnaire with the crucial questions. The archives invited were:

> The BFI National Film & Television Archive (GB)
>
> The (public company) ZDF Archive (Germany)
>
> The INA (Institution National de l'Audovisuel) Depot Legal de la Radio Television (France)
>
> The Teche RAI (public company) Archive (Italy).

The questions we sent to the archivists were:

> What kind of material exists in your Archive?
>
> Are these productions of your television network – have you got the rights? – are there also other kind of materials?
>
> What are the general criteria for selecting the material to place in the Archive?
>
> What kind of catalogue exists?
>
> How and who can gain access to the catalogues?
>
> How and who can gain access to the materials?
>
> How do you face the problem of the materials, standards and formats, which have been changing over time?
>
> How and who can gain access to the materials?

The answers of the archivists delineated a pattern for the overall situation, which is different from one archive to another, but with similar problems. Not all countries have one national television archive, like Great Britain and France. In Germany, for example, there is no centralized archive, but every company – such as the public companies ARD and ZDF – have their own archives.

The first nation which began to archive television sources was Great Britain. The National Film Archive officially became the National Film and Television Archive in 1993, but its first Television Officer was employed as far back as 1960 and it has been archiving television materials since then. In Germany during the 1970s it was realized that there are certain measures that are prerequisites for the preservation and availability of stocks. However it is only during the last 5 years that the situation changed and the broadcasting archives developed in an extraordinary way and found better organizational structures. The French Inatheque was born only in 1995.

Television Archives are structures which have to bear very high costs and they are built by television networks – public or private – only to secure a possible further use in the creation of new programmes. Non-stop programming, satellite and digital television today generate a new importance for the archives in the process of programming. Archive material can be used to meet the increasing demand for programmes and the increasing fear of having nothing to broadcast. What is more, in order to survive in the increasing competition between networks, a cost-reduction in the area of production is necessary. This situation is common to all four archives.

Another very important question centres on the fact that archives are the visual memory of television. But who decides what is going to be kept, secured and thus remembered in the future? Obviously they choose what will be probably useful for further programmes. The archives do not preserve all the television programmes, but they have criteria for selecting material to place in the archive. The BFI NFTVA, for example, is the official archive of ITV, Channel 4 and Channel 5. There is an off-air recording scheme, funded by the ITV companies and Channel 4 and Channel 5. For the time being it keeps 27 per cent of ITV Network output, 22 per cent of Channel 4 and 17 per cent of Channel 5. This proportion corresponds to the size of the grants the Archive receive from the companies. Sometimes (perhaps three or four times a year) the archives record a complete day's output, for documentation. The INA, in order to make a link between all the different kind of selections and programmes, chooses every year, on each channel, on the same day, 7 controlled days named witness days (*Journées témoins*) during which everything is recorded, from the early morning to the end of programming.

The cataloguing rules are obviously influenced by the fact that television archives are made *for internal use only* and every archive has its own rules, often unintelligible to researchers. This is the case, for example, in Italy. Everybody can have confirmation of this when they navigate on the web, where increasingly the archives (in this case Italy, France and ZDF) keep their catalogues. The question of web catalogues is worth a discussion itself. First of all, we often meet only partial selections from the general catalogue and in addition, the data you find has been simplified in comparaison with the original archive data cards.

In the web site of INA this problem is specified and pointed out. I have tried to do a test inside this web catalogue. I selected a programme about Hiroshima and I met some difficulties because the query is split into many fields. You are asked to enter the day and the network which had broadcast the programme (if you are informed about it) and you also have to enter the genre (I could choose among 33 fields, for example Sports, History, Tourism…) and in the end you find a field called au Générique.

When I typed the word 'Hiroshima', nothing had been shown on the screen. I finally found something about Hiroshima when I typed the word 'history' in the query field. The screen displayed 295 items among which something about the topic was present. Moreover, web catalogues represent a contradiction: what is the point of placing a television archives catalogue on the net, available to everyone, if you are not allowed to access the material easily?

Another very important question regards the national legislation about television archives. Some countries, like France, Great Britain and Germany have a law which obliges companies to preserve television sources, but the rules differ from one country to another and many other European nations do not have any regulations. Furthermore the copyright laws are still an unsolved problem. Germany has a good law on copyright, but every broadcasting company regulates the access to its own programmes stocks ie for commercial and non-commercial purposes. However, even with a very liberal practice of use, it would be utopian to believe that the German broadcasting companies would be able to comply comprehensively with the extending requests of the educational and scientific sector. Something special has to be said regarding the archive of the Italian company RAI. Untill two years ago RAI did not have an archive in the strict sense of the word. It did have a storehouse in which everybody who worked in the company could take clips for internal use. Today they are still discussing how to create an archive, what and how to conserve. Furthermore, in Italy legislation about audio-visual sources, does not exist; neither do laws about rights.

We sent a questionnaire also to the historians (with the main questions regarding their relationship to archives):

Why did you decide to make your research in television Archives and use television sources in your work?

What kind of (practical) problems did you face in entering TV Archives?

What kind of (theoretical) problems (selection criteria, description standards etc) did you face?

What about the television rights?

How did you use the visual sources in your work?

Do you think it would be useful to use TV materials in historical research?

Do you think there is something impossible to study without access to TV sources?

I have already tackled the general problems we have to meet and I'll be content with mentioning a few practical questions:

TV archives in Europe are not founded and organized for the academic researchers' use.

Members of universities are a disturbance factor in the daily routine of archivists and the places to view the material in the archives are restricted.

Because of the strict copyright regulations and because of the changing standards over time, it is difficult for a researcher to obtain material.

I shall end by borrowing an image from Joan Kristine Bleicher, from the University of Hamburg. She used in describing the relationship between historians and archivists: in which the famous story by Jorge Luis Borges entitled *The Library of Babel*, both sides take part in an unsolvable conflict of diverging interests. Both sides are forced by the special demands of their work to insist on their positions. On one side researchers crave for material to reconstruct the history of television. On the other side archivists fear the total destruction of their materials by the academic intruders.

At the Istituto Parri, in the time to come, we would like to keep on discussing these subjects. The main purpose is to try to set, with the help of other partners, a sort of interface which can enable different structures and points of view (which belong to historians and archivists) to communicate and understand.

The History of Television through the Internet: A few notes on the project www.histv.net

André Lange

History of television is progressively becoming an academic discipline. There is no doubt about the fact that it will become a major field of investigation for understanding the second half of the 20th century. Resources for such a discipline are however still scarce and fragmented. From this observation, I decided to create a website on the History of Television that may become a focal point for researchers and students, but also for the large public, interested by this emerging field.

At the origin, the project was a modest one: in charge of a lecture at the Free University of Brussels (ULB) and living in Strasbourg, I thought that a website could be a good communication tool with students. The initial website, opened in February 1999, was a bit rough with a lot of technical mistakes and content reduced to some articles and bibliographical notes. Two events decided me to make something more ambitious from this initial modest project. The first one was the almost miraculous discovery in an *alfarabist* (a book antiquarian) in Porto of the very first brochure published on the project of seeing at distance: *La télescopie électrique basée sur l'emploi du sélénium*, published (in French, Portuguese and English) in 1880 by the Portuguese Professor Adriano de Paiva.

The second event was the fact that the site had been selected by the Cité des Sciences et de l'Industrie – the leading French Museum of Education to Sciences – as one of the 50 best educational websites in French for the exhibition in the year 2000 'Plaisir d'apprendre'. With a slow and delayed start the French internet was in 1999 – and still is to a large extent in 2000 – looking for good content in the education area. To be selected together with the Bibiothèque Nationale, L'Musée de l'Homme, the IRCAM and a couple of other highly public supported cultural and educational institutions was an exciting challenge for a hobby-like project .

This is a short description of the content of the site (which is divided into 5 parts).

The introduction (only in French) introduces various aspects of the history of television (the history of television as technological system, a political and social history of television, cultural history, the history of television creators and the history of television works).

For the English-speaking reader the 'On-line anthology of early texts on television' will be the most accessible, as it contains a lot of texts originally published in English or translated into English.

Complementary to the anthology is the section: 'Questions d'histoire de la télévision' (also only in French). This area introduces several articles on some moments in the history of television, in particular on the period prior to the World War II, that are not necessarily well known.

The 'Mary Néant project' found the origin of its title in some lines of James Joyce's *Finnegans Wake*. In Joyce's text, television – as I understand it – is called 'Mary Nothing'. I liked the Philippe Lavergne's translation in French as 'Mary Néant'. This part of the site (far from being completed) is a research project on the television in its relation to the other arts. You will find in it quotations of television by writers such as Jules Verne, HG Wells, Mark Twain, Marcel Proust and F.T. Marinetti. There are also some articles and references to relations between dance and television, television and graphic arts, not to forget television making with reference to television.

The 'Resources' section offers 120 pages of bibliography on research in mass communication, the history of television in its various aspects and a lot of links to interesting sites.

The most developed part of the website is the 'Anthology of early texts on television.' This includes the reproduction of more than 100 texts published before 1900 on the project of 'far-seeing.'

There are at least two excellent reference books on the early technological developments of television: A. Abramson, *The History of Television*, 1880-1941, (Mac Farland & Company, Inc. Publishers, Jefferson, North Carolina and London, 1987) and R.W. Burns *Television – an international history of the formative years*, (IEE/Peregrinus, London, 1998). The two books have been my companions for establishing my collection of early texts on television. Both are written by engineers – one American, the other English – who did an exceptional work of identification of patents and scientific publications, related to publications. Both books have such a level of erudition that they could discourage anybody to undertake further research. However, my attention was drawn to the fact that Abramson's reference to De Paiva's brochure was second hand and a bit imprecise. Getting my own copy of this brochure was like possessing some treasure to share. Which I did by reproducing it in JPEG pictures on my site.

The De Paiva brochure is a quite curious publication: as early as 1878, De Paiva, a Professor of Physics at the University of Porto, published articles in scientific Portuguese publications on the possibility of using selenium to transmit pictures through electricity. He was the first to formulate this proposal, but he never really experimented with it. The final statement of De Paiva is quite prophetic of the world wired society:

'With these two marvellous instruments [telephone and telectroscope], fixed on one spot of the globe, man will be able to extend to the whole of it, his visual and auditory faculties. Ubiquity, from having been utopian, will become perfect reality. Then, conducting wires charged with all important missions will cross and recross at the surface of the earth; they will be the mysterious duets which will bring to the observer the impressions received by artificial organs, which human genius has made to compass any distance. And, just as the complexity of nervous filaments can give an idea of the superior perfection of an animal, those metallic filaments, nerves of another order, will testify to the high degree of civilization of the monster organism – humanity.'

De Paiva's idea was rapidly picked up by other scientists in the world, including the French notaire Constantin Senlecq who is generally hailed – at least in France – as one of the first fathers of the television project. His brochure published in 1880 was nothing else than a claim of paternity, providing evidences and press articles to defend the priority of the idea. In a sense, it is the first publication of the history of television.

I rapidly became aware of the fact that both Abramson and Burns had not identified all the existing early contributions on television. Probably because they are English-speakers, they did not fully investigate the French-speaking and also German-speaking publications. The discovery in the library of Strasbourg University of another brochure by the Austrian Major Benedict Schöffler, *Die Phototelegraphie und das Elektrische Fernsehen* (Wilhelm Braumüller, Wien und Leipzig, 1898) convinced me that a more systematic investigation could reveal further lost contributions. And there were indeed many. After one year of investigation the collection of texts has grown to more than 100 references, making a total of more than 300 html pages of documents in French, Portuguese, English, German, Italian, Spanish and Russian.

The project is not completed yet. The collection of notices is still to be finalised, as well as the analysis of the process of scientific communication leading to the final invention of a 'true' television. But this work in progress already provides – I hope – a first and unique tool for researchers, lecturers and students in the history of television. It also demonstrates how the Internet can change academic historical research and scientific collaboration.

I would like to stress here the role and the importance of the Internet in constituting my collection of texts and creating a network of very efficient correspondents.

The first progress is of course in the incredibly easier access to library treasuries through the Internet. Not only are catalogues accessible from home, the order of photocopies has become simple and also some very rare texts are directly accessible. A special mention should be awarded to the 'Gallica' website of the French Bibliothèque Nationale, which makes possible direct access to publications of the 18th and 19th century such as the *Giphantie de Tiphaigne de la Roche*, *Ignis* by Didier de Chousy, or popular science publications such as *Le Magasin pittoresque* or Louis Figuier's *L'Année scientifique et industrielle*, not to mention the proceedings of the Académie des Sciences. Accessing those texts directly from home, without the costly stand-by in the Bibliothèque Nationale, is an incredible change in the holistic phases.

The Internet has also allowed me to identify rapidly a number of correspondents sharing the same interest for early television. Not only did they encourage me in the project but they also helped me to identify new sources and new texts. Professor Vaz Guedes from the University of Porto provided me with useful material on De Paiva; Karl Beneke, a researcher in the chemistry of celluloid at the University of Kiel, provided me with original information and documents on Raphael Edward Liesegang, the German author of the first book on television and the creator of the German word *Fernsehen*. Jim Zwick, the editor of a wonderful site on Mark Twain, pointed me to the unexpected texts by Mark Twain on Jan Szczepanik, the 'Austrian Edison', inventor of the telelectroscope. I should also mention the friendly contribution of Russell Naughton, from Melbourne University, editor of the site 'Adventures in Cybersound', which, amongst others things, found the astonishing texts by Frank Parsons and Samuel Golden Rule Jones on the future political uses of the telectroscope ('The world will be at our feet'). Those 1899 contributions, probably the first political texts on television, were identified by Russell on the site of the Toledo University, thanks to a powerful search tool. Melvin Rees from the Patent Office spend some time in finding the forgotten W. Gemill 1886 patent on tele-photography, apparently the first one in the world dedicated to a system of 'far-seeing'. Geraldine D'Unger was so happy to find, thanks again to a powerful search tool, a one-line quotation about the 'telephot' of her grand-father Robert D'Unger (a physician better know as Edgar Allen Poe's doctor), that she sent me original material and pictures. Last but not least, the web allowed me to discover and contact the Scottish engineer Don MacLean who has restored and edited on his website (http://www.dfm.dircon.co.uk) the recording of television in 30 lines of John Logie Baird. I was so admiring of Don's work that I translated his site in French in exchange for the right to reproduce the elegant 'Realplayer' picture of Betty Bolton singing for the BBC camera around 1932-1935. I cannot imagine that the pre-Internet academic life could have allowed me to contact so rapidly and precisely such precious and passionate fellows.

The site has rapidly reached the point that I found astonishing myself: more than 15,000 visitors in one year. In August 2000, more than 30 per cent of visitors were from the US, 19 per cent from France, 5 per cent from Australia, 2 per cent from Canada and less than 4 per cent from Belgium. So, I am not quite sure that my students of the University of Brussels are really using the site. The mails I receive from them indicate the perplexity of people in their 20's when confronted with the concept of the history of television. Most of them claim not to watch television – they are students in Film studies and share the French dominant view that cinema is everything and television nothing – and complain about the difficulties of computer access in the University library. I received messages indicating that the site reaches other publics than the target Belgian students: television workers, journalists, children (looking for *the* inventor of television), but also students from France, Canada or North Africa asking for further information. The site is indexed in other academic sites in Belgium, France, UK and US, but also in Canada, in Germany, in Russia, in Spain, in Peru, in Australia. Cultural websites and sites by TV-series fans also link to it, indicating that the academic approach to the history of television transcends the boundaries of the University.

The number of websites in English that are dedicated to the history of television confirms the general interest in this field. They include some academic contributions, but also a quite important number of 'amateur' contributions specialising in the biographical approach to some inventors, dedication to some national or local television company, or the most classical 'fans pages' on a specific series or serial. Strangely enough, the television websites are quite poor on historical material. To my knowledge, RAI is the only European TV company providing archive pictures through the web (http://www.teche.rai.it), going back to the announcement of the election of the 3rd President of the Republic, Giovanni Gronchi, in 1955. The transfer of archive pictures on Real Player does not provide excellent quality of picture, but at least some of the substance of the television from the 1950s to the 1990s is there.

The historian of television, for whom access to the archives remains difficult, would like to see this kind of anthology becoming more general and, of course, of a better technical quality. It is doubtful however that the publication of TV archives on the Internet will soon become a general practice: copyright issues, not to speak of the technical costs, will still be the major obstacle for on-line transmission of such material. As the reissue of TV historical material on video remains limited to some basic cult series, it is not difficult to bet that the access to archives will remain for a long time the privilege of a small number of researchers. A country like France has taken a major initiative with the creation of the Inathèque, providing access to a vast amount of digitalised TV archives, but in a small country like Belgium, where the current television system is in a financial turmoil, the creation of a true system of access is only becoming a structured academic claim, as illustrated by the first conference on the History of television that was organised in October 2000 by the Catholic University of Louvain-la-Neuve.

The Internet as a tool for the history of television is then a paradox: as you cannot use illustrated material – video or still picture – still under copyright protection, you have as the only solution to come back to the written text, JPEG pictures of old scientific magazines in the public domain. You couldn't possibly cover the pre-history of television like this, but it is clear that only major projects with strong funding could propose a sophisticated use of the Internet for using the new medium as a fruitful historical instrument of the true period of television, the second half of the 20th century. In a sense, my fear is that the television organisations will take care of this themselves, without the support of historians or of researchers in mass communication. With a few exceptions, the existing TV programmes on television history have been or are quite disappointing, from a critical point of view. They more often flatter viewers' nostalgia rather than providing enlightenment on the past. The broadcasters' strategy towards the Internet is still unclear, but using the Net to write a critical and documented history of television is obviously the last topic on the agenda. But who knows? In 1900, the French electrician M. Mascart, when opening the International Congress of Electricity in the Paris Exhibition – where the word 'television' had been coined for the first time by the Russian Constantin Perskyi – said that it would probably be indiscreet to ask electricity to transmit pictures. Would it be indiscreet to ask big sister television to use the Benjamin medium for helping us to write her own critical history, and the history of half a century?

The Colour of War: A poacher among the gamekeepers?

Adrian Wood

For the past 25 years I have been privileged to work for, and indeed have been indulged by, some of Britain's best producers and directors. Privileged because they have asked me to find archive film material for some of the most prestigious documentaries and series produced over this period. Indulged because when asked to invest in my lengthy visits to archives on four continents, they have found the resources required.

My work on historical documentaries began in the late 1970s. This was at a time when ITV was obligated to broadcast factual programmes in prime-time hours. At that time I worked for one of the largest contributors of documentary and factual programming to the UK's commercial ITV network, Thames Television. Thames, since its creation in 1968, employed specialist researchers whose sole task was to locate, identify, duplicate and ensure that all appropriate permissions were obtained, from both primary and secondary rights holders, for the reuse of 'library footage'.

My sense then was that, other than in the US, the situation in the UK was unique in so far that these specialist film researchers existed. It also meant that where adequate funding existed we were often able to visit archives and commercial libraries virtually around the globe. This enabled us to acquire a vast knowledge of collections in numerous countries. Historians amongst us were few and far between.

Sometimes, it is easy to overlook that this was at a time when hardly any film footage was held on videotape, when VHS was no doubt only a pipe dream of Panasonic and the Internet was being developed by the Pentagon as a communication system in its 'war' against Communism. The telex was the only means of transmitting text messages rapidly. The only possibility to see material was to have it duplicated based on the basis of textural records. This rarely made any mention of damage to the material or decomposition.

One could hire a local researcher if there was only a small volume but that did not permit qualitative judgements to be made regarding three versions of the same film. It is clearly of importance not just to obtain the right material but obtain it in the best possible quality. If for instance a 16mm dupe exists of a film in the US but there is a 35mm original in Germany clearly one should go to the source. The researcher's skill is to gather this information and acquire material accordingly. This of course then, and now, was not a cheap method of production.

I began my work in German archives, perhaps strangely, not for footage of Germany but material of the then Soviet Union. I was working with Raye Farr on a Thames /WGBH co-production on Stalin's Russia produced by Philip Whitehead and Jonathan Lewis. At that time we had no guarantee of access to the Soviet Archives. We might well have had to be reliant on Soviet materials held at sources such as ETV and the Imperial War Museum in London, DEFA and the Staatliches Arkiv in the German Democratic Republic and commercial sources such as Chronos Film in West Berlin. Chronos, like ETV, had long been a discreet conduit of materials to the West from the Socialist bloc.

For me it was a major challenge, not least because I possessed scant knowledge of the Soviet Union – other than the propaganda I had grown up with. Neither did I speak German, or indeed Russian. When interviewed for the job, I, like the other applicants, was asked how I would cope with my lack of language skills. Apparently I got the job due to my simple reply of 'hiring an interpreter'.

Fortunately, we were able to access the Soviet archives and much material was obtained for use outside the Soviet Union for the first time. I say fortunately because we were only the second 'western' team to have access to the closed Soviet collection at Krasnogorsk.

The production harnessed a large team of internationally renowned historians. Their collective input obtained through meetings in London, Moscow and Boston gave an imprimatur to the production that enabled remarkable access to be obtained to the Soviet archives. The *Glasnost* and *perestroika* of the Gorbachev period had seen the beginnings of an independent Russian television production sector. Thames Television collaborated with one such organisation, American-Soviet Kino Initiative (ASK). ASK's function was not only to arrange permissions for filming throughout the Soviet Union and the necessary travel arrangements but to prise open the door of the film archives.

Following many weeks of discussion, coercion and the occasional bunch of flowers, approval was granted for my first visit to the Archive. The Archive had been described earlier to me by the British researcher who was the first foreigner there. He painted a bleak picture of it being under the control of the KGB. His daunting description of the officer who oversaw all activities in the Archive did little to bring about confidence in my potential for success. This 'KGB Officer' controlled all film screenings and switched off the lamp of the screening table at all times except when the precise fragment of film to be viewed was in the 'gate' of the Steenbeck.

Other people, prior to my arrival in Moscow, insisted that the Archive was only accessible by helicopter. It took little time to discover that the Archive was less than an hour's drive from the Kremlin and the Russian lady charged with screening films for visitors endeavoured to preserve the life of bulbs by only burning them when it was necessary.

The archive at Krasnogorsk was, and to this day is, a veritable Aladdin's Cave: so much had been preserved there and was available in pristine quality. The depth of the collection was astonishing. In all, 66 different newsreels and cinema magazines were produced between 1917 and 1985. All were catalogued and contained in the Krasnogorsk collection. The care lavished on the collection by the State and the Archive staff was breathtaking.

Newsreels and magazine serials were produced for almost every sector of Soviet society. Far richer materials existed than the few materials exchanged for propaganda purposes with occasional Allies in the West. Often overlooked is material shot outside the Soviet Union and used in Soviet newsreels to show the failure of the capitalist system. Wonderful imagery of the early Nazi suppression of the KPD in 1930s Germany lay unused for decades.

Many unique materials, primarily of the pre-Revolutionary period, were obtained from sources both in Germany and the US. The success of my work led to many further visits to Moscow and its archives. It caused me to gain a great insight into the strengths and weaknesses of the collections and indeed of myself. Despite more than ten years of collaboration, some doors to this day appear to remain firmly closed.

Recently I have been endeavouring to locate original source materials contained within post-war Soviet compilation films. These originals are neither held at Krasnogorsk nor in the *Gosfilm* collection at Bielye Stolby. Every endeavour to access the film collection of the former-KGB has met with failure. One is still reliant on the aid of local specialists and archivists whether it is in Russia or elsewhere. It is their expertise, and one's personal relationship with them that cannot be under estimated and should always be remembered when one's successes are measured- either by oneself or, more importantly, by one's peers.

The vast majority of my work since the early 1980s has dealt with either the two World Wars or Soviet history. I grew up in England at a time when many revelled in two victories over Germany. On occasion, television's apparent obsession with these victories leads broadcasters to fail to present so much of recent, but virtually lost, history to a wide and general audience.

My earliest recollections of television after '*The Flower Pot Men*' seem to be '*The Great War*' and '*Victory at Sea*' series'. Both portrayed war as it had been presented to the general public by cinema newsreels – in monochrome. After all, television was black and white until the late 1960s. Indeed, if I recall correctly my first memory of '*World at War*' was in a Common Room on a black and white TV set. It was only when the series received one of its many and justified 'repeats' that I realised some of the episodes contained colour actuality footage. This had been shot principally by the various US armed services. What I then failed to understand was exactly how large a volume of colour film had been exposed and actually existed from World War II.

It was my work in Russia that revealed that it was not merely the German, British and Americans who were recording the war, or aspects of it, in colour but the Soviets too. The 1938 and 1939 Moscow Sport parades were filmed in both black and white and colour. The colour versions utilised a three negative colour system that had first been released in Russia in 1938. Developed jointly by the Mosfilm Studios and the Soviet National Film Institute, *NIKFI*, it was used for the production of seven other documentary productions before the war ended in 1945.

Sadly the 3-strip negatives for all but one of these appear to have been destroyed in the 1960s. It was explained to me in Moscow that a former archive technical director saw no sense in apparently storing three black and white negatives of the same film!

Colour film before the war was an expensive medium. It remained so until the 1970s. Even though Frederik Villiers utilised Charles Urban's Kinemacolor system as early as 1912 in the Balkans War and subsequently in World War I, it was not until World War II that extensive use of colour footage was made. Even then the cost of colour stock, its development and mass duplication kept it reserved for very special events. Available for the 16mm amateur filmmaker from 1928 as Kodacolor or the mid 1930s as either Kodachrome or Agfacolor its extra cost deterred many amateur cinematographers from using it.

Occasionally the cinema newsreel production companies of the 1930s decided to use colour stock for appropriate subjects such as Royal events. Their 'competitors' and fellow members of the Newsreel Association of Great Britain were quick to admonish them for 'setting a dangerous commercial precedent'.

Much of the material that was shot professionally was either blown up to 35mm from 16mm or turned into black and white for general release. One notable exception was the short-lived German wartime propaganda newsreel *Panorama* – with very limited release compared to its black and white counterpart *Deutsche Wochenschau*. Bastinier's stunning colour material shot on the Eastern Front in 1943/44 was used in *Deutsche Wochenschau* in black and white. Similarly, much of the colour gun camera footage of the RAF and USAAF was used for general distribution as 35mm black & white. Many of the fighter aircraft of the Luftwaffe, the RAF and USAAF equipped their aircraft with gun-trigger activated cameras mounted in the aircraft wings. These served the purpose of verifying 'kills'.

It was Lutz Becker's doggedness that brought the Eva Braun home movies back to us in colour in 1970. After much wrangling with archive staff at the US National Archives the original element was finally extracted from the vault and found to be in colour as Becker had maintained. In a *British Pathe* newsreel of March 1947 not only were the camera operators misidentified, they were actually Eva Braun and

Heinrich Hoffman Jr, but the black and white version was 'flipped' prior to distribution to the commercial newsreel companies for use as propaganda.

Before the outbreak of war many amateur filmmakers in Germany had begun to use the German colour stock Agfacolor as well as the Kodachrome stock. Two such people were Hans Feierabend and Josef Eckstaller. Both were members of the *Bund Deutsche Film Amateure* branch in Munich. Membership of the BDFA, at that time, was open only to those who could prove their Aryan purity. The Munich branch contained 40 members, including 3 women.

The material shot by Feierabend and Eckstaller has been inter-cut over the years. These images were first used extensively by Luke Holland's 1993 production for Channel 4: 'Good Morning Mr Hitler'. They reveal the splendour of the Nazi 'Day of German Culture' in Munich in July 1939 and illustrate the seductive 'beauty' of the regime. Neither the colour materials nor the black and white newsreel record portray the horrors that had already begun to fall upon the 'enemies' within Germany.

An article by Craig Brown which appeared in *The Sunday Times* on 23 May 1993 perhaps summed up the effect of this colour film: 'The colour had an uncanny effect, transforming evil back into its original semblance of innocence...days of hope and innocence rendered vile by knowledge...'.

Official policy in the US Armed Forces during World War II stated that 16mm colour was only to be used in an emergency. It was perceived as a far inferior second option. This was despite the fact that many combat cameramen preferred the smaller cameras and the consequently reduced burden with which to wade ashore on an invasion beachhead. A comparison by Col. Frankly Adreon, in charge of the US Marine Corps Headquarters Photo Section, estimated that a 75 per cent reduction in both weight and volume could be achieved by using 16mm colour instead of the recommended 35mm black and white. This was a vital consideration when every roll of film and piece of equipment was to be carried over vital military supply routes. 16mm also enabled a cameraman to shoot for three minutes instead of one without reloading. Despite these advantages, both the US Navy and Army Air Force were formally opposed to the use of 16mm colour for general combat coverage. As late as June 1944, official US Navy policy was to use 'no more 16mm than absolutely necessary'. Between June 1943 and August 1945 the US Army's 3908th Signal Service Battalion exposed 20 million feet of 35mm black and white (3700 hours) and less than 5 million feet of 16mm black and white (approximately 2300 hours). Kodachrome exposure amounted to 70,000 feet (approximately 32 hours). Whilst in 1943 the US Army Air Force shipped to the US over half a million feet of 35mm black and white (around 95 hours) for development but only 40,000 feet of 16mm (less than 19 hours).

In part, this reticence to use 16mm colour was brought about by the apparently poor results achieved by Darryl Zanuck during his work in North Africa for the US Army Signal Corps. Little notice was taken of the fact that Zanuck was supplied with fewer cameramen than he had requested and that some of his best original materials were lost when the Germans sank the ship on which it was being stored.

Two US colour documentary films released in 1944 did much to bring about a change in official attitudes to the utilisation of colour film. *The Fighting Lady*, a US Navy production supervised by Edward Steichen and produced by *March of Time* founder Louis de Rochemont, told the story of the aircraft-carrier based war in the Pacific. Mostly shot aboard the USS Yorktown it contained material from other US carriers. Its aim was to present a microcosm of this aspect of the war in the Pacific Theatre of Operations. The other was William Wyler's film *The Memphis Belle*. Both were released through the US Office of War Information.

Wyler too resorted to the compilation of materials. When he arrived in the UK in 1942, Wyler had no clear idea of the film he wanted to make. A team accompanied Wyler from the RKO Hollywood studios including cameraman William Clothier and sound recordist Harold Tannenbaum.

Wyler relied heavily on footage shot by Detachment B of the 8th Combat Camera Unit (CCU) of the USAAF. This detachment included Daniel McGovern, who had his helmet shot off on his first mission; McGovern was later hospitalised with severe nervous collapse; George Gamble was wounded; Tony Edwards was killed in action; William Wood was shot down but walked back to freedom in six months through France & Spain; David Barker was Missing in Action, presumed dead and Irving Slater was killed in action. Tannenbaum, a 47-year-old Great War veteran was shot down and killed on his first mission for Wyler; Clothier, his RKO colleague, flew a total of 28 missions and ended his wartime service commanding the 4th CCU.

Wyler had enough material after flying four missions. It was rumoured he only flew a fifth merely to gain his Air Medal. On this fifth mission he flew, purely by chance, aboard an aircraft named 'Memphis Belle'. The B-17 was named in honour of the pilot's girlfriend back home in Memphis, Margaret Polk. En-route over the North Sea to the UK the pilot, Robert Morgan, expressed his relief on his safe return – it meant he, and his aircrew, would go back home to the US.

Wyler returned to the US in October 1943 with 20,000 feet of film that was cut down to 3,700ft. Wyler realised the significance of Morgan's comment and decided to call his film 'Twenty-Five Missions'. It was only at the last minute was it re-titled to *Memphis Belle* to make it more appealing to the perceived audience. It was put on general release in April 1944 and, as well as receiving widespread public acclaim, received many awards.

A review in the *New York Times* stated 'every last taxpayer can literally climb aboard a [Flying] Fortress [bomber] and find out for himself how it must feel to plow through a curtain of deadly flak over the target area, at the same time playing a desperate game of tag with the Luftwaffe'. The aircrew went on a nationwide US tour inspiring war workers to contribute to the war effort. Although this was filmed by Wyler nothing was incorporated in the edited film. The unedited rushes, minus the sound languish, remain unused in the US National Archives.

But it was the particular success of *The Fighting Lady* that prompted a massive increase in the volume of Kodachrome being shot. General 'Hap' Arnold, head of the US Army Air Forces Combat Camera Units, immediately set up 'Special Kodachrome Projects' and known as Special Film Projects (SFP). Created in early 1945, one unit alone had shot over 50 hours of material by May of that year.

For those who have been given the opportunity to research in the US National Archives, the colour materials which were shot have been readily available there since the early 1970s. Despite this, budgetary limitations and naiveté lead many television producers to believe that materials can be located via the Internet. Today less than 40 per cent of the US National Archives film holdings is accessible in this way. The majority of material can still only be researched on card indexes or microfilm copies of them.

Much of the German Army's filming for internal purposes was shot using 16mm. Some elements survive at the Bundesarchiv-Filmarchiv but I believe this to be only a small portion of what was produced. During 1942 German Propaganda Companies began work on two films depicting ghetto life. One was in Theresienstadt the other in Warsaw. Both films exist in edited form but neither was released. Interestingly both film units had material shot about the making of the film. The Theresienstadt material is held in the Documentary Film Studio Archives in Warsaw, the material of Warsaw has been deposited in the Bundesarchiv as well as other 16mm black & white material held at the Yivo Institute in New York.

A Moscow based archival film specialist, Victor Belyakov, first alerted me to colour material of the Warsaw Ghetto during my work for the BBC series produced by Laurence Rees, *The Nazis: A Warning from History*. The film shows, only too vividly, the horrors of existence in that place: emaciated children waiting for death on pavements, corpses slung into lime-filled pits, the humiliation of a race.

Filmed concurrently to the German propaganda film, *Das Ghetto*, it also contains multiple takes of purported German Jews entering a butchers shop to buy horsemeat as starving Polish Jews look on. A Soviet intelligence officer took the Agfacolor film original to Russia as private 'war-booty'. The officer was based in Berlin after its liberation by the Allies and was part of a team responsible for the vetting of film materials discovered in the various archives and repositories of the Reich. Luckily it did not meet the fate that most of the captured 16mm materials met in Soviet hands. Lacking 16mm equipment the Soviet solution was simple: if the film could not be viewed and thus categorised it was simply destroyed. Who knows what was lost of the evidence of Nazi barbarity? This perhaps explains the missing original black & white material which apparently shows the second Nazi experiment in mass-extermination at Mogelev, a fragment of which appears in Pare Lorentz film, *Nuremberg and Its Lessons*.

What these colour images of the Ghetto do – like so many of the colour images of this period – is to remove the distance of time. Images appear as freshly as the day they were filmed. The potential to sanitise history through the emotional buffer that monochrome can offer is stripped away.

The colour materials I have found over the years have shown me images that were seen by those who lived and died in those times as they themselves had seen them. British MP Mavis Tate spoke in a 1945 Pathe newsreel edition about the smell of death and suffering in Buchenwald she had experienced on a fact-finding visit. The pictures used by all newsreels produced by the Allies were black & white despite there being colour coverage shot by the SFP's at Buchenwald, Dachau and Matthausen. The colour images convey all but the smell of those places.

I do not believe that the decision taken to release only a black and white print was taken on the grounds of taste. I believe that it was an economic one based simply on the perceived needs of the market. At that time a colour print was approximately five times that of a black and white copy.

For most of the past two decades I have been noting every example of colour film that I encountered which would have relevance for a major presentation of materials relating to World War II. It was in 1983 that I first saw a reference at the Imperial War Museum to the use of Kodachrome by Lieutenant Graham of a British Army Film and Photo Unit operating with the Long Range Desert Group in North Africa. It caused me to ponder how much more colour footage there might be.

By 1990 I was ready to suggest the idea of compiling a film about the Second World War using only colour materials. I was met with much support from those professional colleagues who had seen colour material themselves but was spurned for almost a decade by most producers I mentioned it to. The sole exception was English producer, Jonathan Lewis. The others all doubted that a sufficient volume existed to tell a coherent story. Clearly what the film would not be able to do would be to present a complete narrative account of the entire war in all its theatres. What I did believe was that it was possible to present an overview of the conflict that gave an impression of its scale and horror.

By 1998 I was employed by Trans World International. TWI gave me immense support and encouragement. My colleague Stewart Binns and I set about the development of a 3-hour series entitled *The Second World War in Colour*, a TWI / Carlton Television production for ITV in the UK and for the History Channel in the US. The series for the first time combined officially commissioned colour materials with those of amateur filmmakers. It was broadcast in September 1999. It was followed up in 2000 by a series focussing on Britain during World War II.

These series set out to present an impression of war using authenticated film and textural records. They did not aspire to bring new insight to an academic world. Their simple aspiration was to present an overview of World War II to a modern and as wide an audience as possible.

To date they have received critical acclaim and awards in many of the countries where they have been screened. This success with audiences has led to the commissioning of a further series that demand colour archive footage to be found instead of the standard, and more easlily obtained, black and white version of the same event. This style of presentation combining authenticated pictures with contemporaneous accounts from letters and diaries gives accessibility to history across all age ranges. Many of the audience were surprised and sceptical that all the material was original colour. Whilst we did remove, digitally, the ravages of time in terms of colour fading by regrading the film, no material was 'colourised'.

Television's ability to present history to a mass audience is probably unique. The responsibility of producers and broadcasters is to present factual history. Many individuals have laboured long, hard and unsung in archives so that the fortunate few, such as myself, can bring their work to a large audience.

Fortunately today the work I am doing enables film materials to be deposited in places of safekeeping so that their content can be preserved for future generations. The work we carry out in the course of production allows us to lend financial resources so as to make access copies at many of the archives with which we work. In tandem with my work on colour materials of the Thirties and Forties I am now working on colour materials from before 1920. At the time of writing we can reveal to a wide audience some of the lost colour footage of the 1911 Delhi Durbar.

My journey of discovery continues, due in no small part to the continuing support of my employers, TWI, and broadcasters such as ITV. So much of the colour record of the first half of the 20th century is jeopardised. I believe we all have a responsibility to recover as much of this as possible before it is lost to posterity. I hope I have played some part in awakening an interest in this material.

How to present riots that have not been filmed

Gerda Jansen Hendriks

History programmes for television: what are they? Or more precisely, what laws apply? Should the rules be those of film, ie should there be a dramatic narrative, or those of scholarship, ie that the facts should be correct and verifiable? In my opinion, the two can be combined. I studied history with great pleasure and still am convinced that fairly strict rules of historical scholarship should apply to what I do now. But I have also learned the tricks of the trade that is filming. I still recall that I was more or less shocked when I started making films myself after my history studies. The practice of filming seemed far more arbitrary than I had ever imagined as a student analysing archive footage. By now, 15 years later, it may be that what I do as a filmmaker will in its turn shock historians, but I do think that I am able to combine my responsibility as an historian and as a filmmaker.

To prove my point, I will explain here what I do when I have to show, or rather visualise, events in the past that have not been filmed, or where there is only scant archive footage available. Using examples from three documentaries that I have made, this will be in effect a little catalogue of the tricks that filmmakers use. I will try to clarify why it is necessary to use symbols and technical tricks, to organise reality and to weigh the pros and cons of cheating with archive footage. I think it is important for historians who use film and television in their studies to be aware of these things. Every student learns to read between the lines of written documents and the same applies to films: one has to learn to 'see through the images'. In historical studies, this is facilitated by the use of footnotes and references. Up till now, it was not very easy to do this for films. The arrival of the Internet opens up new possibilities in this area. I will elaborate on this later on.

The three documentaries I will refer to have all been made for the NPS, one of the Dutch public broadcasting organisations. All three are about events that happened after Word War II and have episodes about riots. The first documentary is titled *Bed-Bad-Brood* (Bed-Bath-Bread) and is part of a series of 11 programmes about cases that provoked public opinion in their day.[1] The title refers to the special status that was imposed on the very first group of unorganised asylum-seekers that came to the Netherlands in the beginning of the 1980s. They were Tamils from Sri Lanka, fleeing from the civil war in their country. Their arrival in unexpectedly large numbers caused a lot of problems, including at one point large-scale rioting in the guesthouses where the Dutch authorities forced them to stay. The documentary focuses on a small town in the south of the country, where one of the 12 guest houses for the Tamils was situated.

The focus on a small town is a classical trick in filmmaking. Since film constitutes a very flat and linear way of providing factual information and is not very suited to dwelling on abstract ideas, it often uses *pars pro toto*: a small story with a limited number of characters and a clear location, that nonetheless contains all the elements of the bigger issue at stake, in this case the beginning of the modern phenomenon of refugees migrating to western Europe. To be perfectly clear, using *pars pro toto* soundly means a lot of thorough research. The documentary itself may seem simple, but to be sure that the information it conveys does stand for something grander, one has to have a level of knowledge that far exceeds the story.

The rioting by the Tamils in their guest houses, in April 1986, was not filmed when it broke out. The national news has archive footage of the aftermath, showing one completely burnt out guest house and heavy damage to others. There was no footage of the guest house that my story concentrated on, only some pictures from a local newspaper of the situation the day after. Of course I conducted interviews with the people concerned: several Tamils who were there, the policeman who arrived first on the scene, the mayor who came soon afterwards, the Dutch caretaker. Although interviews with eyewitnesses are usually an essential part of contemporary history programmes, they often cannot tell the whole story. Also, as a trained historian, I am aware of the flaws of memory. Oral history in itself is not sufficient to give a true account of an event. So I also used the police reports that the research had unearthed, including statements from the Tamils taken shortly after the riot. Still, to show written statements, even if you have them read aloud, does not make very exciting television.

To convey the tension of that night of rioting in this film, I opted for rather traditional solutions, mixing the interviews and passages from the police reports with symbolic images, like the blue flashing light of a police car with accompanying sound, night shots of the street where the guest house stood (the building itself had been demolished a couple of years before) that went with the sound of glass breaking and sounds of 'angry mob', as it is called in the index of sound-effect CDs. As far as I am concerned, there is no controversy here. Recently, I was made to realise that one can have a different view. I went out to do some sound recording for a piece of mute archive footage from 1969, showing children playing in a paddling pool. Recording this in the same kind of surroundings, bystanders asked what I was doing. My explanation evoked several exclamations: 'So that's how we are cheated by television!' I was surprised, since combining image and sound from different sources is perfectly ordinary for filmmakers. It apparently is not for the audience.

From the perspective of a historian, I think that there can be no confusion in the episode of the Tamil riot. There is a clear distinction between historical facts, i.e. the police reports, personal memory and symbolic images. At the most, there are some minor details that could be characterised as cheating. For example, in the first shot of the street at night, one sees the church tower in the distance, the illuminated dial indicating nearly 1 a.m., the time that the riot started that night. This is a factual impossibility, since the illumination of the clock and the church stops at midnight. What we filmed was the dial pointing to 10.57 p.m. and then we reversed the image, giving the illusion of 1 p.m. I readily admit that this is cheating, but I also must confess that I do enjoy these small tricks and since this one does not have any influence on the factual content of the story, I do not feel guilty about it. I point it out here, because for anyone who wants to analyse every shot of a film, it is good to know that filmmakers have near infinite possibilities for organising reality. Do not think that this has only become possible with advanced digital techniques. There were a lot of tricks possible before the digital era, the main difference is that it is much more costly and time consuming to do this with film, so you do not see it often in newsreels. Documentaries did make use of it, though.

At this point, it seems fitting to make a small excursion into the world of definitions. I have used the words documentary, film and television without any distinction. First we must define film and television. Of course there is a technical, and even an emotional, difference between film and television or video, as there is between seeing a story on screen in the cinema or on your TV set at home. I have worked in both fields. I still prefer to see a documentary on film in the cinema, but what counts in the end is a good story with fascinating information. From this point of view, it does not really matter on what kind of material a story is recorded or how it is shown. Therefore I will continue to mix up both terms. Then documentary. The word implies non-fiction, which is sometimes interpreted as reality. That is a misunderstanding. Film is never reality. It is enough to say that even live-coverage on TV will only show that very small part of reality upon which the camera is focused. There is an ongoing debate about how much fiction can be allowed into non-fiction, be it in film or in written accounts. I will not elaborate on it here.[2] It is fair, though, to give you my own criteria in this area. I already mentioned organising reality, and that is more or less what I do. To clarify the meaning of this, I will go to the next example, also an episode of the above-mentioned series of 11 programmes.

The documentary unfolds in 1950 in Singapore, which was at that time still part of British Malacca.[3] The story is about a then 13-year-old Dutch girl, Bertha Hertogh. Under her Malay name, Nadrah, she is still very famous in Singapore. Her story is an important part of the permanent exhibition in Singapore's History Museum. In the Netherlands Bertha Hertogh has more or less been forgotten, although her case recently came up again because of the Cuban boy, Elian Gonzalez. Just as with Elian, the story of Bertha is about a custody battle that got out of hand when politics became involved. It was complicated, but it rose to a high in December 1950 when a British judge ordered that Bertha had to go back to her birth parents in the Netherlands and that the custody of her Malay foster mother was no longer valid, nor was her Islamic marriage that had been concluded a couple of months before. The decision of the judge led to large-scale rioting in Singapore, the British authorities declared a state of emergency and 18 Europeans were killed. All because the legal battle between the foster mother and the birth parents by this date had become a symbol for cultural and religious values in east and west, in which not only the parents and foster mother were involved, but also private committees of citizens on both sides and the British and Dutch governments. To tell this story, I went back to Singapore with Bertha Hertogh, who was by now a woman of 60 and had never been back there. This is where organising reality comes in.

For different reasons, I know that Bertha would have never gone back if I had not asked her to do so. One could, with good reason, argue that this goes beyond documenting reality. Of course, I could have done an interview with Bertha at her home in the Netherlands and combined that with some footage of Singapore in the 1950s. But it is not difficult to imagine that it makes much more fascinating television when you see her walking in front of the old Courthouse in Singapore, recalling what happened there. Also, it is my experience that the memory works better when you are at what you'd call the scene of the crime. It's something the police and the judiciary believe in too. Going to Singapore was not the only thing I organised for this film. There also was a reunion with classmates from the Catholic school Bertha went to when she got back to the Netherlands – some nine women, who all remembered her as the girl who did not speak a word of Dutch and who was under constant police-surveillance. Again, this would have never happened if it were not organised. Bertha, by the way, really enjoyed the reunion. I do not consider this as manipulating reality. Every documentary, even every item in TV news, requires a certain amount of organisation, if it is only for the technical point of where to put the camera. Any given angle of the camera can mean a difference in the audience's feelings towards the person who is being interviewed. Decisions like this form an integral part of making television, although the audience may not be very aware of that.

Concerning the riots in Singapore, it was not very difficult to make them visual. There is a newsreel about them, now owned by Reuters. It is short, but enough to convey the tense atmosphere, especially when used with the original voice-over. I do prefer using archive footage with the original soundtrack, since contemporary usage also tells a lot about a given period. Far too often, archive footage is used only for its images. They are there to support a new voice-over. In those cases it is much easier to use the archive footage out of context. In my documentary, I combined the original newsreel with statements from Bertha and passages from the official reports of the Dutch consul-general in Singapore, who happened to write very eloquently, something which is fairly uncommon in diplomatic correspondence.

Organising reality, small tricks, it is all there again in the third documentary, plus a little more, because in this film I did really cheat with archive footage, although I still am convinced that I made a justifiable choice. The title is *Spaghettivreters* ('Eyeties') and it is about the first group of foreign labourers that came to the Netherlands from Italy in 1960, the beginning of the flow of migrant workers who came to do the jobs that the Dutch did not want to do anymore.[4] This first group consisted of young men from the south of Italy. The film concentrates on some of them who worked in the textile industry in the east of the country and were housed mainly as boarders with the local inhabitants. Since they were young, charming Italian men, they got a lot of attention from the local girls, which in turn made the local guys very jealous. This resulted in the first big ethnic riot of the 20th century in the Netherlands. The riot started in the local dance hall (where else, one could ask?) of a small town, where the Italians were refused entry. It went on for two nights and was followed by a one-week strike in the textile factories. The rioting itself had not been filmed, and the quality of the pictures from the local newspaper was so poor that it was hard to see what they represented. So I had a problem.

There were the interviews with the people involved and I had the police reports. The small town itself has been drastically modernised since, except for the dance hall, that still serves the same purpose. For the documentary, we did organise a dance evening there, with the Dutch guys and girls from those days and the few Italians who still live in the town. Of course I could not and did not want to organise another fight. We merely made a lot of jokes about how far one can go in organising something. The interviews were a little problematic, because when it came to the rioting, people were still ashamed to talk about it, even maybe more now than in those days, because ethnic rioting has since become an awkward issue in our society. The factual information of what happened had to come from the police reports. Again, written documents can be terribly boring to show for more than a couple of seconds. What I wanted to show and read aloud required at least a couple of minutes. The research for archive footage had produced, among much else, a fairly unknown report about youth rioting in suburban Amsterdam in the same period. The images bore a strong resemblance to what was written in my police reports: policemen in sidecars swaying their batons, youngsters running away. This was very tempting. It does not happen very often either.

Archive footage seldom fits with a different event, there are always details that do not match the situation. It is not that easy to cheat well. Cheating badly happens often. Recently, I got an American documentary on my desk with the question if this was worthwhile for the NPS to broadcast. It was a story about the beginnings of Russian space travel. It was told with a lot of flair, but I became suspicious very soon. If a voice-over tells me that a Russian pilot crashed in a desert in Inner Mongolia and was saved by a Chinese expedition and that all this was kept secret, while in the meantime images are shown of a deserted landscape with a group of men in the distance, I just won't believe that this Chinese rescue expedition was accompanied by a camera crew. This must be a fake, or to be more precise: this must be archive footage from a different event. It was just one example out of many in this documentary, so you can imagine my advice, even though I am no expert in the field of Russian space travel.

I think that historians who study film and television must be able to discover cheating with images. If they are suspicious enough, they can also recognise in my documentary that the archive footage about the dance hall riot is fake. I deliberately made it that way. After some pondering, I decided to use the footage of the riot in Amsterdam as a background for the texts of the passages from the police reports, but not in a direct way. The footage is slightly distorted by computer. For me, this served as a warning to viewers: watch out, these images are not real, they only have a symbolic meaning. I must admit that I have learned on several occasions that most viewers do not take notice: they simply believe what they see. But I think that historians should not believe what they see, and should be very aware of all the tricks that filmmakers use to tell their stories.

As you have noticed, I am willing to explain my tricks. Not all my colleagues agree, by the way. They think that film should keep its touch of magic. I believe it will stay magic, even if you know all the ins and outs. Up till now, I have not had many opportunities to give account to an audience. Film does not come with footnotes. In the past, I have thought about a system of using some frames at the end of a programme in which I could put a lot of text. Viewers who were interested could see this if they video-taped the programme and used their button for frame-by-frame viewing. It did not seem very handy or elegant.

The Internet and the start of a new, weekly history magazine on Dutch public television, in March 2000, finally brought an opportunity for footnotes. Since this magazine is intended to go on over a longer period, it was possible to create a website for it.[5] Here one can find all the information that cannot be put into the programme itself. It tells you what kind of archive footage is used for each report, it gives much more factual information about the subject, including links to other relevant websites and further reading, it sometimes shows the complete original documents that were used, and so on. I am very happy with this. The historian in me has always been frustrated by the inherent limitations of film, as much as I do love it. The Internet now offers the possibility to share all the information that my colleagues and I collect in order to make a film. Using the Internet for footnotes may become a trend, also for written publications.[6] One can see this as a problem: authors who have no other choice than to put their footnotes on the Internet, because publishers refuse to spend money on extra pages. I think it is not such a bad solution and it can also work the other way around. If this book you are reading now had a website it would be possible for you to view the appropriate fragments of my programmes.

Back to my beginning: should history programmes on television be art or scholarship? For me, history means stories; even modern historians have kept elements of storytelling in their publications. Ideally, history programmes should start as scholarly projects. There should be a thesis and thorough research, using all the historical sources available. There is a difference: television researchers have not only to consider the information they are finding within the context of the thesis, they also constantly have to think about the narrative and visual value of the information, about the way sources (be it documents, artefacts or eyewitnesses) can be useful for the programme. In the end, that is what they are paid for, unlike historians, who may get applause if they come up with a new thesis based on hitherto unknown documents.

In television, it all has to add up to a good story. This implies that there is a dramatic narrative. That is a concept that comes from fiction, but I think it can be applied to non-fiction without distorting the facts. Usually, reality contains enough drama, if you want to see it. It may not be easy if you have to make a programme about the creation of the EU, but I believe it is possible. Good research is a necessity, but in itself does not make a good programme. What is also needed is imagination. This should be based on the facts that the research has come up with, but will often surpass them in order to create attractive television. Surpassing the facts is what any historian will do in establishing a thesis. The form may be very different, but both the serious producer or director and the historian ultimately share the same goal: to give a better understanding of the past.

Notes

1   *Bed-Bad-Brood*, episode 10 of *De Affaire*, NPS, Channel 3, 19 February 1999.

2   The debate is as old as the documentary itself. Recently it has concentrated on the so-called fake documentaries, of which *Relics – Einstein's brain*, made by Kevin Hull for BBC's *Arena*, is the most famous. See for example: Jos van der Burg a.o., *Feit – Fictie - Fake* (Amsterdam, 1997).

3   *Bertha Hertogh*, episode 6 of *De Affaire*, NPS, Channel 3, 22 January 1999.

4   *Spaghettivreters*, episode 13 of *Na de Oorlog*, NPS, Channel 3, 28 March 1995.

5   See *www.anderetijden.nl* The weekly magazine *Andere Tijden* (Changing Times) is produced by NPS/VPRO and broadcast on Channel 3. It started on 12 March 2000 and will continue after a summer break into the summer of 2001.

6   See for example: Jason Epstein, 'The coming revolution in books', *New York Review of Books*, vol. XLVII, nr. 7, p. 55-59.

History without Archives: Simon Schama's *A History of Britain*

*Ian Bremner**

> 'The great story-telling medium of our age is television; perfectly equipped to marry argument with drama, both of which pour from the annals of British history.' (Simon Schama).

It seems to have long been a commissioning adage that the only history that worked on television involved Pharaohs or Nazis. Unless the producer could lay hands upon actual footage of the Waffen SS or peddle some spurious, if graphically enhanced, theory about the astronomic arrangement of the pyramids, there seemed to be no point in making the programme because it would be unwatchable.

Since 1996 a small team of BBC producers has been filming a 16 hour authored series on British history and only the last two episodes contain any archive footage. Starting in Neolithic Orkney, the first transmission run of seven films takes the viewer up to the death of Elizabeth I via the Norman Conquest, the struggle between Henry II, Thomas Becket and Henry's sons, Richard I and John, to the birth of the four nations in the isles, the impact of the black death that left almost half the population dead, to the trauma of the Reformation and the clash between Elizabeth and her cousin, Mary Queen of Scots. It is called *A History of Britain by Simon Schama* and began transmission in October 2000 on BBC2 (with a narrative repeat on BBC1) and on the *History Channel* in the USA from November 1999. Series two, with nine more films will be transmitted in 2001. The series will be supported by just about every medium known to man, from the traditional book, audio book and local exhibitions to a massive and expanding web site (www.bbc.co.uk/history) a CD ROM co-produced with the Victoria and Albert Museum in London, a home video boxed set, a behind the scenes show on the BBC *Knowledge* digital channel and, eventually, an online 'learning journey' that may lead to accredited distant learning history courses.

*(The following piece is entirely Ian's personal opinion – it does not represent the thinking or views of the BBC).

Despite all this new technology, when we call up that footage of Harold getting it in the eye (1066) or Simon de Montfort having his testicles hung around his nose after the Battle of Evesham (1265) we are still met with blank stares. Which leaves us as producers with a fairly big problem. How do you fill an hour of television just with a 'man outstanding in his field,' populated by characters for whom we have no contemporary visual representation, locations that have changed beyond recognition or which now house that great landmark of the 20th century, a Sainsbury's car park? I will do my best to show how we solved some of them and created what we hope will be entertaining but also informative television history, without a frame of archive footage in sight.

But first a little 'history'! Once upon a time the series was going to be a 26 part narrated opus, made in the traditional way of worthy interviews intercut with location filming and the neatly balanced script that producers are so proud of. However, when the great and the good decided it should be shown on BBC1 and BBC2 – as a result of the move between networks of our then commissioner, Michael Jackson, now Channel 4 Supremo – modern protocol demanded that the series have a presenter and the search for one began.

I wish I could do no more than present some profound insight on the great debates that the production team has sat about having to the early hours – should the Peasants' Revolt of 1381 have more time than the Wars of the Roses? It will, by the way. How you do craft a series of this nature? Everything has really boiled down to how the presenter writes about, and we then visualise, *some moments* in the past 2000 years of shared experiences on these islands, which, and I say this only half jokingly, some both within and outside the BBC would have us call the Atlantic Archipelago, for fear of otherwise upsetting someone. Should the 'Britain' word be in the title at all? Can it be called 'Britannia' because of the imperial overtones now associated with a term that began life merely as the Roman word for the bit of land off the north European shoreline, and so on?

HoB is supposed to be a worthy successor to those classic series, *Civilisation* and *The Ascent of Man*. The former, presented by Lord Clark, put man's artistic legacy into context while, in the latter, Jacob Bronowski explained mankind's anthropological evolution. Such comparisons are best avoided for all our sakes and the sad truth is that if you open up the archive and look at those films through modern eyes, they underwhelm. Audience demands and production techniques have moved on and most would find them boring now. Heresy perhaps and as someone who watched both series when they were repeated in my youth, I cannot deny their impact on a whole generation of people. Since then, even the BBC has avoided series of such length. The last, *Triumph of the West*, presented in the mid eighties by Dr John Roberts, passed with little impact and great critical disdain. It did however have one legacy. One viewer, aged about 17, loved it and decided he wanted to do something like that one day. Now I have achieved that ambition and another generation can judge the results.

Our choice to fill the shoes of Bronowski and Clark was Simon Schama, University Professor of Art History and History at Columbia University in New York City. A Brit who moved to the States in 1980, Simon led the charge in writing best selling history, although he is not a specialist in the early history of his native land. As he himself asked at a recent conference: 'What am I doing here?' As usual, he had the answer to hand: 'To provide a mixture of egotism and coyness... .'

The production process has taken over all our lives and has brought its own mixture of problems and rewards. In many ways, it has given me a much more profound insight into Britain and the Britons circa 2000 AD than any study of history could. We filmed the man in Wales who only wanted to bash people with his sword but who I made dress up as a Bishop, only to find that he was still keeping the sword to hand, under his clerical garb. There was the Scottish group who couldn't believe their luck that the BBC would pay them to beat the hell out of each other on camera (or at least look as if they were, all health and safety rules strictly adhered to). We even became involved in the feud between the Evesham Historical Society and their rival splinter group, the de Montfort Society. I think it is safe to say that as soon as one scrapes the surface of the historically interested (or should that be 'challenged'?) in the UK – and history is supposed to be our second most popular past time – one quickly discovers that it is not just academic history departments that are full of strange people!

When the series is broadcast, whatever the hype, it will find itself a much smaller fish in a greatly enlarged television world. The very medium of television – so called because it is neither rare nor well done – will be available to the public through their aerial, both digitally and terrestrially, the digital satellite dish, cable in all its forms, home phone lines, personal computers and the internet, pay-per-view and possibly via the very mains that supply household electricity. As you shall hear, despite all this change and innovation, our series seems a very old fashioned way to make landmark television; shot on film with one author and lots of locations. It is a bold step by the BBC when even its own recent products in this field: – *The Human Body* and *Walking with Dinosaurs* – have depended heavily on massive US co-production money and state-of-the-art graphics: both things that *HoB* is lacking.

The market itself is also more crowded. There has never been more 'history' on television, be it in the form of carefully crafted assessments of some past event, or as repeats of programmes that easily outshine their contemporary equivalents in terms of class and audience. *Blackadder* and *Dad's Army* still regularly feature in both of the BBC's terrestrial channels' top ten lists. They are history in the sense that they are comedies set in the past but were also made a long time ago!

From thrusting young archaeologists promoting truly spurious hypotheses about the mystical and forgotten Black Taj, the fictitious partner to the marble fantasy of the Taj Mahal, to the award winning, *The Nazis – A Warning from History*, television seems to have a limitless appetite for things past. However, the norm in this sound bite age seems to have become at most, a six part series. Indeed, single films within a related strand are common, be they an official strand such as the former *Timewatch* (the main BBC history strand, theoretically covering any period) or *Reputations* (biographies, well over half of which have to be of interest to our American co-producers.) There are also their Channel 4 clones: *Real Lives* and *Secret History*. Or they may come under a series title that links films, such as Channel 4's *Secrets of the Dead* which is actually a product of Channel 4's science commissioner. The films are linked in that they explore how a certain group or person may have died or been killed, be they combatants from the Wars of the Roses or the first British settlers in America, at Jamestown. The format thereby combines sexy science with a 'who-done-it' tease, all set within a historical setting.

Channel 4 is doing well out of history on television at the moment. Recent productions include the stylish series on the work of SOE (a BBC equivalent started months later) and explored the validity of the escape methods devised by POWs to get out of Colditz. Interestingly, despite covering a period where there is some archive footage, these series chose to go the reconstruction route that we ourselves have followed, rather annoyingly using the same Super 8 filming techniques to create material that looks as if it may have been filmed at the time depicted. The line between 'real' and ersatz footage thereby becomes blurred, much as it was by Oliver Stone in *JFK* when he freely mixed actual archive with material he shot and made look exactly as if it were archive film. Our reconstructions clearly show events that could never have been filmed and we do not identify them on screen as reconstructions on that basis. This is not the place to get into a discussion on the dangers of 'misleading' the audience by the use of footage that looks as if it may be 'real,' but it will no doubt merit further debate. Will the film historians argue that we mislead, or are we justified, as producers would argue, by the need to make what is after all television, interesting to watch? Our production techniques will be described below and thus I hope to allow people to draw their own conclusions on our chosen methods.

The surprise recent history hit, which may or may not be good news for *HoB*, was David Starkey's *Elizabeth*, also on Channel 4. With a regular audience of three million, over several weeks it became a top ten hit and proved that there is an audience for history without archive film. Made on a relatively modest budget, with few expensive gimmicks and Dr Starkey lecturing the audience in a way not much different from A.J.P. Taylor's classic talks a generation before. Perhaps the series is evidence that the audience at home don't care about the production techniques we producers agonise over and just want something they can understand and relate to its period. If true, this may have a profound impact upon academics and producers alike.

Another interesting trend is the erosion of the line between who makes history programmes. My colleagues and I form the 'History Unit' of the BBC but are only responsible for a tiny percentage of the Corporation's history output. With the institutional changes planned by Director General Greg Dyke, the unit will stand alone as one part of the new specialist Factual department, within the reformed

BBC, sitting beside Science, the Natural History Unit, Business programmes and so on. This both compartmentalises producers but is also intended to allow more movement within the new bigger parent department. *Reputations*, the biographical strand, is gradually shifting its focus only to people who are alive and a key criterion for subject selection is our old friend: archive availability. Now this is not a bad thing; far from it. Indeed, my point is that colleagues in other parts of the BBC produce most of the half hour history series in the BBC. Science makes *Meet the Ancestors*, Arts make *One Foot in the Past*, Bristol Features produces *War Walks* and those stylish Saturday evening archaeology shows come from an off-shoot of the BBC Manchester based Religious Programmes department, while Education used to produce most of the others. As far as BBC television history is concerned, there is no rulebook or prohibition on who can make what.

One issue of legitimate concern is exactly whose history are we, the broadcasters, promulgating, what objectivity does the audience have a right to be presented with and how free are we, the programme makers, able just to spin a line that interests us, provokes a response and hopefully finds an audience?

Our series has Britain firmly in its title, as does the British Broadcasting Corporation itself. Yet with a new Parliament in Scotland and Assembly in Wales and strong BBC centres in both, is it possible to make a British history series? Interestingly, this reflects one of the hottest debates in current historiography. For the first time professional historians are writing books that they deliberately entitle 'British History.' Penguin's replacement for the venerable *Pelican History of England* has been entitled *The Penguin History of Britain*. Oxford University Press's replacement to its equivalent series remains belligerently *The New Oxford History of England*. If you talk to the authors of volumes in the different series, the bravery of Penguin does cause problems for its writers.

There are two periods where historians have made great strides into meaningful *British* history, the late 13th and mid-17th centuries. This makes great sense. How can you study a period where the England of Edward I tried to make itself overlord of Wales and Scotland, the bloodshed then spilling over into Ireland, without looking at things equally from the perspectives of the non-English nations? The *HoB* film I directed, *Nations*, does its best to reflect this perspective and debate. The seventeenth century, when the King of Scotland becomes King of Britain and the 'English' civil war is in fact caused by events in Scotland and Ireland, provides the second area of rich research. The first films in our second series will reflect this work. However, given the very embryonic nature of the research, even in academic circles, it is no wonder that we mere producers venture there carefully. It can only be hoped that we are judged in this context, not by some well meaning but ignorant, politically correct yardstick. We have done our best to fulfil the self chosen brief of British history, remembering that four countries exist within the isles and trying to explain why they are linked, but different. All of the films cannot do that all the time, anymore than they can all give equal weight throughout to social, economic, cultural, political, military and diplomatic events.

Television and history have rarely, if ever, had a stronger bond. Just as the wider debates within the historical profession about exactly what constitutes history continue, so does the nature, form and trend in history on television. No one associated with IAMHIST needs a reminder that there were very few university based communications or media history courses in the UK as little as 15 years ago or, that when I studied history at Leeds and we used movies, newsreels and other visual sources as evidence, many in the department considered us very unacademic.

And yet within this context of multi-channel homes, limited attention spans and short programme runs that require limited commitment from the audience, the BBC has set out to turn the clocks back and has commissioned us to make the first (and almost certainly last) television history of Britain. In many ways what we are doing is rather old fashioned. Just as *Star Wars* is the future set in the past ('*A long time ago* in a Galaxy, far, far away'), we are the past trying to survive in the future.

In 16 hour-long programmes, shot on super 16 mm film with specially composed music and one lone presenter – the author of each episode – we will attempt to chart British history over the last two Millennia. Following a chronological approach, some films will examine perhaps three decades in detail; the second film on the Norman Conquest, for example. Others cover a century or more in broad brush strokes. The first film takes us from Neolithic Orkney to Anglo-Saxon Kent (a mere 4000 years) the fifth from the Black Death to the eve of the Reformation (only a century and a half) and so on. Each episode has been outlined by the original editor of the series, Janice Hadlow and Simon Schama, our presenter, with a bit of help from Dr Mike Ibeji and myself, the series Associate Producers. Along the way there have been many debates and some revisions. We have all seen favourite moments bite the dust and there will be no equal time rules. Poor old Henry III, who reigned for 56 years (1216 – 1272) will get about five minutes while Henry V (1413 – 1422) will get even less. I am not sure which is more worrying! In a mammoth undertaking Simon is writing, presenting on location and narrating each of the films. There will be no interviews and no other talking heads. It is all about telling good stories.

As Simon says:

> Every so often in the life of a nation it becomes important to step back from the frantic rush of the contemporary and take a long look in the mirror of time. In the life of Britain, this is one of those occasions. What we see may tell us something valuable about ourselves, neither flattering nor distressing, but the truth about how we have arrived at this moment in our shared history. Great story-telling is what makes history live in the minds of the present generation; what connects the past and the future; the historian with the public; learning with imagination.

And so we pass back through time to Stone Age Orkney and meet the first 'Britons'. As Simon says in *Beginnings*, the prelude to the series:

Europe's most complete Neolithic community, miraculously preserved for 5,000 years ... intimate, domestic and self sufficient ... it's not too much of a stretch to image gossip travelling down these alleyways after a hearty seafood supper. We have in other words everything you could possibly want for a village except a church and a pub.

A place like Skara Brae gives us an insight into the minds of our Stone Age ancestors, in fact more information about their lifestyle than we know of succeeding generations until the Romans arrived three thousand years later. Filming in Orkney generally, and at Skara Brae in particular, brings its own challenges. As startling as the 'houses' and 'stone dressers' are, none have a roof and the most precious artefacts reside in the new National Museum of Scotland, in Edinburgh. It is in fact more expensive to fly from London to Orkney than New York and so careful planning is required.

Despite our bests efforts the Gods still have the last say with the weather. We were lucky. Our flight was the first to land that week and this was in July 1998. The lack of scale and ornaments are solved by filming at night with an array of lights and the help of an obliging curator, who brought the stunning artefacts back to their places of discovery. And so the audience will be able to see the gorgeous whale and walrus bone necklace and pin, as well as the carved stone votive objects that look like hand-grenades to me and may have been toys, or some primitive stress-relieving device. The lights and darkness allowed us just to pick out the details that are of visual interest and recognisable as dwellings; a truly wonderful way of seeing the site that can otherwise look a bit like the 18th hole of any fairway. Fortunately for us, Historic Scotland have reconstructed one of the houses, with a roof, fire place and even running electricity, the perfect set for our filming and attempt to evoke the atmosphere of 5,000 years ago.

So we have jumped into the deep end with no archive and one presenter, we are asking the audience to sit through 16 hours, over four months. Can it be any wonder that virtually everyone on the very small production team doubts their sanity from time to time?

Each of the film's is Simon Schama's take on the period, shaped and somehow turned into an hour of television by the production team. But that is just the beginning. In this multi-media age, our colleagues in BBC Education are producing the mother of all web sites to accompany the series and other Millennium output. In a remarkably fruitful co-production, the TV production team are providing the editorial lead to the web producers and have also been commissioned to take as many photographs as we can on location. Combining on-line graphics with a cross referenced data base of these images, for the first time the audience will be able to both ask and answer those questions that arise from each episode: where was that filmed and how do I get there? Or, I want to know more about Thomas More or the forgotten Andrew Murray, the friend and inspiration for one William Wallace of *Braveheart* fame.

In the modern age, the BBC no longer just makes television series. The audience of *HoB* will be able to investigate further through our web site plus those linked to it, to ask what else happened between the death of Thomas Becket and that of Henry II, as there will always be moments in history that an individual film will focus upon before leaping forward, possibly condensing several decades into a sentence. Beyond specific programme related questions they will be able to discover what Roman sites are near their home, to explore how Iron Age Britons lived before the arrival of Rome and possibly even re-fight the battle of Hastings, to see if the Saxons could have won.

The series will also be supported by a host of local exhibitions and projects, working with the libraries and museum services plus a host of heritage organisations that have signed up as partners for the series and the BBC's other Millennium output. BBC Books will publish the illustrated book in Europe and the newly formed publishing arm of Disney/ABC/Miramax will publish it in the US and broadcast the series on their cable station, *The History Channel*. Full publicity is promised through all the tentacles of this media giant. After *Elizabeth* and *Shakespeare in Love*, British history is suddenly big in the States and hopefully now some facts will penetrate the hype.

The most commonly asked question of the series is: 'Why Simon Schama?' Well, it all started in Mickey Mantle's hamburger bar in Manhattan, four years ago. Janice Hadlow had the commission and needed her presenter. For her, the first choice was Simon Schama, the man who was responsible for putting intelligent history back at the top of the best seller lists on both sides of the Atlantic. She pursued him for two years. Faced with his own assertion that he was comprehensively disqualified, she explained that was the point. It is a homecoming for him, someone not steeped in British history day by day and who has lived abroad for the past 23 years, but who now returns with a fresh perspective. Someone who combines excitement with questions and is keen to discover what makes people part of a common allegiance. As Simon told me: 'Over five thousand years of history I've chosen the stories which are most eloquent, moving and instructive about the changing nature of British experience. And we tell them with passion because we know they matter; that in the great argument over where our country is going, history's voices need to be heard.'

The audience can and will trust his judgements, his ability to extrapolate the big picture from a small and illuminating tale, to evoke and re-awaken the voices and characters of our past. It is a risky decision but stands or falls on his perspective. Few professional historians could, or would, have undertaken such an enterprise.

It has always been my personal opinion that some of the greatest documentary series have failed because they refused to hire a writer. For some reason producers assume they can write and for individual films, linking in and out of sync from interviews and archive. To be fair, they usually get away with it. But a big series needs to be just as well written as it is filmed. More people listen to television than really watch it; what they hear determines what they get from it. Great music and pictures just keep their attention. For me, Simon Schama is one of the finest writers of non-fiction English and the series is blessed throughout with his masterly turn of phrase.

For example (in *Conquest!*) we hear about: 'History coming at us like a truck load of trouble ...' That under the battlefield of Hastings, 'We will find bones beneath the buttercups'. That after the Roman invasion, many Briton warlords fell over themselves to don togas: 'For those chieftains sensible enough to reach for the olive branch rather than the battle javelin, [Emperor] Claudius had another plan; give them or rather their sons a trip to Rome and a taste of the *dolce vita* ... If there were sumptuous country villas amidst the olive groves of the Roman countryside, why could there not be equally sumptuous villas amidst the pear orchards of the South Downs?'

In *Dynasty* Simon writes: 'So who exactly was Becket then? Well for a start he was the first commoner of any kind to make a mark on British history. And the possibility that someone like Thomas Becket, a merchant's son with an impoverished Norman knight clanking around somewhere in the family closet could end up as the king's best friend, said something about the possibility of the great swarming city [of London] itself'. As he is about to meet his end in Canterbury Cathedral, confronted by the king's armed knights: 'Becket was, remember, a Cockney, a street fighter, tough as old boots under the cowl. And when he stood rooted to the spot he became physically, as well as theologically, the immovable object. At such times the kind of talk he'd picked up in his Cheapside childhood came back to him, ripe and abusive.'

As we approached transmission all of the production team tried to figure out whether or not we have got it right. Did we make the right decisions about the locations, stories and graphics? Does the music work and are the film's structures clear? Does each episode make a bigger point and collectively paint a fuller picture? That is now for others to judge and it will be interesting to see exactly what the criteria of success is deemed to be: ratings, reviews, column inches or the fact that the BBC can say: 'We still make the epic landmark series that no one else can.' Few would deny that any other organisation in the world would, or could, have embarked on such a commitment.

Most of that is now largely academic. All that is left is to explain some of the thinking behind what we have filmed and how we did it. The bulk of the budgets of these films is spent on location filming. Mike Ibeji and I spent most of our pre-production time finding, 'recce'-ing and then setting up those locations. We have tried to find the unexpected but also not shied away from the well known. The challenge has then been to capture them all in a way that has never been seen before. I went to school in Bath and walked past the Roman baths every day. Mike, our resident Romanist, argued long and hard that we would be foolish to ignore them as a location and I hope that when audiences view (or re-view) the sequence in *Beginnings*, the baths come alive as a space where Iron Age Britain met Rome and two cultures merged to create another stage in the evolution of the British. That session also exploited a night shoot and the use of powerful lights that allowed us to highlight the true Roman features amongst all the Georgian additions. A 30 metre crane gave our cameraman a truly awe inspiring perspective, while that perennial secret weapon of the British, the weather, provided a beautiful evening and then just enough rain to make the naturally warm water in the main pool steam to spectacular effect.

We have filmed on three continents and in nine countries. We have also shot a limited number of generic or stylised re-enactment sequences to bring life to the earlier films. As Richard II is the first king that we know for sure what he looked like, you can understand the problems of illustrating films, which – and this will come as no surprise to anyone who knows Simon's work – are focused upon people, individuals, both named and the forgotten for whom Simon brings life, emotions and motivation. He evokes what a Saxon house-carl might have thought as he saw Duke William's cavalry charge up Senlac hill and explores exactly what motivated Henry VIII during the Reformation.

The scripts have also drawn on chronicle accounts. Through them we will hear the 'voice' of the past and gain a sense of how contemporaries saw the events we describe, not just the neat, objectively assessed accounts of modern historiography. We will honour the relay runners of the past, passing the baton to later generations: the forgotten authors of the Vindolanda letters, the monks Bede and Orderic Vitalis, the chroniclers Geoffrey of Monmouth and Matthew Paris. These are combined with the surviving remains of each period, their artefacts and architecture: bits of knee high rock, a finely carved, if forgotten, Iron Age carved sandstone head in Anglesey, the Bayeux tapestry, the gorgeous abbey of Pontigny where Becket fled in exile, or the remains of 18th century Anglo-French Pondicherry on the Indian Ocean coastline. Through these, combined with all our other locations, we hope to evoke a real sense of the past; to remember the people and places of Britain and assess their impact upon the modern world.

The series tries to identify those moments where something fundamental to the Britain of today happened. If we have got it right, each film tells a self contained story but together they allow us to see why Britain is historically Christian, but Protestant and not Catholic, and why we had the first system of common law but that it was conceived by a king, Henry II, who is remembered only for committing murder in the cathedral. We show how the Normans changed the institutions of the land and the mortality of the Black Death, combined with the arrogance of Richard II that resulted in civil war and left the English country gent in charge.

As already mentioned, the film that I produced and directed, *Nations*, set itself two 'simple' tasks: to explain how and why there are four countries in the isles, that national identity was born at the blunt end of a hammer and that an unexpected side effect was the birth of the first parliaments that contained commoners. Until Edward I tried to take away Welsh and Scots independence, it had no written form. The place of commoners in parliament came not out of the idealism of Simon de Montfort as the Victorians would have us believe, but out of the constant wars that Edward I waged. To pay for the endless marches and mile upon mile of castle walls..., Edward I had to broaden the taxation base and demand the levying of taxes on an annual basis. From this procedure parliament became an irrevocable part of government.

So how did we turn that into a film? First of all I had to convince Simon that this story was worth telling. With that agreed, I read everything I could lay my hands on and went to visit all the surviving locations where key events took place, stopping off along the way to pick the brains of some of the key historians of the period. A structure began to form in my mind, one where we put Edward himself at the centre of events and told the story from his perspective in order to provide a central theme and allow us to jump from England, to Wales, Scotland and Ireland, all in an hour. Simon's narrative took us from the Barons War where the young Edward won his spurs defeating Simon de Montfort by way of Westminster Abbey and Hall. Edward's father, Henry III, built the heart of the abbey we see today and within the Great Hall, his court sat in the medieval Palace of Westminster and represented the restored power of the crown that de Montfort and the barons fought against. With victory over the rebels, Edward became king in his own right and set out to show his neighbours he was their boss as well. Off we go to Wales and then Scotland, via the forgotten tragedy of Edward's expulsion of all England's Jewish population in 1290. The causes of his war with Scotland form a complicated historical moment and one we bring to life with several virtuoso pieces to camera at Norham in Northumberland.

From this point on, Edward's major Scottish foes emerge as key characters: William Wallace and Robert the Bruce. Each is characterised with Simon's usual style. Wallace as depicted on his statue in Glasgow: 'Here he is, the standard freedom fighter of the imagination: the give-em-hell whiskers, the "Save me Jesus" eyes, the ham strings from hell. We've not a clue, of course, whether William Wallace looked remotely like this, any more than we know if he could have stood in as a stuntman for Mel Gibson who immortalised him in *Braveheart*...'

With no historical images of Wallace or Bruce and only a couple of representations of Edward I, the film would have to be given some visual style and impetus. Different directors have tackled this problem in a variety of ways. *Dynasty* uses brilliant visual metaphors of birds of prey to flesh out the Angevin kings and their infighting. *King Death* projects manuscript images onto silk banners displayed in the crypt of the Guildhall in the City of London and then projects moving footage of daily village life before and after the plague, onto a wall of human skulls and bones at Hythe Ossuary to spectacular effect.

The description of Edward I on his tomb as 'Hammer of the Scots' was too good to miss and so a blacksmith hammering at a forge appears throughout *Nations* as Edward hammers his will upon his enemies. He is also described as being like a leopard in one contemporary poem. Brave, but also wily, devious and treacherous. Cue the one pair of leopards in a wildlife park near Winchester. However, with so much fighting and conflict between the nations more literal dramatic reconstructions were also required. We filmed these over two separate but hectic days, one in Scotland and the other in south Wales. I listed all the turning points of the film and we set out to get as many in the can as possible. The Scots group became Wallace's warriors, ambushing invading English columns, gathering for battle, defending and attacking Bothwell castle near Glasgow, a lonely Bruce figure in the wilderness, the schiltrom hedgehog formation of twelve foot spears that stopped the English knights and so on. Semi-professional in their work as extras, the clan came with all the right kit and dozens of weapons; their secret trick of the trade being rubber axes and maces that they could really hit each other with. I found an area of undisturbed medieval peat bog, with not a blade of grass in sight which became the perfect set. We choreographed a sequence of events and shot the whole thing from three different angles, bringing high impact blows to life.

Later in Wales a reconstructed medieval village and Caerphilly castle great hall provided the set for the rest of the reconstructions in the film. In the course of one day we filmed Wallace being captured, the Scots raiding the village, a Jewish family being expelled from their home, the sitting of parliament, Bruce killing a rival in church, his coronation, village life and archers in battle. The re-enactors came with their own kit and so for the cost of hiring one costume in London, we were able to stage a variety of scenes at an affordable documentary cost. At all times safety remained our utmost concern.

After their victory at Bannockburn the Scots raided north England and then took the war against the Plantagenets, now represented by Edward II, to Ireland. A key feature of the film became the texts that the Scots, Welsh and Irish wrote declaring their independence and separate identity. Two of these had never been filmed or photographed before and provide the film with some more original visualised history.

Simon puts the manuscripts firmly into context. On the great statement of Scottish independence as set out in a letter to the Pope in 1320, he writes:

> At the heart of what we call the Declaration of Arbroath was something much more powerful and deeply moving. It is the insistence that the nation lived on, outside and beyond the person of the prince who happened for a time to claim it's government. We have heard some of this before – at Oxford in 1258 – where we came in. But here in Scotland it is much more eloquent; the image of the free born patriot, drawn not as a desperado like Wallace; nor a mighty prince like Bruce, but as a band of brothers ...

The rest of the film comprises location filming, some graphic maps, rostrumed manuscript images, bought in aerial shots and John Harle's fantastic musical score. The series is blessed with its own composer and John, a renowned saxophonist, wrote music that both evoked the period of the films and enhanced their drama and emotion.

Post production of the first series reached its conclusion with the usual mix of problems and bad luck. We seem to have pushed the editing equipment to its extreme in trying to layer shots and get the greatest impact from the pictures. So we have done our best to solve the problems, to make television history without archive that is faithful to its period but still visually exciting. As Executive Producer, Martin Davidson, has written: 'We want *A History of Britain* to become our very own Bayeux Tapestry for the 21st Century, a graphic and gripping account of our place in the British nations, and their place in the world.'

Global narrative and exile culture in *Hawaii Five-O*

Sheri Chinen Biesen

> All through the years of statehood...Hawaii has had a prime-time cops and robbers show on network TV. There is some sort of fascination with the idea of paradise infested with criminal serpents...a lovely shiny society being attacked and corroded around the edges, and maybe at the center too, by corruption...The tube...solution...is a weekly dose of chases, gun play and rapid wrapups. In real life it's always harder, more complex.[1]
> Gavan Daws, *Hawaii*,1989

This study historically examines the global narrative 'reimagining' of local identity, ethnicity, and the unique exoticized 'exile' culture of Hawaii in the American television series *Hawaii Five-0*. This was the first hour-long prime-time crime drama shot entirely in color and on location in Hawaii which ran for 12 seasons from 1968-1980. Produced and packaged by a Hollywood television industry, the CBS television series promoted and exploited the remote multicultural Pacific island 50th state for national and international consumption of a tourist's paradise. Hawaii exists, and has historically existed, in a kind of liminal state – geographically remote, isolated, in exile from the continental United States, yet umbilically connected to the 'mainland' culturally, politically, industrially and economically. In a sense Hawaii is not unlike an exile culture in relation to the mainland U.S. Yet it is not homogeneous but rather a complex amalgam of many different international exile cultures who migrated to this remote locale, often pursuing developing industry in Hawaii: first the Marquesas and Tahitians, then Chinese, Japanese, Okinawan, Korean, Filipino, Portuguese, Spanish, Puerto Rican, Samoan, Vietnamese, Tongan as well as European and American cultures. Hawaii bears the distinction as the only US state with a non-white ethnic majority. By 1900 Japanese residents comprised the single largest population in this diverse island community.[2] The proximity of this chain of Pacific islands to the 'Far East' has also contributed to the cultural reframing of this region as an alluring myth of a far away paradise: unique, other, waiting to be experienced.

Hawaii has a long history as a subject of visual media fascination. Edison photographers W. Bleckyrden and James White, en route from 'the Orient,' shot the first motion pictures on location in Hawaii on May 10, 1898.[3] Since these first moving images were filmed of Hawaii, the 'exotic' Pacific islands have played a variety of roles both on the cinematic screen and televised tube. But, it was *Hawaii Five-0* that transmitted Hawaii globally and brought its reimagining of local culture into millions of living rooms nationally and around the world on a regular basis. *Hawaii Five-0* also initiated Hawaii's burgeoning television industry. The series brought valuable revenue and international exposure to the local Hawaiian economy that suggests a convergence of culture, media and industry that traverses local and global spheres.

Specifically, *Hawaii Five-0*'s representation of this unique 'imagined' regional community provides a national and international glimpse of this remote, liminal island 'state', anthropomorphized as alluring and 'other'. As a 1975 *Los Angeles Times* review of the series explained, the 'real star of *Hawaii Five-0* has always been the islands...There was visual padding here, too – almost the entire Pearl Harbor boat tour, or so it seemed.'[4] The intimate reception circumstances in which global audiences were privy to this 'exotic' narrative related to Lynn Spigel's notion that television offered a 'grand illusion' of the outside world with its 'panoramic vistas and travelogue plots.' Spigel notes an ironic 'discrepancy between the everyday experience of domestic isolation perpetuated by television, and the imaginary experiences of social integration which television programming constructed,' relating the 'utopian discourses which promised that television would connect the home to outside spaces,' to Marshall McLuhan's notion of television as a 'global village' linking the 'obsession with a view of far-away places' within the private sphere of one's own home.[5] In the exotic spirit of a romance narrative, Cecil Smith reimagined a specific cultural space for television audiences in the 1970 *TV Times* article '*Hawaii Five-0*: Crime Series in Lush Surroundings':

> Beyond, the sea slides up the coral beach in waves as gentle as a baby's bath. A sweet and feathery wind rustles through the kukui trees. The tropic sea glistens on the lush green undergrowth. The exotic setting...these incredibly beautiful islands make it a thing apart.[6]

This narratisation of Hawaii capitalizes on the otherness and liminality of its unique cultural space that is not unlike Edward Said's *Orientalism* in depicting a 'feminized' geography of paradise. Said notes the 'separateness of the Orient, its eccentricity, its backwardness, its silent indifference, its feminine penetrability, its supine malleability' often represented as 'a locale requiring Western attention, reconstruction, even redemption.... Thus whatever good or bad values were imputed to the Orient appeared to be functions of some highly specialized Western interest in the Orient.'[7]

Reinscribing history, commodifying culture, and promoting tourism are discourses often found in travelogues. For example, Delta Airlines' *Sky: Magazine of International Culture* weaves a tropical vacation narrative:

> The periodic and unpredictable violence and upheaval that have plagued

the residents of the Caribbean in reality have been critical elements in giving these unique slices of paradise their beauty, character, and charm. For all their fury, hurricanes...scars left by volcanoes, war, slavery, revolts, disease and genocide ironically help account for much of what makes the Caribbean islands alluring and unforgettable...The beautiful mountain you walk on today probably spewed fire and brimstone over helpless villages two decades or a century ago. The old plantation—now a quaint and chic resort—not so long ago was a cruel and vivid symbol of man's inhumanity to man.[8]

Such narratives commodify history and culture to 'capitalize' on tourism; hence, capitalism infuses another narrative in the same issue:

Twenty years ago, Maui was the hot new Hawaiian destination; Lana'i was a 15,000-acre pineapple plantation.... Since then, the economies of agriculture have drastically changed. Growing pineapple is now much cheaper in Guam and the Philippines, where water is abundant and labor costs are much lower. Money can be made on the island by pampering tourists. So The Dole Company, which owns about 98 per cent of the 141-square-mile island, has built a pair of magnificent facilities to attract billionaires and wannabes.[9]

Thus one industry begets another, and culture is appropriated to suit the industrial context: in this case, tourism. I will examine how the alluring representation of Hawaii in the global television media narrative of *Hawaii Five-0* inscribes local culture within a broader effort to commodify 'exotic' exile culture and promote tourism.

In 1968 *Hawaii Five-0* capitalized on the appeal of colour television, location shooting and the exotic allure of Hawaii's unique locale with a savvy production strategy that targeted a broad international market rather than focusing on local reception which was determined by the network not to be substantive enough to economically sustain a prime-time television series. Nevertheless, the show enjoyed surprising popularity with local audiences at home in Hawaii, as well and not only during the remarkable longevity of its 12 seasons on CBS from 26 September 1968 to 26 April 1980, but also in its subsequent syndication market. *Hawaii Five-0* was popular in Hawaii despite its conflation of ethnicity. In a March 1996 *Honolulu Advertiser* article, 'Danno, check every noodle in Chinatown,' local columnist Charles Memminger wrote:

I love *Hawaii Five-0*. Especially now. Watching the old episodes is satisfying on so many levels. It's not just the unintended humor that comes through today...the strange episode where Ricardo Montalban played a Japanese guy.... *Hawaii Five-0* had one of the best opening sequences of any television series ever made. It's not just the theme song...but the pastiche of opening shots ranging from hula dancers to a police car racing through Honolulu presents a feeling of Hawaii that has not been captured on film since.[10]

The series targeted global and national appeal and not only made money for CBS but brought in revenue to local industry and Hawaii's economy by promoting tourism. In adept travelogue fashion, *Hawaii Five-0* presented an alluring 'other' cultural geography as paradise: the natural beauty of the locale, the sea and the mountains, beautiful exotic women, showing you where to stay (hotels), how to get there (planes) while depicting the excitement of it all. *Hawaii Five-0* was tremendously successful in cultivating, advancing and exploiting this mythic tropical ambiance in the name of capital and leisure consumption: the state's tourism industry boomed. Tourism dominated as the primary industry in Hawaii. The State of Hawaii honoured the show's star as Salesman of the Year – especially in aiding the Hawaii Visitor's Bureau's meagre funds to promote Hawaii. Tourists often came *because* of *Hawaii Five-0*. According to the series star and producer Jack Lord, at the end of the show's second season, Hawaii Visitor's Bureau surveys found that 25 to 30 percent of new visitors came to Hawaii specifically because of seeing *Hawaii Five-0*.[11] Yet tourism was not the only local industry influenced by the series' economic success. Simply put, it publicized the region. Whether a local, national or global consumer of the show, how could audiences not conjure up images of Hawaii and the 50th state's fearless crime fighters at the mere mention of the phrase: 'Book, 'em, Danno.'?

Hawaii Five-0 was a crime series set in the lush surroundings of Hawaii involving a plot revolving around a four-man special unit of the Hawaii state police force headed by Steve McGarrett (Jack Lord) who, according to the script, reported only to the Governor. The unit tackled high felony crimes such as espionage and drug traffic. McGarrett's partners in law enforcement were 'Danno' Williams (James MacArthur), Chin Ho Kelly (Kam Fong) and Kono Kalakaua (played by Zulu, a 'Native Hawaiian.')[12] Over the course of the series, the Irish patriarch McGarrett lasted all 12 seasons, his Caucasian comrade Danno lasted eleven, Chinese officer Chin Ho was killed off in the 10th season, and only the Hawaiian character fluctuated in casting: Zulu, tired of saying 'Yes, Steve' and wanting a broader role, left after the first few seasons; he was replaced by another 'local boy' Al Harrington as Ben Kokua who was given more involvement in the fifth season, but who in turn was replaced by Herman Wedemeyer as Duke Lukela in later seasons. Memminger places the show in the tradition of Hollywood film and television detective serials, calling its characters 'so finely drawn that they exist to this day in people's psyches,' noting:

> McGarrett lives among mythical crime-fighters...Charlie Chan, Dirty Harry and Joe Friday. Danno was the kind of underling that any administrator would kill for. He was fearless, uncorruptible and he would do tons of scut work without whining. McGarrett would say, 'Danno, I want you to check every strip joint, bar and restaurant in Honolulu and find out if anyone looking like our guy has been there in the last six months.' And Danno would say, 'Right, Steve.' He was like a heavily armed, anal-retentive cocker spaniel who lived only to please his master.[13]

Chinese actor and former policeman Kam Fong who played detective Chin Ho had spent 17 years as an actual cop on the Honolulu police force. Fong was a solid asset to the program. Producer Leonard Freeman cast Fong for the show because he 'looked right', had amateur acting experience and was 'Hawaii's only Chinese disc jockey'. In 'After 10 Seasons, Kam Fong Expires,' Cecil Smith noted that the local actor helped 'thwart the stigma' locally that *Hawaii Five-0* was a non-local 'halole' show produced outside Hawaii 'stateside' on the mainland US. Yet, even Smith's writing about Hawaii (from Hollywood) marginalizes local culture as 'other' in exile, particularly in referring to the geographic liminality of its cultural space as simply 'the islands' (seemingly recycling tourism jargon) and calling locals 'islanders': 'There's considerable resentment in the islands that the villains are almost always islanders. It is Hawaiians who are the villains in Chin's final show featuring a criminal syndicate called 'kumu' headed by guest star Manu Tupou [notably an actor from Fiji], the local Godfather.' In keeping with *Hawaii Five-0*'s travelogue theme, 'a tourist guide screams' as Chin is 'eliminated.'[14] An interesting regional component of the series is that all the uniformed police officers on the show were actually local off-duty Honolulu Police Department officers.

The series was originally created by executive producer Leonard Freeman; however, following Freeman's death in 1974, the show evolved into a three-way ownership between its star, Jack Lord, CBS, and the Freeman estate who shared in the rich syndication market.[15] Lord admitted that he was the executive producer after Freeman's death, and Lord's contract gave him complete control of material.[16] Freeman's inception for the Honolulu-based show originated when his mother-in-law, who lived in Honolulu, suggested he develop 'something about Hawaii so that he and his wife would visit more often.' This argument certainly corroborates the show's inception being embedded in promoting tourism. There was also a non-fiction source to the premise of the series: 'During a meeting with Governor John Burns, Freeman learned that Burns was planning to start a special police task force to deal with unusual crimes in the islands and was going to call the force "Five-0".' Freeman wrote *Hawaii Five-0* based on that unit.[16]

The cultural geography of Hawaii is reimagined, packaged and marketed to promote tourism in *Hawaii Five-0*, commodified this unique locale much like Hamid Naficy's study of exile culture which cites Edward Said and Benedict Anderson's ideological notion of an 'imaginary geography' as a construction created by exile narratives to produce objects for consumption. While providing economically essential international exposure to this tiny cluster of islands, this cultural depiction by the series is mediated via the specific point of view of a Hollywood narrative. There's a double-edged sword to this representation whereby local culture is rearticulated through the strictures of a broader industrial context by way of the Hollywood mainland. In *The Hollywood Reporter's TV Preview for 1975-1976*, Lord recalls 'defeatist' projections for the show: 'It can't be done. You cannot make a successful series 2,500 miles from home base' outside the Hollywood industry. 'Too many problems – no studio, no equipment, no trained personnel, hardly any professional actors, no costume rentals, no prop houses, etc.' This quasi-colonial relationship between the Hollywood mainland and the Hawaii-based show also permeates its framing of culture in this mix, and the colouring of Lord's statement: 'Since there was never any continuity of motion picture activity before *Hawaii Five-0*, an on-the-job training program was carefully planned by our various department heads. Now our locals are equal in every way to our mainland gang. They are inventive, show enthusiasm and initiative, something which we were warned would never happen with Polynesians.'[18] *Hawaii Five-0*'s production capitalized on exterior shots to 'take advantage of the exotic beauty of the islands.' Freeman and Lord were partners: Freeman 'watching the shop in Hollywood,' developed scripts, hired guest stars and directors while Lord ran the show in Hawaii. During production six days a week, film was flown daily to Hollywood for processing and editing. Yet recognizable island locales and local residents, the majority of them non-professionals, permeated the atmosphere of the show in bit and walk-on parts.[19]

Nonetheless, representations of 'imagined community' in *Hawaii Five-0* perpetuate a fantasy myth of a paradise constructed as commercially viable and accessible for Western and international audiences, nationally and globally transmitted to promote an exotic island destination for tourists and television consumers as 'virtual' tourists. Hamid Naficy's study of exile culture again cites Edward Said's *Orientalism* in noting the ideological dimension of 'an 'imaginary geography,' a construction created by exile narratives' to produce objects for consumption. Naficy argues, 'Such fetish-souvenirs, and the narratives in which they are embedded...authenticate...and simultaneously...discredit' culture. Naficy goes on to posit how these representations of exile narratives are naturalized: 'In the absence of the native habitus – that is the former social, political, familial, linguistic structures, and authorities of home – the exile culture now is forced to seek the structures and the kind of authority that only nature is thought to be capable of providing: timelessness, boundlessness, predictability, reliability, stability, and universality.'

David Morley and Kevin Robins argue in *Spaces of Identity: Global Media, Electronic Landscapes and Cultural Boundaries*, that contemporary mass media/ceremony (eg, film, television) elides conventional divisions between public/private spheres, binding not only an individual region to a broader national context, but inculcating individual, regional, and local concerns within a larger global sphere. This framework provides an interesting method of contextualizing the tradition of American television series set in Hawaii, such as *Hawaii Five-0* which reinscribes local culture and authenticity within a broader global/national effort to commodify an 'exotic' exile narrative and promote tourism.[20]

Naficy's model of exile culture is particularly relevant to a consideration of the global/national and local/regional perspectives inherent in the relationship between international/mainland US culture and the exile/liminal culture of Hawaii, an isolated island state of transplanted exile cultures in the middle of the

Pacific, half way between the Orient and the West. Naficy's analysis of the construction of an 'imaginary geography' in exile narratives is notably significant to the relationship between the mainland/international Hollywood television industry and the liminal/exile state of the television series *Hawaii Five-0*, a 'satellite' show shot on location on an island in Hawaii, then sent to the Hollywood 'mainland' industry for post-production. As a result of this negotiation between global/national and local/regional perspectives, what kind of narrative is being constructed? Further, what issues of ideology are raised in the process?

The liminal exile of this local Hawaiian culture from the U.S. mainland, and the industrial liminality and geographic exile of the *Hawaii Five-0* series from the Hollywood television industry results in a complex tension that mediates the appropriation of exile cultural narrative(s) into the production of global/national mainstream Hollywood television narrative. The conflict dynamic between local Hawaiian exile culture and mainstream Hollywood television narrative negotiates the construction of an exoticized local/regional 'other' for global/national consumption. As Naficy contends, consuming the other evokes a kind of yearning for meaning and self-definition (defining the dominant through one's relation to the other) whereby dominant hegemonies want to capture the threat and allure of the other—coopting difference, effacing history, mapping difference to consume it as a style, similar to the colonial urge for consumption.

In reappropriating a liminal exile narrative, *Hawaii Five-0* signifies a dichotomy between the effort to engage in issues of local regional culture, and the effort to construct, commodify and consume Hawaii as a Western ideal for the purpose of perpetuating an exoticized myth of paradise to sell/promote tourism. *Hawaii Five-0* is distinguishable from *Hawaiian Eye* and *Magnum PI* series in its conflation of authenticity, arguably engaging local culture to a greater degree than either show. Yet this difference of engagement is coopted by mainstream Hollywood consumer ideology to produce a narrative of exotic, feminized cultural geography that is fetishized as 'other.' In *Made In Paradise*, Luis Reyes notes 'a charming, though sometimes confusing, portrait of seduction and corruption, intrigue and greed, using images seeped in stereotype, Hollywood movies and, later, television perpetuated this mythology that combined fact with fiction to form a conflation of Pacific cultures.'[21]

Homi Bhabha explores the notion of cultural identity by foregrounding its ideological ambivalence and liminality to encourage the negotiation of political/cultural authority and national/regional boundaries. This liminal space relates to the issue of television and mass media reimagining, packaging and constructing multifaceted identity amid a multi-ethnic cultural space à la Hollywood narrative and co-opting discourse of marginalized or 'exile' cultures for global consumption. In 'Consuming the Other,' Naficy and Teshome H. Gabriel argue that ultimately, 'a construction of diversity and difference is the democratization of consumption and not of representation. Corporatism nurtures the fundamental transformation that postmodernism is ushering in whereby conscientious citizen is replaced with carefree consumer...if not equal under the law...equal as consumers of products and ideas.'[22]

Although Lord refers to the series as 'not a part of the Hollywood establishment...a non-industry show', suggesting that the show itself exists in a kind of liminal state, *Hawaii Five-0* reimagines a desired, mass-mediated cultural space – a mythic Hawaii à la Hollywood – which reaffirms and naturalizes the promotion of Hawaii's primary economic industry with the infusion of capital into its local/regional 'community' vital to sustain the 50th state.[23] Lord insisted 'against the opposition of a budget conscious network, that the series be filmed in Hawaii in its entirety, using authentic island backgrounds for the action instead of inserting canned scenic footage.'[24] According to Lord: 'We were a breakthrough for TV locations – the first hour-long color series to be made entirely away from Hollywood. The network was aghast when we insisted on shooting in Hawaii. Our early budgets blew their minds. We went over budget more than a million dollars because we had to transfer 60 technicians to the islands.' However: 'Our success isn't due to the different scenery and backgrounds of Hawaii, although they are a factor. We haven't fallen prey to the hype and pressures of the Hollywood miasma.' Instead, Lord asserts, 'We use amateur talent' from the local community and a 'variety of extras of all races. If we need a Chinese gambling house for a scene, we go to an actual gambling house. We don't build a phoney one on a soundstage.... If we need a Shinto priest, we hire a real one. Viewers can tell the difference. We're out on locations six days out of seven. Viewers can smell the trees and flowers, the car fumes, incense and laundries...there's a smell of reality about our show that, along with our refusal to bear the Hollywood imprint, accounts for our longevity.'[25] Is it not true that *Hawaii Five-0* bears Hollywood's imprint?

Cultural influences and industrial mediation intersect in a transcultural process of reinscription (ie Hollywood reimagining Hawaii) which informs its construction of national/regional aesthetic and identity. *Hawaii Five-0* began production in Hawaii in 1967; yet, although shot entirely on location in Hawaii, the crime series was inherently a Hollywood show with pre-production developed and post-production completed in Los Angeles industry studio facilities. In the 1970 article, '"Hawaii Five-0": Crime Series in Lush Surroundings,' for *TV Times* in Honolulu, Smith argued that every 'foot of film' shot for the series 'is sent to the mainland for processing and editing. Jack Lord and his cohorts see nothing they make until it plays on television here – a week later than in the states.' (At that time, everything was televised a week later in Hawaii.) Smith explained that scripts 'are processed through the Hollywood offices of executive producer, Leonard Freeman, Lord's partner. There's criticism that rarely are scripts drawn out of the unique circumstances of island living, that they could happen anywhere. This week's play...deals with a hippie problem – one much less evident here than in the mainland.' Thus, industrial production mediation appropriates local culture and regional identity to perpetuate a Western myth of the exotic. According to Smith, 'Crew and technicians are *haoles* (mainlanders) on subsistence pay and there's been no attempt to develop local people. A new studio has been built for the show at Ft. Ruger near Diamond Head, but it has the feel of a temporary structure, not the center of a burgeoning industry...still the series is Hawaii – 80 per cent shot on actual sites...mountains and plantations and isolated spits of beach.'[26] Records in the Jack Lord Collection indicate the original production facilities were indeed temporary: local residents protested and filed a lawsuit over a zoning dispute forcing the Honolulu city council to move the series' studio location in 1975.[27] Tinker notes that the show did train an army of local people who went on to form the backbone of *Magnum P.I.*'s crew.

A February 23 1976 letter states that CBS Television Network West Coast Vice President, Robert Norvel, defended the proposed facility's renewal following the studio relocation in 1975 and refuted allegations that CBS conned government agencies.[28] As Trumbull explains, 'A few years ago, when an association of residents demanded that the state refuse to renew the studio's lease on a parcel of state land in the Diamond Head area, declaring that the filming upset the calm of the neighborhood, Governor George Ariyoshi intervened to obtain an extension. The studio has since moved to a more sequestered location nearby.'[29] An April 2, 1976 letter from the State of Hawaii Department of Planning and Economic Development Director, Hideto Kono, to Rudy Pacarro of the Honolulu City Council and Chairman of the Planning and Zoning Committee (with a copy also sent to Hawaii Governor George Ariyoshi) addresses the issue of *Hawaii Five-0's* permit for a studio at 18th Avenue and Diamond Head Road. 'I write to you to stress the seriousness with which the State Administration views a possible delay in the granting of this permit,' Kono states. He goes on to assert:

> The issue is simple but very serious: Shall permission be granted in a reasonable time to a vitally needed segment of a major industry to operate in Hawaii for a limited period, providing jobs and related major economic benefits to our people? Or shall negativism, delay, and an excessively critical and carping attitude drive this industry from our shores to competing Mainland states?

Further, in an overwhelming gesture of support for the series (and either referencing its wholesomeness or its lack of environmental detriment) Kono argues:

> What is involved here is a responsible, 'clean,' cooperative industry which has leaned over backwards to meet environmental, planning, aesthetic and other demands made upon it. This motion picture and television industry—represented so prominently by CBS and Hawaii Five-0 film production activities—provides millions of critically needed dollars to Hawaii's economy.

Hence, tourism and the implications of the possible removal of its promotion apparatus ie the televised location shooting for the show – welded considerable power. The State letter integrates discourses of 'democracy' and regionalism in appealing:

Certainly, the Hawaii Five-0 people have been eminently fair to the people of Hawaii. More than 20 potential sites were examined to find the one most suitable for meeting all the various concerns of the State and City and our people, as well as the technical needs of the producers...due to the State's commitments...a complex of decisions is now in danger of going *kapakahi* [out of control], to the detriment of many worthwhile State goals.

These goals are not only strictly industrial, but also related to the domestic sphere of the family. As Kono asserts, 'Foremost among these goals...is the State's economic health. Hawaii is desperately in need of various types of new industry, as well as an expansion of present industries. Our unemployment rate is extremely high. Any loss of jobs and employment income is a very serious blow to our island families who live in a State which has the second highest cost of living in the Nation.' Further, he warns, 'There is nothing permanent about the Hawaii Five-0 production operations. Their request is for a five-year lease, under a conditional use permit. In return, Hawaii receives an outstanding portion of the television industry.'

Kono rolls out all the state's economic ammunition directly relating to the show's integral position to the tourism industry and, in his State letter to Pacarro, relates it to the personal sphere of Hawaii's people:

> Hawaii Five-0 has introduced more than $30 million into Hawaii's economy. It has an average weekly audience of more than 30 million persons in the United States alone, and is distributed in 66 foreign countries. The series obviously has a tangible effect upon Hawaii's tourism industry. The loss of this segment of the film industry to Hawaii will hurt Hawaii's people. It is imperative that the City Council consider the urgency of the time-factor involved. The Hawaii Five-0 producers are pledged to vacate their present premises at Fort Ruger. Plans must be made now because of the extremely short deadline.... It is our urgent request that you do all you can to assist.[30]

Trumbull's 1979 *New York Times* article "Hawaii Five-0," at Age 11, Is an Island Institution' examines the style of consumption of Hawaii: 'How do the crime and violence in "Five-0" affect Hawaii's image?' *Honolulu Advertiser* editor George Chaplin contends viewers often mistook the show's crime fighters as 'real people,' quoting a man in Israel: 'With such a fine police force, then Hawaii must have a low crime rate.' Chaplin argues, 'The story fades from memory quickly, but the image of the beautiful scenery remains...The effect of the series has been a significant plus for Hawaii.' According to a Honolulu Police Department spokesperson, 'Most people must know we can't have that kind of crime here.'[31] But, if TV cops are going to crack a case, why not do it in a beautiful locale with a 'rescue narrative' involving the 'saving' of paradise? Of course, this narrative rearticulates and appropriates local culture for global consumption.

Just as 1950s Hollywood films capitalized on wide-screen colour images of spectacle shot at faraway locations in stereophonic sound to lure a growing TV audience away from black-and-white small screen television, *Hawaii Five-0* capitalized on location shooting in Hawaii as a strategy for showcasing colour television by the late 1960s – tapping in to the travel and colour film market. Invoking the formal experimentation of late 1960s avant-garde inspired cinematic *mise-en-scene*, in particular exploiting Hollywood's co-opting of European art cinema as an industrial media strategy to target a 'hip' baby-boom audience. *Hawaii Five-0* also promoted travel as an expanding consumer leisure activity. Accentuated by its incredibly popular theme song, 'Hawaii Five-0,' composed by Morton Stevens which gained significant radio air play in recording cross-promotion. The frenetic pace of the show's opening is basically a deft hyper-travelogue. It advertises and commodifies the myth of the exotic to consume local culture as 'other' via mediation of dominant ideology of global/national Hollywood genre narrative.

Selling excitement and geographic/psychic 'escape' for would-be tourists through an adrenaline rush, the progressively rapid movement of the show's visuals open with the beautifully blue Pacific ocean: a surfer's paradise. As a perfectly sublime and phallic wave swells, powerfully lifts, curves, tilts and crashes behind the flaming red title 'Hawaii Five-0' zooming in exhilarated acceleration toward the camera, quickly cutting to numerous swish pans of the water and zooms of the ocean waves, followed by a series of split-second aerial shots of Diamond Head, scenic landscapes, the city skyline, the mountains, a helicopter shot of Aloha Tower, and shot after shot of *hotels* – culminating in a careening helicopter zoom to the penthouse of the Ilikai Hotel lanai/balcony where Lord stands. Cut to Lord turning toward the camera, numerous swish pans, a shot of a car careening headlong down a tree-lined street, followed by an avant-garde shot of the moving car at a reverse, upside-down "Dutch angle" which turns completely over, as it juxtaposes an 'exotic' Polynesian island girl running along the ocean. Cut to multiple Freudian shots of water, followed by a plethora of zooms of scenery, sculpture, countless beautiful 'exotic' women, a young boy (possibly a gay reading?), more 'island' women, followed by another avant-garde truck/tracking shot at a "Dutch angle" with a fish-eye lens along the underbelly of a jet. Cut to an extreme angled fish-eye shot directly up panning under the jet engine on the plane's wing, across the front of another turbine, then an extreme shot straight upward towards a moving plane crossing the sun, numerous epileptic zooms of sunsets and oceans, the notable close-up from breast to hip of a gyrating female Tahitian dancer (as in tourist luaus, conflating Polynesian culture and readily being used because of its rapid rhythms and faster pace to signify a Hawaiian hula dancer), followed by countless zooms into neon lit landmarks and city lights at night, sirens, then Danno through cracked glass, a crashing car engulfed in flames. Cut to Chin Ho with walkie-talkie on the roof, zoom to Duke/Zulu with binoculars amid the lush green mountain scenery, then flashing sirens. All in less than 60 seconds. Out of these multiple points of contention, there emerges an instability and heterogeneity permeating the influence of this 'dominant' Hollywood narrative of local culture.

Noting the 'exotic Pacific setting' of the series, Brooks Robards argued *Hawaii Five-0* lent itself to 'romantic fantasies.'[32] And the series' solid ratings reaffirmed its popularity with audiences. According to figures in the Jack Lord Collection, by the opening of its sixth season, *Hawaii Five-0*'s ratings in its Tuesday, 9:00-10:00pm time slot for the episode 'I'll Kill 'Em Again' on September 24, 1974 were a respectable 27 rating with a 40 share for the first half hour from 9:00-9:30pm (following *M*A*S*H.*'s popular 29.4 rating/44 share from 8:30-9:00), and a 27.7 rating/41 share for its final half hour from 9:30-10:00pm.[33]

In cultivating a local television industry along the slopes of Diamond Head *Hawaii Five-0*'s success also meant a significant financial input for local business in Hawaii. By the late 1970s, the series certainly aided the state's economy by promoting tourism. A small Pacific island seen globally on a weekly basis by 300 million viewers in 83 countries affected the image of the 50th state in other faraway locales internationally. In its 12 seasons, *Hawaii Five-0* was the longest-running drama series on the air and the third longest in television history, behind *Gunsmoke* which ran 20 seasons and *Bonanza* which ran 13; it even displaced *Dragnet* as the longest-running police show during that era. (The 1980s prime time 'soap' melodrama *Knots Landing* would later run 14 seasons.) Lord attributed *Hawaii Five-0*'s longevity to its 'ambience.' The show's star and producer asserted that "Hawaii" still conjures up romance, with visions of the trade winds and palm trees, especially in places' where the 'snow is six feet deep.'[34]

In "Hawaii Five-0,' at Age 11, is an Island Institution' *The New York Times* indicated that besides nearly $500,000 spent producing each of the 24 annual segments of the series, Honolulu families of married staff members spent at least another $500,000 on personal expenses per season in the local economy with maintenance of the unit's motor vehicles and constructions costs adding another $500,000 or more. *The New York Times* promoted the show's economic benefit for Hawaii and estimated that during *Hawaii Five-0*'s first 11 years, 20,000 local people were used as extras (at $65 a day plus lunch) receiving a total of nearly $1 million, with a similar amount going to local actors. The Hawaii-based series put more than $100 million into circulation in production costs and indirectly aided the state's economy 'by an incalculable amount through its contribution to the promotion of tourism.'[35] Indeed, tangible economic benefits from *Hawaii Five-0*'s global reimagining of Hawaii's cultural space and its productive infusion of capital back into the community provided tremendous opportunity. According to the State Department of Business, Economic Development and Tourism and the State of Hawaii Film Office, not only did the show inject $100 million into Hawaii's economy; it also provided 8,000 jobs a year.[36]

On the show's 10th anniversary, *The Honolulu Star-Bulletin* acknowledged Hawaii's 'heavy debt to the series' while expressing ambivalence about its sensationalized mixture of beauty with crime and violence. Nonetheless, the local Honolulu newspaper conceded, 'There is no denying that the 'Five-0' show has brought more people to a fascination with Hawaii than even the strains of 'Sweet Leilani' or 'Aloha Oe'.[37]   Ultimately, *Hawaii Five-0*'s production and representation signifies a dichotomy between the effort to engage in issues of local culture/regional industry, and the effort to construct, commodify and consume Hawaii as a feminized and fetishized Western ideal of 'Oriental' island exile and regional ethnicity as 'other' ie to perpetuate the exotic myth of the travelogue, of a remote tropical Pacific paradise promoting tourism via global Hollywood television narrative.

Notes

1   Gavan Daws, *Hawaii 1959-1989: The First Thirty Years of the Aloha State*. Honolulu: Publishers Group Hawaii, 1989, p.102.

2   Eileen H. Tamura, *Americanization, Acculturation, and Ethnic Identity*, Urbana: University of Illinois Press, 1994. Roger Bell, *Last Among Equals*. Honolulu: University of Hawaii Press, 1984.

3   Robert C. Schmitt, *Hawaii in the Movies, 1898-1959*. Honolulu: Hawaiian Historical Society, 1988, p.vi.

4   'Hawaii Five-0,' (Review) *The Los Angeles Times*, September 15, 1975.

5   Lynn Spigel, 'Installing the Television Set: Popular Discourses on Television and Domestic Space, 1948-1955,' in *Private Screenings: Television and the Female Consumer*, eds. Lynn Spigel and Denise Mann. (Minneapolis: University of Minnesota Press, 1992), pp.9-13.

6   Cecil Smith, 'Hawaii Five-0: Crime Series in Lush Surroundings.' *TV Times*. (Honolulu) January 1, 1970.

7   Edward W. Said, *Orientalism*. New York: Vintage Books, 1978, p.206.

8   Jim Gilbert, 'Off the Charts,' *Sky: The Magazine of International Culture*, Delta Airlines, January 1996, p.50.

9   Joshua Shapiro, 'Forever Hold Your Peace,' *Sky: The Magazine of International Culture*, Delta Airlines, January 1996, p.89.

10   Charles Memminger, 'Danno, check every noodle in Chinatown,' *The Honolulu Advertiser*, March 22, 1996, p.C-1.

11   'Visitors to Hawaii,' Hawaii Visitor's Bureau Market Research, April 18, 1996. State of Hawaii Department of Business, Economic Development and Tourism correspondence from the Hawaii Film Office, Note to History Files Re.: Series production and expenditure statistics, April 19, 1996. Jack Lord in Gene Tinker, 'It began with 'Hawaii Five-0,'' *Hyatt's Hawaii*, vol.6, no.3 (1984), p.12.

12   Luis I. Reyes, with contributions by Ed Rampell, *Made In Paradise: Hollywood's Films of Hawaii and the South Seas*. Honolulu: Mutual Publishing, 1995, p.319.

13   Charles Memminger, 'Danno, check every noodle in Chinatown,' *The Honolulu Advertiser*, March 22, 1996, p.C-1.

14   Cecil Smith, 'After 10 Seasons, Kam Fong Expires' *The Los Angeles Times*. April 4, 1978.

15   Bettelou Peterson, 'McGarrett's Still on the Beat.' *The Detroit Free Press*, from the Jack Lord Collection, University of Southern California Cinema-Television Library, Los Angeles, California, April 4, 1979.

16   Robert Trumbull, ''Hawaii Five-0,' at Age 11, is an Island Institution.' *The New York Times*. February 11, 1979, p.61.

17   According to Bernie Oseransky as cited in Luis I. Reyes, with contributions by Ed Rampell, *Made In Paradise: Hollywood's Films of Hawaii and the South Seas*. Honolulu: Mutual Publishing, 1995, p.319.

18   Jack Lord, 'It Can't Be Done.' *The Hollywood Reporter's TV Preview for 1975-1976*, reprinted in Gene Tinker, 'It began with 'Hawaii Five-0,'' *Hyatt's Hawaii*, Vol.6, No.3 (1984), p.13.

19   Benedict Anderson, *Imagined Communities*. London: Verso, 1991.   Luis I. Reyes, with contributions by Ed Rampell, *Made In Paradise: Hollywood's Films of Hawaii and the South Seas.* Honolulu: Mutual Publishing, 1995, p.319.

20   David Morley and Kevin Robins. *Spaces of Identity: Global Media, Electronic Landscapes and Cultural Boundaries.* London: Routledge, 1995. Hamid Naficy, 'The Poetics and Practice of Iranian Nostalgia in Exile,' *Diaspora*, Vol. 1, #3, 1991, pp.289-291. Hamid Naficy, 'Exile Discourse and Television Fetishization,' *Quarterly Review of Film and Video*, Vol. 13, 1991. Hamid Naficy, Exile Cultures. Minneapolis: University of Minnesota Press, 1993. Hamid Naficy and Teshome H. Gabriel. 'Consuming the Other,' University Of California, Los Angeles, 1991. In 'Discourse of the Other: Postcoloniality, Positionality, and Subjectivity' *Quarterly Review of Film and Video*, Vol. 13, May 1991.

21   Luis I. Reyes, with contributions by Ed Rampell, *Made In Paradise: Hollywood's Films of Hawaii and the South Seas.* Honolulu: Mutual Publishing, 1995, p.3.

22   Hamid Naficy and Teshome H. Gabriel. 'Consuming the Other,' University Of California, Los Angeles, 1991. In 'Discourse of the Other: Postcoloniality, Positionality, and Subjectivity' *Quarterly Review of Film and Video*, Vol. 13, May 1991, p.i. Homi Bhabha, *Nation and Narration*. Routledge, 1990.

23   Jack Lord quoted in Vernon Scott, "Five-0' Rode in With Tide but it Still Hasn't Ebbed.' *Memphis Press-Scimitar.* September 30, 1978, p.6.

24   Jack Lord quoted in Robert Trumbull, "Hawaii Five-0,' at Age 11, is an Island Institution.' The New York Times. February 11, 1979, p.61.

25   Jack Lord quoted in Vernon Scott, "Five-0' Rode in With Tide but it Still Hasn't Ebbed.' *Memphis Press-Scimitar.* September 30, 1978, p.6.

26   Cecil Smith, 'Hawaii Five-0: Crime Series in Lush Surroundings.' *TV Times.* (Honolulu) January 1, 1970.

27   Hideto Kono, '...the City Planning Commission on March 31 voted to recommend against granting a permit...' Letter from State of Hawaii Department of Planning and Economic Developent Director (Kono) to Rudy Pacarro, Honolulu City Council and Chairman, Planning and Zoning Committee [cc: to Governer George Ariyoshi] from the Jack Lord Collection, University of Southern California Cinema-Television Library, Los Angeles, California, April 2, 1976, p.1.

28   Hideto Kono, '...the City Planning Commission on March 31 voted to recommend against granting a permit...' Letter from State of Hawaii Department of Planning and Economic Developent Director (Kono) to Rudy Pacarro, Honolulu City Council and Chairman, Planning and Zoning Committee [cc: to Governer George Ariyoshi] from the Jack Lord Collection, University of Southern California Cinema-Television Library, Los Angeles, California, April 2, 1976, p.1.

29   Robert Trumbull, "Hawaii Five-0,' at Age 11, is an Island Institution.' *The New York Times.* February 11, 1979, p.61.

30   Hideto Kono, '...the City Planning Commission on March 31 voted to recommend against granting a permit...' Letter from State of Hawaii Department of Planning and Economic Developent Director (Kono) to Rudy Pacarro, Honolulu City Council and Chairman, Planning and Zoning Committee [cc: to Governer George Ariyoshi] from thc Jack Lord Collection, University of Southern California Cinema-Television Library, Los Angeles, California, April 2, 1976, pp.1-3.

31   *Honolulu Advertiser* editor George Chaplin, a man from Israel, and Honolulu Police Department spokesperson quoted in Robert Trumbull, "Hawaii Five-0,' at Age 11, is an Island Institution.' *The New York Times.* February 11, 1979, p.61.

32   Robards, Brooks. 'The Police Show.' In Brian Rose, Ed. *TV Genres: A Handbook and Reference Guide*. London, England/Westport, Connecticut: Greenwood Press, 1985, p.16.

33   "I'll Kill 'Em Again' Hawaii Five-0 Episode Ratings' from the Jack Lord Collection, University of Southern California Cinema-Television Library, Los Angeles, California, September 28, 1974.

34   Jack Lord quoted in Robert Trumbull, "Hawaii Five-0,' at Age 11, is an Island Institution.' *The New York Times*. February 11, 1979, p.61.

35   Robert Trumbull, "Hawaii Five-0,' at Age 11, is an Island Institution.' *The New York Times*. February 11, 1979, p.61.

36   State of Hawaii Department of Business, Economic Development and Tourism correspondence from the Hawaii Film Office, Note to History Files Re.: Series production and expenditure statistics, April 19, 1996. 'Visitors to Hawaii,' Hawaii Visitor's Bureau Market Research, April 18, 1996. Gene Tinker, 'It began with 'Hawaii Five-0',' *Hyatt's Hawaii*, vol.6, no.3 (1984), p.12.

37   *Honolulu Advertiser* editor George Chaplin quoted in Robert Trumbull, "Hawaii Five-0,' at Age 11, is an Island Institution.' *The New York Times*. February 11, 1979, p.61.

Bibliography

Anderson, Benedict. *Imagined Communities*. London: Verso, 1991.

Bagott, Dan. 'Series: 'Hawaii Five-0' On Location in Singapore' CBS Television Network Trade News Press Release from the Jack Lord Collection, University of Southern California Cinema-Television Library, Los Angeles, California, April 24, 1978.

Bell, Roger *Last Among Equals*. Honolulu: University of Hawaii Press, 1984.

Bhabha, Homi K., ed. *Nation and Narration*. New York: Routledge, 1990.

Butzel, Marcia, and Ana M. Lopez, Eds. 'Mediating the National,' Special Issue, *Quarterly Review of Film and Video*, Vol. 14, No. 3, 1993.

Cassin, Jean M. 'After years and years...' Letter to Jack Lord from the Jack Lord Collection, University of Southern California Cinema-Television Library, Los Angeles, California, January 2, 1980.

Daws, Gavan. *Hawaii 1959-1989: The First Thirty Years of the Aloha State*. Honolulu: Publishers Group Hawaii, 1989, p.102.

Dixon. 'Hawaii Five-0 Expenditures' Budget from the Jack Lord Collection, University of Southern California Cinema-Television Library, Los Angeles, California, November 11, 1974.

Finnegan, William. 'In order to keep you advised on 'Father'...' Memo to Doug Green, from the Jack Lord Collection, University of Southern California Cinema-Television Library, Los Angeles, California, September 12, 1973.

Gaines, Jane, and Michael Renov, Eds. 'Female Representation and Consumer Culture,' Special Issue, *Quarterly Review of Film and Video*, Vol. 11, No. 1, 1989.

Gilbert, Jim. 'Off the Charts,' *Sky: The Magazine of International Culture*, Delta Airlines, January 1996, p.50.

Gitlin, Todd. 'Prime Time Ideology: The Hegemonic Process in Television Entertainment.' In Horace Newcomb, Ed. *Television: The Critical View*. New York: Oxford University Press, 1994.

Hawaii Five-0. Leonard Freeman Productions for CBS Television, September 26, 1968 to April 26, 1980. (Videotaped Episodes): 'A Bullet for McGarrett.' October 29, 1969 (second season), 'Killer Bee.' January 21, 1970 (second season), 'Two Doves and Mr. Heron.' October 12, 1971 (fourth season), 'The Hostage.' March 11, 1975 (seventh season) from the University Of California, Los Angeles Film and Television Archive; 'Tsunami.' December 22, 1977 (tenth season), 'East Wind, Ill Wind.' December 29, 1977 (tenth season), 'Tread the King's Shadow.' January 5, 1978 (tenth season), 'A Big Aloha.' January 12, 1978 (tenth season) Videotaped June 13-16 1995, Channel 'K5' TV, Honolulu, Hawaii. 'All the King's Horses.' November 26, 1969 (second season), 'Leopard on the Rock.' December 3, 1969 (second season), 'The Devil and Mr. Frog.' December 10, 1969 (second season), 'The Joker's Wild, Man, Wild.' December 17, 1969 (second season), 'Which Way Did They Go?' December 24, 1969 (second season), 'Death Wish on Tantalus Mountain.' September 19, 1972 (fifth season) 'You Don't Have to Kill to Get Rich But It Helps.' September 26, 1972 (fifth season), 'Pig in a Blanket.' October 3, 1972 (fifth season), 'The Clock Struck Twelve.' October 10, 1972 (fifth season), 'Journey Out of Limbo.' October 31, 1972 (fifth season) Videotaped January-April 1996, Channel 54, Austin, Texas.

'Hawaii Five-0.' (Review) *Daily Variety*. September 18, 1970.

'Hawaii Five-0.' (Review) *Los Angeles Times*. September 15, 1975.

'Hawaii Five-0.' (Review) *Variety*. September 23, 1970.

'Hawaii Five-0.' (Review) *Variety*. September 15, 1975.

'Hawaii Five-0.' (Review) *Variety*. September 16, 1980.

'Hawaii Five-0 – Expenditures.' Budget from the Jack Lord Collection, University of Southern California Cinema-Television Library, Los Angeles, California, July 17, 1975.

"'Hawaii Five-0' Thriller Unfolds in Singapore...' CBS Television Network, Television City, Press Release in the Hawaii Five-O Clipping File, University of Southern California Cinema-Television Library, Los Angeles, California, February 27, 1979.

Holmlund, Christine Ann. 'Displacing Limits of Difference' in 'Discourse of the Other: Postcoloniality, Positionality, and Subjectivity' *Quarterly Review of Film and Video*, Vol. 13, May 1991.

"'I'll Kill 'Em Again' Hawaii Five-0 Episode Ratings' from the Jack Lord Collection, University of Southern California Cinema-Television Library, Los Angeles, California, September 28, 1974.

Jameson, Fredric. 'Reinfication and utopia in mass culture,' *Social Text*, 1, (1979) pp.130-148.

Joyrich, Lynne. 'All that Television Allows: TV Melodrama, Postmodernism, and Consumer Culture' In *Private Screenings: Televisdion and the Female Consumer*, eds. Lynn Spigel and Denise Mann. Minneapolis: University of Minnesota Press, 1992.

Kono, Hideto. '...the City Planning Commission on March 31 voted to recommend against granting a permit...' Letter from State of Hawaii Department of Planning and Economic Developent Director (Kono) to Rudy Pacarro, Honolulu City Council and Chairman, Planning and Zoning Committee [cc: to Governer George Ariyoshi] from the Jack Lord Collection, University of Southern California Cinema-Television Library, Los Angeles, California, April 2, 1976.

Lipsitz, George. 'The Meaning of Memory: Family, Class, and Ethnicity in Early Network Television Programs' In *Private Screenings: Television and the Female Consumer*, eds. Lynn Spigel and Denise Mann. Minneapolis: University of Minnesota Press, 1992.

Lord, Jack. 'It Can't Be Done.' *The Hollywood Reporter's TV Preview for 1975-1976*, reprinted in Gene Tinker, 'It began with 'Hawaii Five-0," *Hyatt's Hawaii*, Vol.6, No.3 (1984), p.13.

Lord, Jack. 'Re: Death with Father - Revised Second Draft dated June 14, 1973.' Memo to Bob Sweeney, from the Jack Lord Collection, University of Southern California Cinema-Television Library, Los Angeles, California, July 9, 1973.

Memminger, Charles. 'Danno, check every noodle in Chinatown,' *Honolulu Advertiser*, March 22, 1996, p.C-1.

Morley, David and Kevin Robins. *Spaces of Identity: Global Media, Electronic Landscapes and Cultural Boundaries*. London: Routledge, 1995.

Naficy, Hamid. *Exile Cultures*. Minneapolis: University of Minnesota Press, 1993.

Naficy, Hamid. 'Exile Discourse and Television Fetishization,' *Quarterly Review of Film and Video*, Vol. 13, 1991.

Naficy, Hamid. 'The Poetics and Practice of Iranian Nostalgia in Exile,' *Diaspora*, Vol. 1, #3, 1991.

Naficy, Hamid and Teshome H. Gabriel. 'Consuming the Other,' University Of California, Los Angeles, 1991. In 'Discourse of the Other: Postcoloniality, Positionality, and Subjectivity' *Quarterly Review of Film and Video*, Vol. 13, May 1991.

Newcomb, Horace, Ed. *Television: The Critical View*. New York: Oxford University Press, 1994.

Nichols, Bill. *Ideology and the Image*. Bloomington: University of Indiana Press, 1981.

Norvel, Robert W. 'On February 10, 1976, you forwarded a copy of a letter...' CBS Television Network letter from West Coast Vice President, Norvel, and George Koga, Honolulu City Council defending proposed facility renewal, documenting studio relocation in 1975 and refuting allegations that CBS 'conned' government agencies; from the Jack Lord Collection, University of Southern California Cinema-Television Library, Los Angeles, California, February 23, 1976.

'Notes on Publication Information Meeting Re Request for Conditional Use Permit,' from the Jack Lord Collection, University of Southern California Cinema-Television Library, Los Angeles, California, February 5, 1975.

'Passport Travel Guide, Journey to Adventure: 'Hawaii – A Place of Magic." Travel video hosted by Gunther Less, GLL TV Enterprises, Inc., 1990.

Peterson, Bettelou. 'McGarrett's Still on the Beat.' *Detroit Free Press*, from the Jack Lord Collection, University of Southern California Cinema-Television Library, Los Angeles, California, April 4, 1979.

Reyes, Luis I. with contributions by Ed Rampell, *Made In Paradise: Hollywood's Films of Hawaii and the South Seas*. Honolulu: Mutual Publishing, 1995.

Robards, Brooks. 'The Police Show.' In Brian Rose, Ed. *TV Genres: A Handbook and Reference Guide*. London, England/Westport, Connecticut: Greenwood Press, 1985.

Said, Edward W. *Orientalism*. New York: Vintage Books, 1978.

Schmitt, Robert C. *Hawaii in the Movies, 1898-1959*. Honolulu: Hawaiian Historical Society, 1988.

Scott, Vernon. "Five-0' Rode in With Tide but it Still Hasn't Ebbed.' *Memphis Press-Scimitar*. September 30, 1978, p.6.

Shapiro, Joshua. 'Forever Hold Your Peace,' *Sky: The Magazine of International Culture*, Delta Airlines, January 1996, p.89.

Shohat, Ella. 'Gender and Culture of Empire' in 'Discourse of the Other: Postcoloniality, Positionality, and Subjectivity.' *Quarterly Review of Film and Video*, Vol. 13, May 1991.

Smith, Cecil. 'After 10 Seasons, Kam Fong Expires' *The Los Angeles Times*. April 4, 1978.

Smith, Cecil. 'Hawaii Five-0: Crime Series in Lush Surroundings.' *TV Times*. (Honolulu) January 1, 1970.

Spigel, Lynn. 'Installing the Television Set: Popular Discourses on Television and Domestic Space, 1948-1955.' In *Private Screenings: Television and the Female Consumer*, eds. Lynn Spigel and Denise Mann. Minneapolis: University of Minnesota Press, 1992.

Spigel, Lynn. *Make Room for TV*. Chicago: University of Chicago Press, 1992.

State of Hawaii Department of Business, Economic Development and Tourism correspondence from the Hawaii Film Office, Note to History Files Re.: Series production and expenditure statistics, April 19, 1996.

'Studio Chronology,' Hawaii Film Office, April 19, 1996.

Tamura, Eileen H. *Americanization, Acculturation, and Ethnic Identity*, Urbana: University of Illinois Press, 1994.

Tinker, Gene. 'It began with 'Hawaii Five-0,'' *Hyatt's Hawaii*, vol.6, no.3 (1984), pp.11-12.

Trumbull, Robert. "Hawaii Five-0,' at Age 11, is an Island Institution.' *New York Times*. February 11, 1979, p.61.

'Visitors to Hawaii,' Hawaii Visitor's Bureau Market Research, April 18, 1996.

Zalburg, Sanford. 'Lights! action! camera!: The film biz is big biz in Hawaii,' *Honolulu Advertiser*, June 20, 1978, pp.B-1,B-2.

'Bigger on the inside...' *Doctor Who* as British cultural history

Nicholas Cull

It all began around teatime on Saturday, 23 November 1963. Throbbing electronic music and swirling graphics summoned British television viewers to their screens. The titles announced *Doctor Who*, a quirky science fiction serial about an eccentric time traveller, wandering the galaxy in a space ship disguised as a London police telephone box. This ship – known as the TARDIS (the acronym stood for Time and Relative Dimension in Space) – was necessarily bigger on the inside than it appeared on the outside. Within a few weeks the Tardis had brought the Doctor face to face with the most evil life form in the galaxy: the Daleks – ruthless mutant creatures encased in pepper pot shaped robotic bodies, committed to conquest. The Daleks were an instant success, and kick-started what became the longest running drama serial in British television history, outside the soap operas. Given its sustained popularity, *Doctor Who* provides the cultural historian with a window on the culture that created and embraced it: Britain, between 1963 and 1989. The origins of *Doctor Who* illuminate a transitional moment in the history of the BBC as the corporation searched for a programme format to beat commercial competition. Moreover the shape and development of *Doctor Who*'s character and adventures reveal both sustained national obsessions and the path of social changes. The shifting tone of *Doctor Who* also tells a story as the programme drifted away from its part in the BBC's mission to educate and became a mischievously subversive expression of camp in British popular culture.

Origins: The space on a Saturday night

The origins of *Doctor Who* lie in a battle as enduring as the struggle between the Doctor and the Daleks: the struggle for ratings between the BBC and its commercial rival, ITV, launched in September 1955. By September 1960 there were no BBC programmes in the British top 10.[1] One of the few BBC success stories during these years was a seven-part 1961 science fiction drama called *A for Andromeda* co-written by the astronomer Fred Hoyle and starring the then unknown actress Julie Christie. With this in mind, the corporation contemplated a cycle of one-off sci-fi short story adaptations. In early 1962 the veteran BBC executive Eric Maschwitz (then Special Assistant and Advisor to the Controller of Television) asked the Script Department, Television (then run by Donald Wilson) to 'survey the field of published science fiction, in its relevance to BBC Television drama.'[2] An initial report of April 1962 raised many problems with sci-fi, including the lack of character-driven stories in a genre that, as Kingsley Amis famously noted, preferred 'the idea as hero'. The writers found no existing stories suitable for immediate adaptation but suggested further research.[3] Two members of staff, Alice Frick and John Braybon, spent the next eight weeks reading as much science fiction as possible, searching for suitable material for a series. Their brief was to find imaginative character-driven stories that 'did not include Bug-Eyed Monsters' (abbreviated as BEM's) or elaborate spacecraft, for fear that contrived costumes and effects would prevent the audience from suspending their disbelief.[4] They found several stories that fitted the bill. The most promising was a 1960 novel by Paul Anderson called *Guardians of Time* in which time travellers from Earth's future – the Time Patrol – enrol a protagonist from the Twentieth Century to help prevent other time travellers from tampering with the past. Their report in July 1962 noted the potential in such a scenario for 'individual plots... tackled by a variety of screen writers' thereby creating 'the *Z Cars* of science fiction.'[5] The seed for *Doctor Who* was in place.

As part of its effort to regain ground on ITV, the BBC hired a number of star players from the world of independent broadcasting, including the Canadian-born head of drama at the ABC (Associated British Corporation), Sidney Newman. A veteran of the National Film Board of Canada, Newman was best known for his work on *Armchair Theatre* and as the creator of *The Avengers*. Newman joined the BBC on 9 December 1962 as 'Head of Drama Group, Television' and immediately began the process of reorganization. He hoped to make an impact on ratings by the autumn of 1963.[6] Newman's first problem was the massive loss of viewers on a Saturday evening between the end of the BBC's sports programme *Grandstand* at 5.15 and the start of the popular pop music review show *Juke Box Jury*. Neither classic serials nor imported cartoons had worked in this slot. Clearly the BBC needed a programming bridge, specifically aimed, as Newman later put it 'at a state of mind generally fitting Saturday afternoons.'[7] A lively science fiction serial appeared to fit the bill perfectly.

Newman set about the task of designing a suitable serial. He put together a small team including the former Head of Scripts, Television (now Head of Serials, Television), Donald Wilson, a writer named C.E. 'Bunny' Webber and the two researchers who had produced the science fiction survey of 1962. On 26 March 1963 the group met in Wilson's office to consider the central device for the series. Wilson favoured a time machine which would also be capable of moving out into space or down into a single molecule. Alice Frick suggested a flying saucer carrying a regular cast of characters and although the saucer was rejected as 'not based in reality and too Sunday press' her idea of a regular core cast immediately fell into place.[8] As the concept developed over the weeks that followed, Newman suggested that the time machine should look like an ordinary object 'to shock audiences not to take for granted the world around them.'[9] Webber toyed with the idea that it might take the shape of a night watchman's hut. He then suggested an invisible machine, but this didn't meet Wilson's need for a 'visual... tangible symbol'. By 16 May the shape was fixed as a police box.[10] The team resolved to keep the outward appearance of the Doctor's ship a secret to increase its impact when the programme aired that autumn.[11]

As the whole point of the serial was to secure viewer loyalty, the next order of business was to arrive at a balance of regular characters likely to interest the target audience. Wilson felt that at least one of the major characters should be a teenager, with whom the *Juke Box Jury* audience could directly identify. Frick preferred two young adult characters as a focus for teenager aspiration. In a document of 29 March Bunny Webber set out character needs for the as yet un-named 'loyalty' serial at length. He recommended a central young male and female provide the heroic and romantic tension, and an additional character: 'Men are believed to form an important part of the 5 o'clock Saturday (post-Grandstand) audience. They will be interested in the young hero; and to catch them firmly we should add: THE MATURER MAN...WITH SOME CHARACTER TWIST.' Webber felt, however, that this character should be aged around '35-40' as: 'Nowadays, to satisfy grown women, Father-Figures are introduced into loyalty programmes at such a rate that TV begins to look like an Old People's Home: let us introduce them *ad hoc*, as our stories call for them.'[12] His colleagues disagreed and soon the proposed line-up of travellers included a 'with-it' girl of 15, the two heroes (her teachers) and the owner of the space craft, 'a frail old man lost in space and time' nick-named by his comrades: 'Doctor Who'. As originally planned the Doctor was more mysterious than heroic: 'he is suspicious and capable of sudden malignance... he is searching for something as well as fleeing from something.' Webber even speculated that as the programme developed he might be revealed to be a scientist who had 'opted out' and now tried to stop scientific progress when he encountered it. Others declined to see the Doctor as a 'reactionary'.[13]

As the early concept documents makes clear, Newman, Webber and Wilson also hoped that *Doctor Who* would have academic integrity and play its part in the BBC's mission to educate:

> The series is neither fantasy nor space travel nor science fiction. The only unusual science fiction 'angle' is that four characters of today are projected into real environments based on the best factual information of situations in time, in space and any material state we can realise in practical terms.[14]

Hence the two young adult characters became a science teacher and a history teacher to explain the 'real environments' as the adventures developed. Newman,

Wilson and Webber imagined stories dealing with visits to other worlds and the earth's past, and a first adventure in which the crew of the Tardis would be accidentally miniaturized, to give audiences a new perspective on their own world.[15] No adventure would last more than four to six weeks, to avoid an unpopular scenario causing too much damage to ratings. The series was intended to run for 52 weeks.[16] Finally, in keeping with the terms of the original Script Department report into science fiction, Newman was determined that the show should not feature 'Bug-Eyed Monsters'. [17]

In order to give the programme the sense of 'today' necessary to retain the *Juke Box Jury* generation, Newman recruited a promising twenty-seven year old production secretary from ABC named Verity Lambert to produce the series. Lambert joined the team in June 1963. Lambert and script editor David Whitaker set about the task of commissioning scripts. One of their first recruits that summer was Terry Nation, who developed a storyline that brought them into direct conflict with Sydney Newman's prejudice against Bug-Eyed Monsters. The story, dealing with the Doctor's adventures 'in a world stricken by an atomic explosion', developed into much more as Nation imagined mutants encased in robotic shells: the Daleks. Lambert justified the story educationally as a way to teach children about the potential of nuclear war to cause genetic mutation.[18] In later September 1963 the story was moved up the 'running order' to become the second Doctor Who adventure.[19] Dalek 'costumes' were speedily developed by BBC designer Raymond Cusick and as late as October the production team still had no idea exactly how Dalek speech could be synthesised.[20] This was television flying 'by the seat of the pants.'

The first episode of *Doctor Who* attracted an estimated 4.4 million viewers: 9 per cent against ITV's 8 per cent. Audience research found viewers generally positive about what one called a 'cross between Wells' *Time Machine* and a space-age *Old Curiosity Shop*', and particularly engaged with the use of 'radiophonic' effects to create an 'out of this world atmosphere'.[21]

By the end of the first adventure the figure had grown to 6.4 million. By the end of the first Dalek adventure 10.4 million people tuned in each week. Initially the producers did not expect the Daleks to return and gave away two of their four machines to a Dr. Barnado's children's home. But return they did. On Boxing Day 1964, 12.4 million viewers watched the climax of the second Dalek adventure '*The Dalek Invasion of Earth*'. For the next year Dalek merchandise dominated the toyshops of Britain.[22] The battle for Saturday teatime had been won, for the time being at least.

Alongside reports from the audience research unit, the *Doctor Who* production team had a bulging postbag to keep them in touch with the audience. Dalek related mail ranged from adult complaints about the element of horror to an invitation from a decidedly un-horrified child who wanted the Daleks to attend his birthday party. The BBC arranged for Daleks to open fetes. One spent a season with the flesh-and-blood animals in Manchester's Belle Vue zoo. When a director of Marks and Spencer asked to buy a Dalek his request was politely declined for fear that 'his friends seeing his Dalek and asking him where he got it' might begin 'obtaining others and using them for the *wrong purposes*.'[23] One child wrote in to ask 'how the Daleks get up and down steps.' His letter survives with the pencil annotation from the script editor: 'Do we know?'[24] Occasionally viewers wrote in asking the production team what happened in an episode they had missed. Lambert, or the script editor David Whitaker, dutifully replied, filling in the missing action.[25]

The format of time and space travel allowed astonishing creative freedom albeit within the limits of pitifully small BBC effects budget, which for the first Dalek adventure amounted to £200 an episode.[26] When the lead actor, William Hartnell, retired the producers decided that the Doctor and his species had the ability to regenerate to allow a new lead to join the programme. When the show ended its run in 1989 seven actors had played the part. The story developed as the series progressed. John Tulloch and Manuel Alvarado, the leading cultural critics to study the series have hence spoken of *The Unfolding Text*.[27] We learned in 1969 that the Doctor was a member of a race called the Time Lords from the planet Gallifrey; that he disagreed with their policy of never intervening in the affairs of other worlds and had stolen his Tardis and begun a career as an inter-galactic wanderer. Despite this extra-terrestrial origin the Doctor remained quintessentially English and his adventures dealt with the British historical experience in a very direct way.

Doctor Who and British-ness

Doctor Who arrived at a time of great British cultural uncertainty and brought a reassuring message. The country was in the midst of its retreat from Empire. The big story was the dawn of the 'Space Age' from which the British were emphatically excluded. Only Americans or Russians (and their chimps and dogs) got to go into space. The *Doctor Who* format enabled the British to imagine themselves in space by leaping over the problem of the spacecraft. The Tardis required neither expensive special effects nor a complex plot to imagine a British space programme. The Tardis looked like a police box, the audience eventually learned, because it had a 'chameleon circuit' allowing its shape to change to blend in with each new environment, and this circuit had broken when the Doctor first arrived in London. This back-story is not present in the early production documents. While directing the first Dalek adventure, Richard Martin suggested that the Tardis needed to maintain a form tied to a specific time and place as an anchor to ensure the sanity of its occupant, but might change shape at some point in the future of the series.[28] But the Tardis remained a Prussian blue 1929-pattern London police box for the next 30 years, and hence served as a metaphor for the persistence of mid-twentieth century British-ness within the series. It carried all the cultural baggage of the picture postcard London 'bobby'. Britain had led the world with the foundation of a civic police force in the nineteenth century, and conceptions of British-ness consistently stress values of fair-play, law, order and 'decency'. The idea of a vehicle that was 'larger on the inside that it appeared on the outside' had its analogue in the country as a whole. Britain clung to the idea that it too was larger than it appeared in the world of the 1960s.

The character of the Doctor incorporated a number of British types including H. G. Wells' time traveller[29]; Sherlock Holmes;[30] Van Helsing in *Dracula*; and the ever-resourceful back room boffins who according to British popular culture had won World War Two by inventing bouncing bombs. The boffin had become part of British science fiction in the 1950s thanks to the BBC television series (and spin-off Hammer films) *Quatermass*.[31] Moreover, the Doctor's adventures repeatedly showed the triumph of brains over brawn, a national trope that could be found everywhere from school fiction to prisoner of war drama. The Doctor always wore some form of 'retro' costume, which gave the whole programme a flavour of projecting something from a better past into an uncertain future.

Each actor brought his own emphasis to the part. The first Doctor, William Hartnell (1963-66) played the part as a crotchety professor who used his ingenuity to 'muddle through.' When Patrick Troughton took over the role in 1966, he became what Newman called the 'Charlie Chaplin tramp of outer space', puncturing the pomposity of the authority figures he encountered. The 1970 incarnation brought new dash to the role along with the shift to colour. Jon Pertwee played the Doctor as an Edwardian dandy, with a suave elegance that owed much to *The Avengers* with a dash of *James Bond*. He spent most of his time marooned on Earth as a scientific advisor to something called the United Nations Intelligence Taskforce (UNIT) a secret military organisation dedicated to defeating alien invasion. The British army enjoyed the public relations boost. Pertwee's successor, the most long-lived Doctor, Tom Baker (1974-1981) was modelled on a bohemian student. His trademark was a floppy hat and trailing scarf. Baker brought a number of specifically British references to the part including a bag of 'jelly babies', which, on occasion, he used to threaten an enemy unfamiliar with the limited explosive potential of British confectionery. During these years, producer Philip Hinchcliffe and script editor Robert Holmes developed the series as a pastiche of classic Gothic horror and adventure stories. Material appropriated included: *Dracula, Frankenstein, Dr Jeykel and Mr Hyde, the Beast with Five Fingers, the Mummy, the Prisoner of Zenda, Fu Manchu* and even Victorian tales of cursed light-houses. According to BBC audience research, this was the show's golden age.[32]

Doctor number five, Peter Davison, (1981-1984) was the most obviously nationally marked of the set as he appeared in an Victorian cricket outfit and cultivated the air of a gentleman adventurer. Doctors six (Colin Baker, 1984-1986) and seven (Sylvester McCoy 1986-1989) seemed variations on the same theme of frock coats, floppy hats. Colin Baker 's coat was 'motley' which perhaps echoed older traditions of a harlequin dancing around authority. McCoy carried one further particularly British prop: an umbrella, with a handle in the shape of a question mark. Thus elements of a national self-image were preserved and projected into space, where this reassuringly British character encountered a succession of British cultural and historical obsessions.

Doctor Who and the British historical experience

If *Doctor Who* reflected one historical experience, it was the Second World War, especially when it came to the Daleks. These regimented creatures were thinly veiled re-incarnations of the Nazis. Their catchphrase – 'Exterminate, Exterminate' – echoed the vocabulary of the holocaust, topical in 1963 as a result of the Adolf Eichemann trial. Through the Daleks, *Doctor Who* relived Britain's 'finest hour', resisting and defeating the Nazis. In the first story the Doctor was a Winston Churchill in space, rallying the pacifist co-habitants of the Dalek world of Skaro to resist their oppressors. The link between the Nazis and science fiction was logical. Churchill's rhetoric during the summer of 1940 echoed apocalyptic science fiction. He spoke of the Nazis as a sort of robotic enemy whose victory would bring 'the abyss of a new Dark Age made more sinister, and perhaps more protracted, by the lights of a perverted science.'[33] Hitler eventually attacked Britain with robot weapons in the form of the pilot-less V-1 and V-2 flying bombs. The links to World War Two developed along with the Daleks. In 1964 the Daleks invaded Earth. The BBC went to great lengths to film them gliding through the streets of London, with the House of Commons in the background, playing with the awareness that Britain had come perilously close to invasion in 1940. In 1975 the Daleks were revealed to be the creations of a culture whose uniforms and salutes echoed the Nazis.

The need to explore this territory was such that numerous other races followed the Dalek example. Other totalitarian invaders included the Cybermen, created by London medical academic Kit Pedler in 1966; the Ice Warriors, who arrived in 1967 and the Sontarans, first seen in 1973. Most of these species at some point hatched a plan for the conquest of Earth requiring a stop-off in London on the way. Often the invader lurked on the London Underground or emerged from the sewer system, like Nazis rising from the national unconscious.[34] In the 1988 adventure *Silver Nemesis* the Cybermen shared the limelight with a real Nazi, back from hiding in South America. Such stories readily became a vehicle for British army heroics and the character of the Brigadier (played by Nicholas Courtney and a regular figure in the Pertwee years) unflappable in the presence of marauding aliens became a favourite character in the series. But *Doctor Who*'s earth invasion stories were more than a reassuring return to the known terrain of World War Two; they also opened difficult issues such as the level of violence justifiable to destroy the Daleks, and such taboo issues as the question of whether British people would have collaborated. In *Day of the Daleks* (1972) the Doctor accuses a Dalek collaborator (the human 'controller') of being a 'Quisling'. Even in the 22nd century this World War Two term derived from the name of the Nazi's puppet governor of Norway causes offence. In 1972 the writer Malcolm Hulke explicitly proposed an adventure in which aliens had defeated Britain and a collaborationist 'Vichy government' had been established in Harrogate. He imagined 'the Doctor's goal is to find the aliens' master plan and so prove to the world's population that they are all doomed unless they work together. It is Churchill vs. the appeasement policy.'[35]

The centrality of World War Two should not obscure the more subtle historical traces within the series. The received account of British history shared by the writers and audience of *Doctor Who* drew on a number of key historical experiences: resisting invasion, establishing democracy, opposing slavery, and advancing the Protestant Reformation. All these concerns surfaced in *Doctor Who*. In resisting invasion by Daleks and Cybermen, the Doctor was conforming to a defensive narrative of British-ness established in the days of Elizabeth I and refreshed by the historical encounters with Napoleon and other foreign despots.[36] The Doctor's arch-enemy – a fellow Time Lord called The Master, who arrived in 1971 to act as 'front man' for various invading species – was initially played by half-Spanish actor, Roger Delgado. With his pointed black beard and hypnotic dark eyes, the renaissance tradition of the Spanish villain was alive and well.[37] *Doctor Who* also displayed a suspicion of radicals worthy of Edmund Burke. He narrowly escaped getting executed during the French Revolution in a 1964 adventure called *The Reign of Terror*.

The Doctor matched his opposition to totalitarianism with a faith in the ability of liberated societies to get on with ruling themselves. He was never averse to helping a monarch and claimed to have been present at the coronation of both Elizabeth I and Victoria.[38] Any fault generally lay with the monarch's advisors. From the sixteenth century it was commonplace to identify Britain with liberty and by the mid-1700s with opposition to slavery. Numerous *Doctor Who* stories explored this territory both on other worlds, and on earth in the past (*The Highlanders*, 1966-67) or future. The Doctor became an inter-galactic William Wilberforce spreading liberation to slaves who were generally white, as though to allow British audiences to explore the notion of racial subjugation.

Historically, British-ness was also constructed in opposition to Roman Catholicism, and echoes of this can also be found within *Doctor Who*. Beyond being a survivor of the Massacre of Saint Bartholomew's Eve (*The Massacre*, 1966) the Doctor emphasised self-reliance and the individual rather than the community. The Doctor is revealed to be a dissenter from the ancient but moribund society of the Time Lords, who eventually appear in the programme wearing flowing robes and skull-caps like a cosmic Vatican. In a wider religious context, *Doctor Who* inhabited the Manichean universe of a perpetual struggle between good and evil. Numerous episodes rested on oppositions between the Doctor and the Master or the White Guardian and the Black. The programme preached a neo-Christian ethic of self-sacrifice. The Doctor 'died' to save this or other worlds on multiple occasions, and several companions followed suit without the benefit of regeneration into a new body.

Doctor Who as a text of its time

As well as reflecting and perpetuating the values of Britain's past, *Doctor Who* became an arena for exploring emerging issues of British life between 1963 and 1989. Cold War fears were implicit in the original conception of the Daleks as nuclear mutants. Subsequent adventures dealt with all the Cold War themes familiar from American science fiction: the threat from an enemy within; villains like The Master, skilled in brain-washing/hypnotism; super bombs capable of destroying whole worlds.[39] Stories in the early 1970s reflected the era of détente. In both *Mind of Evil* (1971) and *Day of the Daleks* (1972) the Doctor has to save international peace conferences. In *Frontier in Space* (1973) he uncovers a Dalek conspiracy to sabotage the fragile peace between long-term adversaries Earth and the reptile planet Draconia. In the era of Ronald Reagan and the Second Cold War the adventure *Warriors of the Deep* (1984) dealt with an attempt by a monstrous third party to precipitate nuclear war between two 21st century power blocs.

Doctor Who also engaged the issue of race and Empire. On the surface the programme took a determinedly anti-imperialist stand. The Doctor himself was an alien, and his adventures regularly set him against brutal military types oppressing other races on far away planets.[40] *The Mutants* (1972) had the additional element of a sub plot dealing with the process of de-colonisation. Imperial issues got an unusual twist during the early 1970s, in two stories by Malcolm Hulke in which creatures – *The Silurians* (1970) and *Sea Devils* (1972) – who had once ruled the earth, awoke from hibernation and attempted to reclaim the planet. The dilemma reflected contemporary issues then coming to a head in the Middle East and Northern Ireland. The Doctor was sympathetic until these species resorted to violence. Although none of the Doctor's incarnations or assistants were 'ethnic' in British terms, the programme had no shortage of sympathetic 'others' whether on earth or in space.[41] Yet set against this were the recurring alien invasion stories and plots that reworked tropes familiar from Imperial adventure stories, as when a companion is captured by primitive aliens who practise human sacrifice (*Death to the Daleks*, 1974). Earth-bound ethnic enemies included a murderous Egyptian (*Pyramids of Mars*, 1975) and an evil Chinese magician (*The Talons of Weng-Chiang*, 1977). There were allusions to the lost Raj in dressing The Master in a Nehru suit. Hence the programme reflected Britain's mixed feelings at becoming a cosmopolitan country.

In the early days Sydney Newman hoped that the programme might help shape British attitudes to technology. He wrote to Verity Lambert suggesting she might 'do something in future episodes of Dr. Who to glamorise the title, occupation etc., of engineer.' He felt that applied science had 'lost prestige' and felt that a few judicious mentions in *Doctor Who* might boost the profession and 'do the country a lot of good.'[42] There is no evidence that Lambert responded to this; rather the programme displayed mixed feelings in its presentation of science (applied or otherwise) and technology. For all its celebration of science with marvels like the Tardis, the Doctor's sonic screwdriver and trusty robotic dog K9

(1977-81), the series also displayed fears of the technological Pandora's Box. *Doctor Who* played on concerns over robotics and computerization. In stories like *The War Machines* (1966), *Green Death* (1973) and *Face of Evil* (1977) the villain is revealed to be an out-of-control computer. The programme seemed particularly wary of the industrial application of science. Villains included several mining corporations (*The Colony in Space*, 1971; *Vengeance on Varos*, 1985), chemical firms and a businessman eager to market a killer pesticide (*Planet of Giants*, 1964). But as one might expect in the nuclear age, there was no shortage of mad scientists planning to wipe out human life and give the world back to the plants (*The Seeds of Doom*, 1976), or to conquer the world with dinosaurs. Mad scientist plots were as common as Earth invasion stories. In the 1975 adventure *Genesis of the Daleks*, audiences learned that a mad scientist called Davros created the Daleks in the first place. Davros thereafter became a perennial character in Dalek adventures.

The social politics of *Doctor Who* were in some ways inclusive. The presence of travelling companions allowed a little class and regional diversity, and included a cockney sailor and a Scottish highlander, Jamie, rescued from the aftermath of the Battle of Culloden. The original series plan called for the Doctor's youngest travelling companion to be 'working class'.[43] Yet the Doctor remained upper middle class. Working class people were generally represented as being in need of leadership, or at the very least technical assistance: a good cause for the Doctor's whiggish interventionism. If there was a critique of the British class system, it lay in the portrayal of the Doctor's own civilisation. The Time Lords were by their very name an aristocracy and a decadent one at that. As an enraged sixth Doctor pointed out to them: '10 million years of absolute power. That's what it takes to be really corrupt.'[44]

The social politics of *Doctor Who* remained remarkably static over the programme's 25 year run, except in the area of gender. The treatment of female companions shifted considerably during the three decades of the series. Despite the early efforts to include women with intellectual authority like the teacher Barbara, the show repeatedly slipped back into allowing the Doctor's female companions to be 'screamers'. Later shifts in casting and writing did, however, mirror the social changes of the time, and the Doctor's more capable female companions included a space agent (1965-66),[45] a computer programmer (1968-9) scientist (1970), a reporter (1974-1976), a defiantly self-sufficient but skin-clad savage, Leela (played by Louise Jameson, 1977-78), who to the delight of a generation of British girls dispatched a succession of monsters with her trusty dagger. Two incarnations of a female Time Lord followed (1978-81), but in the end the writers steered away from companions who too closely matched the Doctor in intellect as this denied them the invaluable narrative device of his explaining exactly what was going on in laymen's terms. No less significant is the rise of the female villain in *Doctor Who*. From being rarities in adventures like *Galaxy Four* (1965), which featured the Drahvins, a race in which females were dominant, or *The Stones of Blood* (1978), villainous women became standard fare. In the era of Margaret Thatcher it was only to be expected that the Doctor would encounter women like the wicked space ship captain in *Enlightenment* (1983), the planetary dictator Helen A., in *The Happiness Patrol* (1988) and the legendary Morgaine La Fey in *Battlefield* (1989). In 1985 the writers Pip and Jane Baker created the show's first female super villain 'The Rani' (played by Kate O'Mara in *The Mark of the Rani*, 1985 and *Time and the Rani*, 1987). The Rani's scientific speciality was chemistry, coincidentally the subject in which Margaret Thatcher earned her undergraduate degree.

Doctor Who as camp

Thatcherite characters like Helen A. or the Rani were not the only elements of satire in *Doctor Who*. *Vengeance on Varos* (1985) dealt with the issue of violence in the media by positing a world in which the population is kept happy through regular broadcasts of executions and *The Sun Makers* (1977) made fun of Britain's Inland Revenue system. More generally *Doctor Who* frequently included philosophically subversive ideas. Many episodes dealt with the danger of an enemy within. Other plots turned on the coincidental resemblance between the Doctor and an evil doppelganger or included a villain attempting to take the Doctor's form.[46] *The Inferno* (1970) went so far as to posit an evil parallel universe in which usually sympathetic characters reveal their murderous side, and Britain is ruled by home-grown fascists. Through such stories, *Doctor Who* suggested that evil was not necessarily far away and in an unsympathetic shape, but could be within the self and one's own culture. Adventures such as *The Armageddon Factor* (1979) in which the Doctor discovers that the power for good – in this case the 'White Guardian' – was actually evil also had subversive implications.

Doctor Who also became playful with the notion of historical causality. Despite Sydney Newman's belief that the Doctor should not intervene in real events, by the 1970s it had become commonplace to use events in *Doctor Who* to 'explain' the course of history. In the 1971 adventure *The Daemons* the Doctor discovered that all human history was an alien lab experiment. Explosions in the course of *City of Death* (1979) and *Earthshock* (1982) trigger the development of life on earth and the destruction of the dinosaurs respectively. In the 1982 story *The Visitation*, a fight with aliens accidentally starts the Great Fire of London in 1666. Such stories explicitly subverted the grand historical narratives. Hence, as with the darker elements in the World War Two borrowings, while recycling ethical and historical certainties *Doctor Who* was equally capable of raising doubts about them. This subversive element increased as the series developed, and eventually became part of the fabric of the programme. Although many plot elements within *Doctor Who* remained remarkably stable, the tone changed greatly over the course of its run. *Doctor Who* became camp. British culture has long used camp to engage the more challenging features of life in a socially constricted society. In the world of camp the markers of gender, sexuality and class roles are broken down, made ironic and thrown back at the audience: repeated with a twist.[47] During the 1960s and the *Carry On* films, the *Avengers* and the *Monty Python* team all drew on this heritage, albeit in different ways. *Doctor Who* was also part of the tradition.

Doctor Who's debt to camp was much deeper that just casting *Carry On* regular Peter Butterworth as its first recurring villain, The Monk in *The Time Meddler* (1965) or, as the writer of *The Romans* episode admitted, drawing on *Carry On Cleo* as inspiration.[48] Like all camp the world of *Doctor Who* affirmed self-expression and was a clarion for eccentricity and distinctiveness. In the 1968 *Doctor Who* adventure, *The Mind Robber*, the Doctor is trapped in a world in which words and stories became real; in *The Three Doctors* (1973) and *Castrovalva* (1982) entire worlds are created by the mind of one individual. Such ideas affirmed the power of the imagination. The Doctor was beyond sex, and able to transcend his body when necessary, and continually re-invent himself. Given the freedom implicit and explicit within the programme and its characterizations, and its defiance of convention, it is perhaps not surprising that the programme attracted a gay and lesbian fan-base.[49] More than this, camp became central to the content of *Doctor Who*. In *Doctor Who*, the key elements in the British behaviour, manners and mission to the world – including resistance to Fascism in World War II – were repeated and made ever more knowing. By the time the producers actually dressed the creators of the Daleks in Gestapo uniforms or had Peter Davison's Doctor play cricket in *The Black Orchid* (1982), it was quite clear that they 'knew' what they were doing. At some point it became important to joke about British-ness and 'having to save the world again', in order to create space for imagining a new future. But self-parody would prove a hard joke to sustain for a mass audience.

The Decline of *Doctor Who*

As *Doctor Who* developed the programme displayed an awareness of its place as a British institution. Cast changes were debated in the press, and special anniversary episodes brought the multiple incarnations face to face.[50] Script editors like Eric Saward (1981-86) paid particular attention to series continuity. Some of the sixth Doctor's adventures referred back to events and characters from two decades previously in the life of the series.[51] In *Remembrance of the Daleks* (1987) the Doctor actually visited the original airdate of the series: 23 November 1963. His companion, Ace, was seen watching television as a new BBC science fiction serial is announced. She turned off before the programme could begin. The 'canon' of *Doctor Who* adventures was well known to many children watching thanks to a growing shelf of novelisations of adventures published by Target books from 1973 onwards; 1976 saw the foundation of a major fan organisation: the Doctor Who Appreciation Society. The series generated a fan magazine *Doctor Who Monthly*, and a spin-off comic, *Doctor Who Weekly*, launched in October 1979. A comprehensive guide to the series, Peter Haining's *Doctor Who A Celebration: Two Decades through Time and Space* appeared in 1983.[52] Writers could play to a gallery of long-term fans who enjoyed the idea of a coherent *Doctor Who* universe. But this level of self-awareness within the programme created the danger that *Doctor Who* could come to be about *Doctor Who* and part-company with the wider audience necessary to sustain production. It came as a shock for fans when in 1985 the BBC suspended *Doctor Who* for a year. Despite being a landmark of British television, its days now seemed numbered.

As with the death of any national hero, accounts of the demise of Doctor Who have long ago fallen into an orthodox pattern. Villains abound including Mary Whitehouse of the National Viewers and Listeners Association who led a long-running campaign against violence in the programme; Michael Grade, the BBC's head of drama who effectively sacked the sixth Doctor (Colin Baker) in 1986, and even John Nathan-Turner, the programme's producer, who alienated fans by allowing the series to become a showcase for such unlikely guest stars as comedian Ken Dodd and game show host Nicholas Parsons.[53] The truth is that *Doctor Who* was destroyed by the same force that brought it into being: the quest for ratings.

Although *Doctor Who* appeared to have a life of its own, production decisions were always related to ratings. To Sydney Newman's chagrin William Hartnell's Doctor drifted away from educational adventures in earth history to please the audience.[54] Hartnell was able to sustain average audiences of 8.4 million viewers. Despite a shift towards the popular, space-based, adventures his successor Patrick Troughton averaged only 6.9 million. Shifting to colour, Jon Pertwee restored the ratings to an average of 8.2 million viewers. Tom Baker took *Doctor Who* to unprecedented heights of popularity with audiences peaking at 16.1 million for *City of Death* (1979); Tom Baker's average weekly audience across his run as the Doctor was 9.3 million viewers, but his final season slipped to only 5.8, and one episode of *Full Circle* (1 November 1980) was watched by only 3.7 million. ITV had won back the Saturday slot with the expensive effects of the imported *Buck Rogers in the 25th Century*.

It was time for a change. Audiences warmed to Peter Davison, and he attracted an average of 8.2 million, despite moving to weeknight transmission. Although the programme still commanded a loyal following of 25-35 year olds, audiences began to slip again with Colin Baker. Whether in the mid-week slot in 1984 or on competing with *The A-Team* on Saturday nights in 1986, he averaged only 6.5 million viewers. The final Doctor, Sylvester McCoy, averaged 4.8 million, with his final season (scheduled against an equally venerable British television fixture, Granada's soap *Coronation Street*) netting only 4.2 million. The final adventure, *Survival*, transmitted in November and December 1989 averaged 4.9 million viewers, exactly a million less than the average for the first adventure in 1963.[55]

Part of the problem was that in the world of *Star Wars* audiences no longer accepted the low-tech, low-budget BBC special effects, but more than this *Doctor Who* had out lived its cultural purpose. Britain still craved the cosy virtual community of *Coronation Street* but had a diminished need or desire to re-live the Second World War in either straight allegory or camp parody. The country was now well used to both technological and ethnic diversity and didn't require *Doctor Who* as a space to explore fears around these issues. Moreover, for better or worse the sort of assertion of British identity and history implicit in *Doctor Who* was now unfashionable anywhere except in the die-hard corners of the Conservative Party. Britain in 1989 was less homogenous, more cynical (or sophisticated) and less willing to suspend disbelief than it had been in 1963. The Doctor's age, paternalism, intellect, innocence and wide-eyed optimism were all as out of place in 1989 as a 1929-pattern police box. A more flexible programme could have moved with the times, but *Doctor Who*'s self-awareness and the continuity that was so important to fans mitigated against this. For the casual viewer, continuity seemed like predictability and jokey self-parody merely undermined the programme's dramatic rationale. It was a battle the Doctor could not win. At the end of the 1989 season the BBC auctioned the right to make *Doctor Who*. They did not receive an acceptable bid for a television series. In 1996 the BBC and Universal collaborated in a *Doctor Who* TV movie starring Paul McGann as the Doctor's eighth regeneration. No further films followed. Rather, a succession of camp parodies joked about a programme that had tried to stay alive by joking about itself. *Doctor Who* seemed like a cultural dead end.[56] And yet *Doctor Who* lives on in public memory and a lively fan culture. In 1999 the Post Office issued a stamp featuring a Dalek, photographed by Lord Snowden, and readers of *Radio Times* voted the entrance of the Daleks as the second greatest moment in the history of television drama. Classic episodes regularly appear on video and satellite television, and fresh adventures continue to emerge in spin-off novels and elaborate audio productions, featuring original cast members. An enterprising group of independent filmmakers has even produced its own spin-off videos featuring characters and creatures from the show.[57] As with all national heroes, the faithful believe he will return and pick up where he left off in 1989 when, in the guise of Sylvester McCoy, he exited with a final, self-parodic appeal to the imagination, fair play and the British national drink: 'There are worlds out there where the sky is burning, where the sea's asleep and the rivers dream, people made of smoke and cities made of song; somewhere there's danger, somewhere there's injustice, and somewhere else the tea is getting cold. Come on, Ace, we've got work to do!'[58]

Notes

1   Ralph Negrine, *Television and the Press Since 1945* (Manchester University Press, Manchester, 1998), p.24.

2   BBC Written Archives Centre, Caversham Park, hereafter BBC WAC, T5/647, Script Department to Maschwitz, Science Fiction Report, 27 April 1962 (by Alice Frick and Donald Bull).

3   BBC WAC, T5/647, Script Department to Maschwitz, Science Fiction Report, 27 April 1962 (by Alice Frick and Donald Bull).

4   BBC WAC T5/647, Braybon and Frick to Head Script Department Television, 25 July 1962.

5   BBC WAC T5/647, Braybon and Frick to Head Script Department Television, 25 July 1962. The report also noted the potential for stories dealing with telepaths as per Eric Frank Russell's novel *Three to Conquer*, (Ace, New York, 1957). The realistic police drama *Z Cars* had been launched that year to considerable success.

6   BBC WAC, T31/67/3, Newman to Controller Programmes, Television, 11 February 1963.

7   BBC WAC, C.103, Sydney Newman to Jeremy Bentham, 13 April 1984; T5/638, *Doctor Who*: General notes on background and approach for an exciting adventure-science fiction drama serial for children's Saturday viewing. Circa June 1963.

8   BBC WAC, T5/647, Discussion of Science Fiction Series, 26 March 1963.

9   BBC WAC, C.103, Sydney Newman to Jeremy Bentham, 13 April 1984.

10   BBC WAC, T5/647, "Dr. Who" General Notes on Background and Approach, undated. T5/638,

Doctor Who: General notes, Wilson/Webber/Newman, 16 May 1963. The Tardis was un-named until Anthony Coburn wrote the pilot episode of the series. It is used in programme documentation from 16 September 1963.

11   BBC WAC, T5/648, Amendment to promotional material, V. Lambert, 1 November 1963.

12   BBC WAC, T5/647, Webber to Wilson, 29 March 1963. Emphasis in original. The time travel scenario was still not fixed at this point. Webber suggested that his three characters be a group of scientific trouble-shooters facing new villains every week in TV western style. Wilson's response to this idea was a marginal note: 'corny'.

13   BBC WAC, T5/647, "Dr. Who" General Notes on Background and Approach, undated, c. April 1963 written on Webber's typewriter. Although the Doctor did not develop into an anti-progress' character many stories reflected a concern over scientific innovation, which will be discussed below.

14   BBC WAC, T5/638, *Doctor Who*: General notes, Wilson/Webber/Newman, 16 May 1963.

15   BBC WAC, T5/638, *Doctor Who*: General notes, Wilson/Webber/Newman, 16 May 1963. In T5/647, Newman to Wilson, 10 June 1963, Newman rejected the synopsis of the Giants story as 'thin on incident' and beyond 'the realms of practical live television.' The team switched to a time travel story featuring Cavemen and used the giants idea in the autumn of 1964.

16   BBC WAC, T5/638, *Doctor Who*: General notes, Wilson/Webber/Newman, 16 May 1963.

17   BBC WAC, C.103, Sydney Newman to Jeremy Bentham, 13 April 1984.

18   BBC WAC, C.103, Sydney Newman to Jeremy Bentham, 13 April 1984; T5/648, Amendment to promotional material... V. Lambert, 1 November 1963; On original slot for the Nation serial see T5/647, summary of projected serials circulated by Whitaker 31 July 1963 to avoid duplication of themes in BBC scheduling.

19   BBC WAC T5/647, Memos by David Whitaker, 31 July & 16 September 1963.

20   BBC WAC, T5/648, C. Barry to Post Office Joint Speech Research Unit, 18 October 1963.

21   BBC WAC, T5/647, Audience Research Report, 'Dr Who', 30 December 1963.

22   BBC WAC, C.103, Samantha Beere, Doctor Who Audience Research Data, 1963-1989, Broadcasting Research Information Services Report, (hereafter, Beere, 1989), p.11-13. On Barnado's see T5/648, Memo 3 January 1964. For 'Dalekmania' and Terry Nation see *Daily Mirror*, 1 December 1964 and T5/647.

23   BBC WAC, T5/648, Memo to V. Lambert, 7 May 1964. Also T5/647.

24   BBC WAC, T5/649/1 letter from M. J. Wright, age 8. c. 1964.

25   BBC WAC, T5/645/1, Lambert to Miss G. Knight, 26 November 1964.

26   BBC WAC, T5/648, Production Secretary to C. Barry (director), 25 November 1963.

27   John Tulloch and Manuel Alvarado, *Doctor Who: The Unfolding Text* (Macmillan, London, 1983).

28   BBC WAC T5/648, Memo Richard Martin: *Doctor Who* Serial B, 22 October 1963.

29   On the role of George Pal (dir.) *The Time Machine* (1960) in *Doctor Who* see John R. Cook, 'Adapting telefantasy: Doctor Who and the Daleks' in I. Q. Hunter (ed.), *British Science Fiction Cinema* (Routledge, London, 1999), pp. 115-116.

30   Holmes' humour was intended to be part of the second doctor's style (BBC WAC, T5/647, 'The New Dr. Who', undated, c. 1966). The Master was imagined as a 'Moriarty' to the Doctor's Holmes (T65/20/1) and during Tom Baker years the Doctor actually wore a deerstalker hat in Victorian London adventures.

31   *Quatermass*, created by Nigel Kneale, first aired on the BBC in 1953. The three Quatermass films were *The Quatermass Experiment*, (1955), *Quatermass II*, (1957) and *Quatermass and the Pit*, (1967). The relationship between Doctor Who and Bernard Quatermass was especially obvious during the years when Jon Pertwee played the Doctor.

32   BBC WAC, C.103, Beere, 1989, p. 39.

33 The quote is from the climax of the 'Finest Hour' speech of 18 June 1940, see Nicholas J. Cull, *Selling War* (OUP, New York, 1995), pp.71-72. On Churchill and science fiction see Paul K. Akron, 'Shall we all commit suicide' in *Finest Hour*, No. 94, Spring 1997. Churchill also compared Soviet Foreign Minister Molotov to a 'robot.'

34 *The Web of Fear* (1968); *Invasion* (1968); *Attack of the Cybermen* (1985).

35 BBC WAC T65/17/1, Hulke to Dicks, 18 December 1972, proposal for 'Bridgehead from Space'. The eventual story, *Invasion of the Dinosaurs* followed a different path, but did include the revelation that a regular military character – Captain Yates – had thrown in his lot with the enemy, in this case a mad scientist

36 The 3rd Doctor claimed to have been a cellmate of Walter Raleigh (*Mind of Evil*, 1971) and a personal friend of Nelson (*The Sea Devils*, 1972).

37 In *Colony in Space* (1971) it is noted that the Spanish ambassador had been mistaken for the Master and arrested. In *The Sea Devils* (1972) the Master was sent to prison, like Napoleon he was the sole prisoner on an island jail.

38 As in *The Curse of Peladon* (1972), *The Androids of Tara* (1978) or *Delta and the Bannermen* (1987).

39 *The Dalek Masterplan*, 1965-66, *Colony in Space*, 1971, *Earthshock*, 1982.

40 This aspect of *Kinda* (1982) is in Tulloch and Alvarado, *Doctor Who: The Unfolding Text*, p.150; for a detailed description of this adventure as a Buddhist allegory see pp. 247-303.

41 Black actors appeared periodically in sympathetic if stereotyped supporting roles such a noble slave in *Tomb of the Cybermen* (1967) or a kindly soldier, Cotton, in *The Mutants*, 1972.

42 BBC WAC, T5/647/1, Newman to Lambert, 10 April 1964.

43 BBC WAC T5/638, *Doctor Who*: General notes, Wilson/Webber/Newman, 16 May 1963.

44 *Trial of a Time Lord* (1986)

45 The path-breaking character, Sarah Kingdom (Jean Marsh) was an agent of the Space Special Security Service. She appeared in the twelve-part story *The Dalek Master Plan* which ran from 13 November to 21 January 1966, but died saving the world in the final part.

46 *The Massacre* (1966); *Enemy of the World* (1967-68); *Meglos*, (1980); *Arc of Infinity*, (1983).

47 In the world of camp (from the French verb *se camper*: to posture or flaunt) the signs of sexual identities are repeated with a twist, exaggerated until they can be recognised to be not facets of nature but the constructs of culture. Received identity is revealed as artificial and transformed into a mask of performance. A space for existence is created behind that mask and a means of expression is established through the medium of the performance. When one has acknowledged that all life is theatre, one can both enjoy the performance and, perhaps, begin to change the script. For an introduction to camp see Philip Core, *Camp: The Lie that Tells the Truth* (Plexus, London, 1984) esp., p. 115. Indispensable discussions may be found in Jack Bubuscio, 'Camp and the Gay Sensibility' in Richard Dyer (ed.), *Gays and Film* (BFI, London, 1980) pp. 40-58 and Susan Sontag, *Against Interpretation and Other Essays*, (Farrar, Straus & Giroux, New York, 1961) pp. 275-292.

48 The producers considered *Carry On* leading man Jim Dale for the part of the Doctor, see Adrian Rigelsford, *The Doctors: 30 Years of Time Travel* (Boxtree, London, 1994), p.99 and Tulloch and Alvarado, p.157.

49 Gay *Doctor Who* fan culture was affectionately featured in writer producer Russell T. Davis' path-breaking drama of gay life in Manchester, *Queer as Folk* (Red Production Co. for Channel 4, 1999).

50 *The Three Doctors*, (1973); *The Five Doctors*, (1983).

51 *Attack of the Cybermen*, 1985 referenced *The Tenth Planet*, 1966 and *The Two Doctors*, 1985 featured the second Doctor and Jamie from 1966-69. Rigelsford, *The Doctors*, p.139 notes that Saward also planned to bring back The Celestial Toymaker from the 1966 story of that name.

52 The BBC's own *Radio Times* published 10th and 20th anniversary special issues devoted to the

background to the series. Peter Haining, *Doctor Who A Celebration: Two Decades through Time and Space*, (W. H. Allen, London, 1983).

53   See Peter Haining, *Doctor Who: A Time Traveller's Guide*, (W. H. Allen, London, 1987), pp. 206-9 and Rigelsford, *The Doctors*, pp. 140-141, 149. On hostility to Nathan-Turner see *The Stage*, November 1988 and John Tulloch and Henry Jenkins, *Science Fiction Audiences: Watching Doctor Who and Star Trek*, (Routledge, London, 1995), pp. 159-163.

54   BBC WAC, C.103, Sydney Newman to Jeremy Bentham, 13 April 1984.

55   BBC WAC, C.103, Beere, 1989, esp. pp. 18, 25, 31, 39,42, 46, 50. Figures during the 1979 season were boosted by a strike at ITV during the transmission of the early episodes, including *City of Death*. The viewers stayed for the rest of the season.

56   *Doctor Who* (BBC/Universal, 1996). Comedians using Doctor Who material include the drag queen Lilly Savage, whose imagined cosmetic saleswomen as Daleks barking the order: 'exfoliate'. Victor Lewis Smith developed a running sketch featuring gay Daleks; Harry Hill featured Doctor Who in sketches and had the Brigadier (Nicholas Courtney) singing and dancing with Cybermen. In 1999 the Comic Relief team produced a full-scale spoof adventure featuring Rowan Atkinson, *Doctor Who and the Curse of Fatal Death* (1999) in which the Doctor encounters a race who communicate only by breaking wind. He regenerates into Joanna Lumley (among others)

57   For coverage of Doctor Who spin offs including the BBV (Bill and Ben Video) productions see 'Regenerate', *Daily Telegraph*, 5 August 1999.

58   *Survival* (1989).

Blackadder Goes Forth and the 'Two western fronts' debate

Stephen Badsey

Introduction

It is certainly unusual, and it may well be unique, for a television light comedy series to be cited repeatedly as evidence in a major historical debate. Yet this is the case for the BBC series *Blackadder Goes Forth*, first shown on British television in 1989, and set among British troops on the Western Front of the First World War 1914-1918 (or 'Great War', as historians are increasingly returning to call it). Specifically, the image of the Western Front evoked by the series has been used by historians as a focus for what has recently become known as the 'Two Western Fronts' debate. This debate, which is presently one of the most important in British historiography and historical education,[1] reflects the recognition that in the last quarter of the 20th Century two distinct views have developed of the Western Front and its experience for the British. One view, which is based chiefly on analysis of cultural artefacts and literature, tends to support the stereotype of the Western Front which is manifest in late 20th Century popular culture, and which is also still evoked by more traditionalist British military historians.[2] The other view, which may broadly be described as revisionist, is based on extensive research into the political and military history of the Western Front in the last quarter of a century, and questions many of the assumptions of this stereotype.

As a highly successful television light comedy, *Blackadder Goes Forth* is not only an excellent example of mass popular culture but is also set firmly in the context of the traditional stereotype, and it has become a particular target for revisionist historians. Hugh Cecil and Peter H. Liddle, the editors of the published proceedings of the landmark 1994 Leeds University conference on the Great War, which marked the emergence of the revisionist perspective as a mainstream position in British historical studies, cited the *Blackadder* series specifically as perpetuating 'myths which persist in the face of strong contrary evidence', regarding *Blackadder* and other television programmes as 'the greatest influence in moulding opinion today'.[3] Other critics of the influence of *Blackadder* include the revisionists G.D. Sheffield and Brian Bond,[4] while Jeremy Black has taken a wider view of the series' popularity, coupled with its relentlessly cynical view of the futility of warfare, as evidence of a 'decline of deference' and late 20th Century anti-militarism, drawing parallels with the American comedy television drama series *M★A★S★H* (1972-83) set in a military field hospital during the Korean War.[5]

As a further example of its importance, *Blackadder Goes Forth* had within a decade of its first transmission become well enough established in the British popular consciousness to become itself part of television history. In 2000 a British television programme *'100 Great Television Moments'* presented clips based on viewers' votes for the most memorable television events of the century. The top of this poll was dominated by factual episodes (the winner was the 1969 moon landings); but the final 'over the top' scene from the last episode of *Blackadder Goes Forth* was voted in at number nine, one of only two fictional pieces to make the top 10.[6] In his 1999 BBC television series *The Western Front* of six half-hour episodes, Richard Holmes, in the episode dealing with the Battle of the Somme (1916), used in commentary a recognisable paraphrase of one of the more memorable *Blackadder* lines, 'Clearly, Field Marshal Haig is about to make another gargantuan effort to move his drinks cabinet six inches closer to Berlin',[7] on the assumption that the phrase had achieved almost proverbial status. Most interestingly of all from the perspective of the use of television as an aid to teaching history, a 1996 BBC television documentary on the revisionist view of the Western Front, *Haig: The Unknown Solider*, used scenes from *Blackadder Goes Forth* intercut with the commentary of historians in order to establish the stereotype before subjecting it to scrutiny.[8]

As a light comedy, *Blackadder Goes Forth* was naturally not created with any deep historical intentions, and it may seem strange that revisionist historians have taken it so seriously. The reason is that it provides an unusually good example of what Sellar and Yeatman's jovial classic of bad history, *1066 And All That*, called 'all the history that you can remember';[9] a comic expression of a version of the Western Front that has become accepted in late 20th Century culture and that is now seen by revisionists as profoundly unhistorical. As such, *Blackadder Goes Forth* contains moments of deliberate seriousness which have led to its being taken as a realistic – or at least only partly satirical – representation of the Western Front. It has evoked responses concerning the real events of the war quite unlike those of comparable British light or farcical comedies set in a historical context, such as the BBC series *'Allo, 'Allo* (1982-1992) ostensibly portraying the French resistance during the Second World War, or the less successful Channel Four series *Captain Butler* (1997), featuring 18th century piracy.

By way of illustration of the issue, and as a fine example of the 'Two Western Fronts' of history and of popular culture, as part of the commemoration of the eightieth anniversary of the Great War's end in November 1998 the newspaperman Max Hastings wrote for the London *Evening Standard*:

Let us start with *foie gras*. And then perhaps a *piece de boeuf a l'os*... [We are] in that most delightful of hostelries the Château de Montreuil…You still do not care for champagne? The men who presided for four years over the greatest of military disasters had no such qualms. For here, between 1916 and 1918, was the headquarters of Field Marshal Sir John Haig, commander-in-chief of the British Army, who like most of his fellow generals dined nightly off china and crystal among the finest fare that Montreuil could provide.[10]

This example is chosen from many, with neither mockery nor hostile intent, but as having appeared in a major British newspaper, by an author who also enjoys no small reputation as a military historian. In fact, General Sir *Douglas* Haig (Field Marshal from late 1916) was Commander-in-Chief of the British Expeditionary Force in France from late 1915 to 1919 (the post of Commander in Chief of the British Army was abolished in 1904). His headquarters took up the entire town of Montreuil, but his own residence was a nearby simply furnished country house called the Château de Beaurepaire. This house was used as a base and to meet important visitors. Otherwise Haig was at least as likely to be at a forward headquarters (or, by 1918, in a headquarters train). Haig suffered from both asthma and a stomach malady, and both drank and ate sparingly, preferring water with meals. His staff could indeed provide hospitality for important guests and for rare formal occasions (as could the staff of the American General Dwight D. Eisenhower at his headquarters in the sumptuous Palace of Versailles in late 1944, or almost any general in a comparable position throughout history). But Haig's normal regime involved a working day of about eighteen hours, with both a brief lunch and dinner taken up by visitors. In this Haig was in no way exceptional when compared to other British general officers on the Western Front, many of who suffered illnesses from overwork, including members of Haig's own staff. Also, despite positive orders (issued in October 1915) not to risk their lives in the front lines, some 78 British generals were killed in action or died on active service in the course of the war.[11]

It might be argued that such detail is only important for specialists in the field. But if, for example, a modern newspaper article had argued that in 1911 the wicked King Edward IX had practised the *droit de signeur* and ruled without parliament, the average educated reader, without necessarily knowing about the constitutional crisis faced that year by George V, would nevertheless be confident that what was written was nonsense. It is hard to imagine such a divergence between the known facts and the popular image in any other aspect of 20th century British history than that of the Western Front; and it is trying to understand this image and its origins that has led historians to *Blackadder Goes Forth*.

The series as television

From the perspective of the average British television viewer of the late 20th century the series *Blackadder Goes Forth* is immensely familiar; but this may not be true for everyone interested in the 'Two Western Fronts' debate.[7] We need therefore to deal first (with due apologies) with the series and its origins as a television cultural artefact.

Altogether four main *Blackadder* series were made for BBC television at two year intervals from 1983 onwards, each of six 30-minute episodes; and together they represent one of the more important world-wide popular and commercial successes for British television of recent times. Light, farcical comedies linked together by continuity of production, cast and style (and allegedly described by one participant as 'situation tragedy'), each series was set in a deliberately fictionalised past, featuring a cynical and scheming member of the Blackadder family and his inept servant Baldrick, in each case played by Rowan Atkinson and Tony Robinson respectively. After an initial pilot episode that was never shown on British television (but was shown in the United States in 1983), the first series starring Atkinson as Prince Edmund, younger son of a fictitious late mediaeval English king, and known as *The Black Adder*, was transmitted in 1983. The second series, *Blackadder II*, featured Lord Edmund Blackadder as a favourite at the court of Queen Elizabeth I. This was followed by *Blackadder The Third*, featuring Mister Edmund Blackadder, butler to Prince George in Regency England. The fourth series, (hence the punning title *Blackadder Goes Forth*), was also the last, and featured Captain Edmund Blackadder of the British Army (the gradual slide of the scheming and ambitious Blackadder character down the social scale through history, from prince to harassed Army captain, was part of the humour). In addition, a one-hour Dickensian parody special *Blackadder's Christmas Carol* was shown on television in 1987. Since then, the principal actors have appeared as *Blackadder* characters for charity benefits, including twice on BBC television in 1998, once for the charity Comic Relief in a short sketch called *The Cavalier Years*, and once for the 50th birthday of Prince Charles in another cavalier sketch, *The King's Birthday*. In January 2000 the London Millennium Dome included a specially made short film, *Blackadder Back and Forth*, in which the characters journey by time machine back to important moments in British history.[13]

All four series have been repeatedly shown in syndication around the world, they have been released on audio and video, and the complete published scripts have appeared in book form.[14] There is also an official BBC *Black Adder* website,[15] several unofficial websites, and at the time of writing persistent rumours of another series or a feature film being planned. In short, the collected *Blackadder* series and characters have taken on a much wider cultural life than the relatively small number of original episodes would suggest; and given the diversity of forms in which they are available no estimate of a total viewing audience is possible, except to say that it is substantial.

The sixth and final episode of *Blackadder Goes Forth* was appropriately entitled *Goodbyee!*, the title being taken from a popular music hall song of the Great War, made familiar to modern audiences through its use in the 1963 stage production *Oh! What a Lovely War* by Joan Littlewood, and the 1969 Richard Attenborough film of the same name. The setting is a dugout in a British front-line trench, somewhere on the Western Front during the First World War, home to Captain Blackadder, late of the (fictitious) 19th/45th East African Rifles, and to the anonymous and seldom seen company of British soldiers that he commands. Captain Blackadder shares his dugout with other two main characters: Private S. Baldrick, late of the 'Turnip Street Workhouse Pals' (a joke at the expense of the real British 'Pals Battalions' of 1914), and Lieutenant the Honourable George Colthurst St. Barleigh, played by Hugh Lawrie as an typical British 'silly ass' of the Bertie Wooster type. (Lawrie would later play Wooster in the short-lived television series *Jeeves and Wooster* 1990-1993, opposite Stephen Fry as Jeeves). The exact date and location are irrelevant, but various (and often contradictory) references place the dugout as somewhere in the Somme region between 1916 and 1918. The 'Big Push' is looming in a few days, as it has been throughout the series, and Blackadder is determined not to take part in it. The two other main characters in the series do not share the life of the trenches. Ensconced at headquarters in a sumptuous château at least a hundred miles to the rear, they are General Sir Anthony Cecil Hogmany Melchett, played by Stephen Fry, and Blackadder's arch-enemy, the sneering staff officer Captain Kevin Darling, played by Tim McInnerny, whose principal ambition is to survive the war and keep wicket for the Croydon Gentlemen's cricket team. Throughout the series, the main interaction is between the front line dugout and headquarters, with the German enemy only rarely making an appearance.

At the end of this last episode, General Melchett orders Captain Darling to join Blackadder's company at the front, and together with Lieutenant George, Baldrick and the rest of the company they charge 'over the top' to certain death. Despite the rest of the series, this final moment is anything but comic, with the scene of the figures moving in slow motion through the mud of no-man's-land slowly mixing to a green field with waving red poppies, backed by sombre music instead of the series' normal jaunty theme tune.

With its disregard of time, space and authenticity, *Blackadder Goes Forth* may be seen as the quintessential representation of the postmodernist Western Front, first described and popularised in Paul Fussell's very influential book of 1975, *The Great War and Modern Memory*,[16] which has played a major part in the teaching of the war's literature. In particular, Fussell and his followers argue that the Western Front can only be understood as a uniquely *unhistorical* event, taking place outside time. Fussell's work has since been subject to considerable criticism by revisionist historians pointing out his lack of historical rigor, and has to some extent been discredited.[17] But the persistence of his influence, and the basic method of approach to the Great War through literature and cultural artefacts, has contributed greatly to the existing 'Two Western Fronts'. As an expression of the Western Front as eternal, unchanging and futile, the *Blackadder* view might almost have been taken directly from Fussell. At one point Captain Blackadder describes how the war 'would be a damn sight simpler if we just stayed in England and shot fifty thousand of our men a week', a more than tenfold exaggeration of the real death rate coupled with the assumption that the losses are all for nothing.[18] In a curiously gratuitous scene in the last episode, Field Marshal Haig (played by Geoffrey Palmer) is shown at his own headquarters, casually knocking over toy soldiers on a terrain model with his hand to represent his own side's casualties, and then sweeping them into a dustpan.

All four of the *Blackadder* series owed much (and much of their success) to a variety of British comedy traditions, including an acknowledged debt from *Blackadder Goes Forth* to the long running BBC comedy series *Dad's Army* (1968-1977), based on the Home Guard of the Second World War. But what was new about the series was the fusion of comic talent from two styles that appeared together in the early 1980s. One of these was a revival of 'Oxbridge' satire, a style traceable ultimately to the 1960s *Beyond the Fringe* review by undergraduates from Oxford and Cambridge Universities. Atkinson himself and fellow Oxford graduate Richard Curtis together scripted the first *Blackadder* series, while Hugh Lawrie and Stephen Fry were products of the famous Cambridge University 'Footlights' company. John Lloyd, who produced all four series, also added a strong element of continuity. The remaining three *Blackadder* series were co-scripted by Curtis with Ben Elton, a leading exponent of the rather more aggressive and politically orientated 'Alternative Comedy' style, which emerged in London in the same period. Rik Mayall, another prominent exponent of Alternative Comedy, made guest appearances in all the series except the first, as various incarnations of the flamboyant 'Lord Flashheart'. Atkinson had first come to prominence in the BBC satirical series *Not the Nine O'Clock News* (1979-1982), on which Curtis – barely out of university for a year – had also worked as a writer; and this had been followed immediately by the first series of the anarchic situation comedy *The Young Ones* (1982-1984) which established Mayall and the 'Alternative' style as viable television material.

In terms of themes and general *mise en scene*, the first series, *The Black Adder*, was to some extent the exception among the four, particularly in being set in a completely fictitious reign (the premise was that King Henry VII had managed to falsify all history books, and that one of the Princes in the Tower in fact reigned for 13 years as Richard IV, with Prince Edmund 'The Black Adder' as his younger son). Thereafter, the Curtis/Elton scripts used a broad-brush approach based on the fictional and feature film version of history. The second and third series, set in Elizabethan and Regency times, represent the earliest and latest dates respectively for a 'Romantic Age' of swashbucklers, identified by George MacDonald Fraser as existing rather more in Hollywood than in history itself.[19] So, inevitably, *Blackadder II* includes a Sir Walter Raleigh episode with jokes about potatoes; and other episodes involving a venal clergyman and some puritans. Similarly, one episode of *Blackadder The Third* features Dr Samuel Johnson (died 1784) in conversation with Percy Shelley (born 1792); while others include the Duke of Wellington, and 'Pit the Younger' played as a precocious and squeaky-voiced adolescent.

Partly because of the success both of *Blackadder* itself, and of various cast members as their careers flourished through the 1980s, the series developed something of a repertory theatre company feel. The repeated appearances of Rik Mayall as Lord Flashheart have already been noted. Miranda Richardson, who played Queen Elizabeth I as a self-obsessed teenager in *Blackadder II*, also made guest appearances in the third and fourth series. Tim McInnerny appeared regularly in the first two series as incarnations of Lord Percy, Blackadder's inept assistant, before playing Captain Darling in *Blackadder Goes Forth*. Stephen Fry played Lord Melchett, the Queen's advisor, as a regular character in *Blackadder II*; while Hugh Lawrie played Prince George the Prince Regent, again as a regular character, throughout *Blackadder The Third*. To this should be added a number of running jokes and conventions established for *Blackadder Goes Forth* from the earlier series, including one followed faithfully in every series: that the leading characters should by some contrivance die together in the last scene of the last episode.[20] By the time that *Blackadder Goes Forth* was made, the comic relationships between the characters governing it, and a certain amount of its structure, had already been established by the preceding series.

The series as history

Many of the images and features of the stereotype Western Front lent themselves in a very natural way to the *Blackadder* treatment, especially the battle of wits between the *Blackadder* character and higher authority, and the idea that everyone should die at the end. To this existing base of established conventions and interpersonal relationships, the scriptwriters for *Blackadder Goes Forth* added some familiar clichés from the late 20th century popular perception of the Western Front. The first episode, 'Captain Cook', introduces the characters and their surroundings, stressing the difference between the front-line dugout and the general's château. Next, 'Corporal Punishment', deals with the court martial of Blackadder by General Melchett, and his consequent escape from near death by firing squad. This theme of the rigged court martial and firing squad has preoccupied late 20th Century views of the war, including the feature films *Paths of Glory* (1957) and *King and Country* (1964) as well as the BBC television drama series *The Monocled Mutineer* (1986). The third episode 'Major Star' features a concert party, with Gabrielle Glaister reprising her role from *Blackadder II* of 'Bob', the girl who has dressed up as a soldier to follow her fortune. The next two episodes, 'Private Plane' and 'General Hospital' are vehicles respectively for Rik Mayall as Squadron Commander Lord Flashheart of the Flying Corps, and for Miranda Richardson as Nurse Mary, the suspected spy. There are strong echoes here of two other BBC drama series, the 1979 dramatisation *Testament of Youth*, based on Vera Brittain's experiences as a VAD nurse in the war, and *Wings*, the 1977 drama series about a Royal Flying Corps squadron. (The stockshots of aircraft flying that appear in 'Private Plane' were taken from the *Wings* series, at conveniently low cost to the BBC).

In the final episode, *'Goodbyee!'* Blackadder, while waiting for the final order to attack, outlines to George and Baldrick the reason for the war's outbreak:

[T]he real reason for the whole thing was that it was just too much effort not to have a war… You see, Baldrick, in order to prevent a war in Europe two super blocs developed: us, the French and the Russians on one side, and the Germans and Austro-Hungary on the other. The idea was to have two vast opposing armies, each acting as the other's deterrent. That way there could never be a war… [But] there was one tiny flaw in the plan…[21]

As should be apparent, historical authenticity is not very high on the series' order of priorities[22] *Blackadder Goes Forth* is not the historical Western Front of the Great War, and it was never meant to be; and it derives part of its humour from trading on the clichés of popular or schoolbook versions of history. But this version of the outbreak of the Great War is recognisably the 'failed deterrent' or 'war by timetable' popularised in the early 1960s by A.J.P Taylor in Great Britain and Barbara Tuchman in the United States, drawing a parallel between the events of 1914 and the nuclear standoff of the 1960s (and made even more topical by the brief revival in Great Britain of the Campaign for Nuclear Disarmament in the early 1980s).[23] In short, this is the kind of explanation for the outbreak of the Great War that the average educated British television viewer of the 1980s might have learned at school or possibly even university. A similar explanation for the outbreak of the war appears in the successful Tom Stoppard stage play *Travesties* (1974). Together with a liking for Alternative and Oxbridge comedy, this view of the Great War was in Great Britain simply part of the cultural inheritance of the early 1980s 'Yuppy'[24] generation.

From tragedy To farce

As with the previous Blackadder series, the episodes *of Blackadder Goes Forth* largely stand alone, and may be taken in almost any order. But unlike the previous series, the fact of inevitable and pointless death from the final act of attacking 'over the top' is established early in the first episode, and then features as a reference point throughout the series. In each episode the chief motivation of Atkinson's 'Captain Blackadder' character in seeking to create a concert party, or join the Royal Flying Corps (and so on) is a desire to find a posting away from the front before the attack is ordered. This dark idea of waiting to die, which gives the series its underlying structure, comes directly from one of the most famous fictional versions of the Western Front: R.C. Sherriff's *Journey's End*; and both the difference between the two works, and the path from one to the other, are revealing ones.

Journey's End first appeared in 1929, as a stage play by Sherriff playing simultaneously in London, New York and Chicago (with touring companies taking it to 20 other countries) and a BBC radio play; followed by a 1930 Hollywood feature film (for which Sherriff did not write the adaptation) and a novel written in collaboration with Vernon Bartlett.[25] Its frequent revivals have included a 1984 London West End stage revival (starring Jason Connery), and a 1988 BBC television production. Indeed, taking this production of *Journey's End* together with *Wings*, *Testament of Youth* and *The Monocled Mutineer*, it is instructive just how frequently dramas related to the Western Front appeared on British television in the decade preceding *Blackadder Goes Forth*.

In contrast to the timelessness and lack of specific location for the Western Front of *Blackadder Goes Forth*, Sherriff based his play on a very specific event which was utterly familiar to many members of his original audience in 1929: a British front-line battalion on the Saint Quentin sector of Fifth Army front in the last few days before 21 March 1918, waiting not to advance but to receive a major German attack. The action is set, like *Blackadder Goes Forth*, chiefly in the officers' dugout of a company. But at the end of the play, as the Germans attack, the implication clearly exists that the officers will all die doing their duty. Although many of the front-line battalions would be overwhelmed, the German defeat in this battle was one of the major turning points in the war, leading to an Allied victory, and this was well known to contemporary audiences.

Sherriff served with the 9th East Surrey Regiment, which fought hard in this battle, although not initially in the very front line. He was not himself present, due to being wounded in the Third Battle of Ypres ('Passchendaele'). Nevertheless, *Journey's End* was regarded by its first audiences as highly realistic, earning praise from Winston Churchill, and Sherriff a standing ovation from a specially invited audience of Victoria Cross holders, as well as support from pacifists and many others who saw the play as anti-war. In fact, Sherriff's view of the Great War, like that of many others who had served in it, was complex and ambivalent. He did not believe that it should have started, and hated the idea of fighting it; but he also believed that it had to be fought and won. Himself a public schoolboy who had been promoted from the ranks, Sherriff also meant *Journey's End* as a monument to the young men from public schools who had officered the Army at a junior level. His company commander in *Journey's End*, 'Captain Stanhope', is himself barely out of school and already holds the Military Cross; while the new addition, Lieutenant Raleigh (corresponding to the 'Lieutenant George' of *Blackadder Goes Forth*) is a naïve newly-commissioned schoolboy, but is far from being a comic figure.

As the literary historian I. F. Clarke showed in 1966,[26] for a generation before the Great War popular culture and imaginative fiction in Britain and Europe had predicted a war that would be technological in nature while being dependent on the heroic individual for its conduct. It is also a relevant fact, in the expectation of the next war being like the last one, that the experience of many British volunteers in the South African War (1899-1902) had been on the whole quite a pleasant one, not unlike a giant scouting and riding holiday for adults. (Indeed, Colonel R. S. S. Baden-Powell had improvised just such a body of 'boy scouts' for his defence of Mafeking, an experience which led directly to his founding of the Boy Scout movement on his retirement from the Army in 1907.) Away from the Western Front the experiences of individuals like T. E. Lawrence ('Lawrence of Arabia') closely fitted these expectations. But on the Western Front only half the promise was delivered. The principal objection of the 'trench poets', writers such as Sassoon, Blunden, Aldington and Graves, was to the impersonal nature of mass industrialised warfare which cramped, or removed or simply had no place for their individual humanity before it finally maimed or killed them.

In this context it is surely not a co-incidence that the first stories about Flight Commander Lionel Bigglesworth were published in 1932, in *Popular Flying*. William Earl Johns, the author of the 'Biggles' stories, was a 40 year old former grammar school boy and sanitary inspector, whose military flying career had been five weeks flying DH4 bombers on the Western Front in summer 1918 before being shot down. But Johns, displaying the same attitudes as the ex-ranker Sherriff, unhesitatingly made his hero a teenage public schoolboy and fighter pilot, promoting himself to 'Captain' Johns in the process.[27] As George Orwell noted in his classic article on 'Boys Weeklies' in 1940, the heroes of boy's stories of the 1930s set in the Great War were either secret agents or pilots, never infantry.[28] On the Western Front only the pilot 'aces' with their single combat achieved the pre-war ideal of the heroic individual, and Sherriff's play remains one of the very rare enduring examples of the British infantry subaltern of the Great War as hero (although also very definitely as victim). It is doubtful if any British play, film or television dramatisation of the Western Front since perhaps 1950 has depicted something that was actually a commonplace of the war: a competent officer bravely and successfully leading his troops.[29] The most recent British television portrayal of the Great War, the BBC drama *All the King's Men* (1999), set in the Gallipoli campaign, cast David Jason as a brave but elderly and under-trained officer, whose misplaced faith in the wisdom of his superiors leads to his own death and those of his men.

Remarkable confirmation of the attitude already identified by Orwell amongst a younger generation looking at the Great War came in 1976, when a film version of the *Journey's End* story was released, with the plot transferred to a Royal Flying Corps scout squadron on the Western Front as *Aces High* (starring Malcolm McDowell as 'Captain Gresham' – the 'Stanhope' figure). Additional material for the film came from C. Day Lewis' autobiographical *Sagittarius Rising*, written about his own Western Front flying experiences.[30] Whereas the action of the theatrical version of *Journey's End* remained completely within the dugout, *Aces High* enjoyed rather more freedom. In particular it includes a scene in which Gresham is invited to a 'planning lunch' at an unspecified 'headquarters', the only purpose of which appears to be to emphasise the gulf between the front-line and high command. As might have been predicted, this scene belongs very much to the Western Front described in Hastings' *Evening Standard* article cited earlier. In a sumptuous château, a table laden with delicacies and crystal is peopled by well-fed staff officers making idle or salacious gossip, presided over by an impossibly elderly brigadier-general (Ray Milland, who was 70 years old, compared to the 35-45 years old for those actually serving in the war). The contrast with McDowell's gaunt and almost skeletal Gresham with his boy-like deference could not be greater.

In 1930 Journey's End had been a success both as a stage play and as a film. But in 1976 with *Aces High*, acceptance of the main themes of Sherriff's story by a commercial cinema audience was judged as being dependent on the film's simultaneous reinforcement of the image of the heroic pilot, château generalship, and other clichés of the Western Front. By the late 1980s, despite the BBC revival of the original *Journey's End*, Sherriff's portrayal of the behaviour and attitudes of officers and men in the trenches was so remote from popular cultural understanding of the Western Front that it could only be understood by a mass British television audience as the farce of *Blackadder Goes Forth*. In innocently providing entertainment for a further new young generation, *Blackadder Goes Forth* helped shape their future attitudes towards the Great War. In attracting the attention of historians of the conflict, it has also helped bring into sharp focus the nature of the debate regarding the Western Front of literature and popular culture against the Western Front of history.

Notes

1 Although focussed on the British experience, this is an international debate, and some of its contributors have been Australian, Canadian and American historians writing on the British and wider Imperial experience. See for example: Modris Eksteins, *Rites of Spring: The Great War and the Birth of the Modern Age* (London: Black Swan, 1990); Gerard DeGroot, *Blighty: British Society in the Era of the Great War* (London: Longman, 1996); Tim Travers, *The Killing Ground: The British Army, The Western Front, and the Emergence of Modern Warfare 1900-1918* (London: Unwin Hyman, 1987); Trevor Wilson, *The Myriad Faces of War: Britain and the Great War 1914-1918* (London: Polity Press, 1986); Jay Winter, *Sites of Memory, Sites of Mourning: The Great War in European Cultural History* (Cambridge: Cambridge University Press, 1995).

2 For example by Sir John Keegan, *The First World War* (London: Hutchinson, 1998), who rejects without debate an entire body of findings on the Western Front.

3 Hugh Cecil and Peter H. Liddle (editors), *Facing Armageddon: The First World War Experienced* (London: Leo Cooper, 1996, p. xix and fn 1.

4 G.D. Sheffield, '"Oh! What a Futile War": Representations of the Western Front in Modern British Media and Popular Culture,' in Ian Stewart and Susan L. Carruthers (editors) *War, Culture and the Media* (Trowbridge: Flicks Books, 1996) pp. 54-74; Brian Bond, 'A Victory Worse Than Defeat? British interpretations of the First World War', Liddell Hart Centre for Military Archives Annual Lecture, Kings College London, 20 November 1997.

5 Jeremy Black, *War and the World: Military Power and the Fate of Continents 1450-2000* (London: Yale University Press, 2000) p. 275.

6 '100 Great Television Moments' first broadcast in Great Britain by Channel Four Television, April 2000.

7 This is the line as given in the published version of the *Blackadder* scripts, [Anon.] *Black-Adder: The Whole Damn Dynasty* (London: Michael Joseph, 1998) p. 350; compare with the video release version of *The Western Front* (1999), Episode 3: '*Feeding the Front*'.

8 *Haig: the Unknown Soldier*, part of the BBC *Timewatch* series, first transmitted on British television July 1996; video version released May 2000.

9 W.C. Sellar and R.J. Yeatman, *1066 and All That: A Memorable History of England* (London: Methuen, 1930) Introduction (n.p.)

10 Max Hastings, 'I do not believe our generation could have borne the martyrdom of World War One', *Evening Standard*, 2 November 1998, pp. 8-9.

11 John Hussey, 'Portrait of a Commander in Chief' in Brian Bond and Nigel Cave (editors) *Haig: A Reappraisal 70 Years On* (London: Leo Cooper, 1999) pp. 12-36; Frank Davies and Graham

Maddocks, *Bloody Red Tabs: General Officer Casualties of the Great War 1914-1918* (London: Leo Cooper, 1995) pp. 1-44.

12   At the 18th IAMHIST Conference in 1999 at which a version of this paper was first presented, the present writer was surprised that, despite worldwide syndication of the *Blackadder* series, a contingent of distinguished American historians deeply interested in the television and film portrayal of the Western Front had never encountered the series before.

13   At the time of writing a useful source of information for all these appearances is the unofficial *Blackadder* website http://www.blackadderhall.co.uk

14   For scripts of *Blackadder Goes Forth* see *Black-Adder: The Whole Damn Dynasty*, pp. 348-438; for video see *The Complete Black Adder Goes Forth*, BBC Enterprises 1992.

15   At the time of writing this is to be found at http://www.comedyzone.beeb.com/blackadder. As may have been noticed, the designation of *Black Adder*, *Black-Adder* or *Blackadder* is to some extent arbitrary; the BBC shows a slight preference for the first version.

16   Paul Fussell, *The Great War and Modern Memory* (London: Oxford University Press, 1975).

17   See, for example, Robin Prior and Trevor Wilson, 'Paul Fussell at War', *War in History* I (1) March 1994 pp. 63-80.

18   *Black-Adder: The Whole Damn Dynasty*, p. 414. The figure for official military dead for the whole British Empire in the course of the war was 947,023, and most historians would accept a round figure of 1-1.25 million. Given that the war lasted 223 weeks, this produces a weekly average of between 4,000 and 4,500 British and Empire dead on all fronts. This is itself a horrifying figure, but quite unrelated to the *Blackadder* view of the war.

19   George MacDonald Fraser, *The Hollywood History of the World: From One Million Years BC to Apocalypse Now* (New York: Beech Tree Books, 1988) p. 104.

20   Strictly, at the end of *Blackadder III* only Prince George dies, and Blackadder is mistakenly accepted by mad King George III as his son and heir.

21   *Black-Adder: The Whole Damn Dynasty* p. 442.

22   The series' attitude to historical accuracy is well conveyed by Captain Darling's uniform, which mixes the red tabs of a Great War Staff officer with a Guards Brigade officers' hat and tunic of the Second World War, and which includes, entirely against the conventions of the character, both the Military Cross and George Medal for bravery.

23   A.J.P Taylor, *the First World War: An Illustrated History* (London: Hamish Hamilton, 1963) pp. 11-15 (note that Taylor dedicated this book to Joan Littlewood); Barbara Tuchman, *The Guns of August* (New York: MacMillan, 1962).

24   An acronym from 'Young Upwardly-mobile Professionals'.

25   Andrew Kelly, *Cinema and the Great War* (London: Routledge, 1997), pp. 66-75.

26   I.F. Clarke, *Voices Prophesying War: Future Wars 1763-3749* (Oxford: Oxford University Press, 2nd Edition, 1992) originally published 1966.

27   See Peter Berrisford Ellis and Jennifer Schofield, *Biggles: The Life Story of Captain W.E. Johns* (Godmanstone, Veloce, 1993) passim.

28   George Orwell, 'Boys Weeklies', in *Inside the Whale and Other Essays* (London: Penguin, 1962) p. 192. The essay originally appeared in *Horizon* Number 3 of March 1940.

29   A related partial exception is the portrayal of the war in Australian television and cinema in the 1980s, at a time when elements within Australian politics were self-consciously attempting to create a national image independent of Great Britain. The Australian television drama series *ANZACS* (1985) follows the fortunes of Australian officers and men from Gallipoli to the end of the war on the Western Front. Even then, the hero – portrayed as a highly competent and caring officer – is killed in action; and this series, like its various British equivalents, has a marked and largely unhistorical anti-British high command bias. Another Australian film of the same period, *The Lighthorsemen* (1987) portrays a competent Australian officer successfully

commanding his troops in Palestine in 1917, with slightly less of an anti-British high command bias. *Gallipoli* (1981), another Australian production, is much more in the tradition of soldiers as victims, British high command as incompetent, and the (unseen) British troops as not much better.

30 Cecil Lewis, *Sagittarius Rising* (London: Peter Davies, 1936).

The World at War: **Television, Documentary, History**

James Chapman

The World at War is widely and justifiably regarded as a landmark in the history of television documentary. It has routinely attracted epithets such as 'monumental' and 'magnificent' from journalists and academic commentators alike.[1] Perhaps the most significant aspect of the acclaim lavished upon the 26-part Thames Television series is indeed that the plaudits have come from both television critics and professional historians – constituencies who often hold very different views about the televisual representation of history. Clive James, reviewing the series for the *Observer* in 1973, realised that after only two episodes 'it has already established itself as a documentary series of central importance'.[2] Ten years later and the reputation of *The World at War* had been even further enhanced. 'It will always rank as one of the finest achievements since the dawn of television,' one critic declared when the series was repeated on Channel 4.[3] Historians, temperamentally less inclined to hyperbole, have nevertheless been lavish in their praise. For Donald Cameron Watt, *The World at War* could be considered one of 'the great historical television series'.[4] Even that most exacting proponent of historical probity, Arthur Marwick, accepts that it 'set new standards for prodigious research and integrity of presentation'.[5]

From these comments – and many more could be quoted in a similar vein – it would seem that *The World at War* is highly regarded both as good television and as good history.[6] This chapter sets out to consider what makes *The World at War* 'good television' and 'good history'. The qualities identified in the series by television critics and professional historians provide different sets of benchmarks against which the genre of television historical documentary continues to be judged. *The World at War* is a prominent example of television history, but it is television history in two different senses: the series is not only an example of the representation of history *on* television, but is also part of the history *of* television. Here, therefore, we will explore both the production history of the series and its representation of history. Iin particular, we look at the tensions that arise between television producers and professional historians in the genre of historical documentary, and suggest how these tensions were (for the most part) resolved in the production of *The World at War*. As part of the genre of television historical documentary, *The World at War* needs to be considered in relation to the three

127

separate constituents which come together in that generic categorisation. By examining the topic in three parts – 'television', 'documentary' and 'history' – there emerges both a contextual framework for analysing the series and a nexus of concepts and ideas which inform and even to some extent determine the form and nature of a series like *The World at War*.

Television

The production personnel involved in *The World at War* have suggested various reasons why the series came to be made when it was. Jeremy Isaacs, who at the time was Controller of the Features Department at Thames Television, recalled that early in 1971 he approached the senior management at Thames with the idea of making a documentary series about the Second World War.[7] Jerome Kuehl, who was to be associate producer of the series, has gone on record to the effect that '[t]here's an official history and there's an unofficial history of the origins of the Second World War series'.[8] The details of these 'official' and 'unofficial' histories provide a fascinating insight into the rationale and motives of television producers. A combination of various circumstances and no small degree of opportunism determined the origins of *The World at War*.

Kuehl's 'official' history suggests that 'the series was made when it was for technical and ... psychological, moral and political reasons'. In this account, a combination of circumstances in the late 1960s and early 1970s created the conditions under which a highly ambitious series like *The World at War* could be produced:

> The technical reasons [he continued] were that an enormous amount of film was shot during the Second World War, but once the war was over it was forgotten. It was put into archives and left there, uncatalogued and forgotten. Even when people knew of the material there was no public access to it. ... Only when the archive footage was made publicly available was it possible for anyone to make a film using material which had not been seen before, and you can situate that point at about the late 1960s. Thus only from about 1965-1970 onwards was it technically feasible for an ambitious company, or an ambitious production unit, to set about using material which was novel, by which I mean had not been widely seen by anybody other than the cameramen who filmed it, the lab technicians who processed it, and the people who had put it in the archives.[9]

This account needs to be nuanced slightly, for it is not strictly accurate to suggest that all the actuality footage of the war was laying forgotten in archives or that none of it was publicly available. The main source of archive film for *The World at War* was the Imperial War Museum (IWM) – the end credits of each episode include a caption 'in co-operation with the Imperial War Museum' – which acts as the official repository for British and Commonwealth actuality footage shot by service cameramen, as well as official documentary and propaganda films produced or sponsored by the British government. Documentation in the Ministry of

Information (MOI) files in the Public Record Office reveals that even during the war itself there was discussion over what to do with the vast amount of actuality footage being shot by official cameramen. In April 1941, for example, Ian Dalrymple, the Supervising Producer of the Crown Film Unit, wrote to Jack Beddington, the Director of the MOI's Films Division, suggesting 'the compilation of an exhaustive history of the war on film'.[10] Although nothing was to come of this initiative, the actuality footage was handed over to the IWM at the end of the war for preservation and cataloguing.

The World at War was indeed praised for its extensive use of archive film, but it would be wrong to assume that all the footage used was being brought into the public domain for the first time. A cautionary note was sounded by one of *The World at War*'s directors, David Elstein, who, reacting against 'the hubristic claim about "rare archive film, much of it never seen before on British television"', remarked that 'rarity is in the eye of the beholder, and there is not much new to me - in the battle scenes particularly'.[11] There is a difference, of course, between what is familiar to experienced film researchers on the one hand and what is familiar to the general public on the other hand. 'Isaacs's team modestly point out that it is embarrassing to be praised for discovering film which is easily accessible in the Imperial War Museum,' observed the historian Douglas Johnson. 'Nevertheless, it is true that the series is showing some remarkable excerpts from films which have never been seen before.'[12] Other archival sources used in the series include the US National Archives in Washington, and the archives of the newsreel companies, especially Movietone, Pathé and Visnews, all of which had provided material for earlier film and television documentaries. But television audiences in Britain and America were far less likely to be familiar with the material which came from European archives such as the Bundesarchiv in Koblenz or Film Polski in Warsaw.

According to Thames Television's own publicity, the team of film researchers on *The World at War* watched some three and a half million feet of film in the course of 1971-72.[13] This probably represents the most thoroughgoing and systematic job of film research undertaken anywhere in the world up to that point. Even so, however, there were lacunae in the coverage. In particular, the researchers were denied access to Soviet and East German film archives. Most of the film of the war on the Eastern Front, therefore, is either material of German origin which was accessible in West Germany or a small amount of Soviet film held by the IWM. Film researcher Raye Farr testified that the series 'was done entirely from material available in the West'.[14]

If the technical resource to cope with millions of feet of archive film was one reason why *The World at War* came to be made when it was, the other factors that were part of Jerome Kuehl's 'official' history of the series' origins were what he grouped together as 'the moral/political/psychological explanation'. *The World at War* was to make extensive use of oral history through interviews with actual participants in the war. Kuehl recognised that it was only with the passage of time that people were prepared to speak candidly about their wartime experiences. Those who had been young men or women during the war had now reached middle age and 'could look back with a certain distance on the events of their young manhood or womanhood', while for those who had already been middle-aged during the war the time was ripe to record their recollections as it may have been their last opportunity to do so before they died. 'The raw material for the interviews was there,' Kuehl remarked, 'and Thames had the wit and the foresight to see that this was the time to make the series.' [15]

So much for the official account of the origins of *The World at War*. In this account the series was made when it was due to a combination of circumstances which made it technically possible and historically viable. From a purely historical point of view, the 1970s was probably the best time to make the series anyway. On the one hand, the war was still recent enough that a large number of participants were still alive and able to contribute, but on the other hand sufficient time had passed so that the events of the war could be treated with a degree of objectivity and detachment. But this explanation still leaves certain questions unanswered, not least how and why *The World at War* came to be made by an independent television company when, traditionally, it had always been the BBC which produced the 'big' documentaries on British television.

'The *unofficial* history,' according to Kuehl, 'is that everyone knew there was going to be a series made about the Second World War for just these reasons'. The BBC, he suggested, 'thought they had a moral monopoly on these kinds of programmes, and they assumed, along with everyone else, that when the series on the Second World War was made, it would be made by the BBC'.[16] Indeed, the BBC had already produced one historical documentary series which some commentators have regarded as a forerunner of *The World at War*. In 1964, to commemorate the fiftieth anniversary of the outbreak of the First World War and also to help launch BBC2, the corporation had produced *The Great War*, which ran for 26 forty-minute episodes and which, like *The World at War*, made extensive use of both archive film and eye-witness accounts. *The Great War* was intended to be more than purely military history, though it employed the services of the distinguished military historian Captain Basil Liddell Hart as its chief adviser. The aim of the series, according to its producer Tony Essex, was to 'produce a developing philosophy on war and to give an account of the political, social and economic history of the early 20th century'.[17] The series was narrated by Michael Redgrave, while other distinguished actors provided the 'voices' of historical personalities, including Ralph Richardson as Field Marshal Haig and Emlyn Williams as David Lloyd George. The BBC had followed *The Great War* with a 'sequel' covering the 1920s, *The Lost Peace* (1966), and even while *The World at War* was in preparation at Thames, broadcast a series of eight programmes under the series title *Grand Strategy of World War II* (1972), presented by historian Michael Howard. The notion that the BBC was somehow the natural home for a series like *The World at War* was apparently quite widespread among television viewers. 'It is a sad commentary,' observed Douglas Johnson, 'that many of those writing to Thames

Television should express surprise that ITV, and not the BBC, has made this achievement.'[18]

So how did *The World at War* come to be made by Thames? Kuehl's explanation is worth quoting at length for the way in which it exposes the economic imperatives that were paramount in the world of independent television:

> The Independent Television Authority, as it was at the time, closely controlled not only the *nature* of the programs [sic] made by the contractors, but the profits made by the contracting companies. When these profits got too large, a kind of excess profits tax was imposed, and when profits were thought to be too small, then the tax was lowered. This is a crude description of the 'levy'. What happened, I believe, is that in 1971 the levy was unexpectedly reduced. So literally from one day to the next, Thames had quite a large sum at its disposal, which no one had budgeted for. Then the controller of the Features department, Jeremy Isaacs, in effect, went to the senior executives of Thames Television and said, "I know what to do with that money. We will make the history of the Second World War."

> The Board was delighted with this suggestion for several reasons. One is that, as he explained it to them, it would have a large archive film component. That meant library film and a less expensive series than using live actors. The second reason was that because the series was about the war, it would have a lot of gunfire. It would be a kind of heroic shoot-em-up which could compete successfully for audiences against westerns and other forms of violent movies. And because it was about a great public event, the Second World War, it would also count as public service broadcasting. They could kill three birds with one stone. So they approved the series.[19]

In this version of events, therefore, the immediate origins of *The World at War* are attributed to an act of sheer opportunism on the part of Isaacs himself. It is, in effect, an example of the 'great man' interpretation of history in which Isaacs is presented as the bold visionary who acts swiftly and decisively to take control of favourable circumstances and persuades the philistines of Thames Television to commission a project which he will then transform into something of an altogether different order. Kuehl, indeed, offers precisely this reading of events, remarking that 'Jeremy's skill was in translating a mandate to make a shoot-em-up into a populist, popular and popularizing visual history of the Second World War.'

Kuehl admitted that his unofficial explanation 'is just speculation on my part', but on closer inspection it does not seem entirely fanciful. Under the terms of the Television Act of 1954, which established the framework for the introduction of independent television in Britain in 1955, the Independent Television Authority (ITA) was empowered to lay down guidelines for the nature and content of programming across the ITV network. The ITA was a public body which in organisation and constitution was not unlike the BBC's Board of Governors. Indeed, the Reithian values which still pervaded broadcasting were apparent in the ITA's policy that its contractors (the four companies which held regional ITV franchises) should be required to inform, educate and entertain – the very essence of the concept of public service broadcasting that had underpinned British television since its inception. The franchise holders raised revenue through selling advertising space, but part of this revenue was used to support the ITA through a levy on their profits.

While independent television quickly became a success with viewers, winning audiences from the BBC so that by the late 1950s it enjoyed a lead of over two-to-one in the ratings war, it attracted criticism from both politicians and cultural commentators for the perceived low-brow nature of its programming which was derided as comprising nothing more than 'wiggle dances, give-aways, panels and light entertainment'.[20] These criticisms came to a head in the report of the Pilkington Committee on Broadcasting, a body set up in 1960 'to consider the future of the broadcasting services in the UK' and whose members included Richard Hoggart, author of *The Uses of Literacy* (1957) and a critic of what he perceived as the decline of moral seriousness in the provision of popular culture for the masses. In 1962 the Pilkington Committee delivered a stinging verdict on independent television, declaring that 'the service falls well short of what a good public service of broadcasting should be'.[21] The main consequence of the Pilkington Report was that the third channel was awarded to the BBC rather than to ITV. Another consequence was that, under the terms of the Television Act of 1964, the ITA was allowed to 'mandate' certain kinds of serious programmes and to require all franchise holders to broadcast them at the same times. The result of the Pilkington Report, in the words of one recent commentator, was that 'ITV's programming over the next two decades became more like the BBC's'.[22]

It is entirely possible, therefore, that Thames saw *The World at War* as being a means through which it could fulfil its public service remit and provide the kind of 'serious' programming that was required of it by the ITA. The public service remit (inform, educate, entertain) is apparent in Jeremy Isaacs's 'mission statement' to his production team, which concluded with the expressed objective of producing 'programmes worth watching which might also help us understand the times we live in'.[23] The television critic Peter Fiddick, moreover, was firmly of the opinion that 'Thames has proved to its network colleagues that a serious programme can sustain the demands of peak-time'.[24]

The popular success of *The World at War*, which attracted audiences of up to 15 million throughout its first transmission on British television in 1973-74, is all the more remarkable given that it was by no means the first television series to chronicle the history of the Second World War. There had already been any number of series which, through a combination of archive footage and interviews with participants, had recounted the events and personalities of the war. The most famous of these was the American NBC network's *Victory at Sea*, a 26-episode half-hour documentary series first broadcast in 1952, but other, similar examples included *Crusade in Europe* (ABC, 1949), based on General Eisenhower's account of the European campaign, and the BBC's *The Valiant Years* (1961), based on Sir Winston Churchill's history of the war.[25] But *The World at War* was different from these predecessors in several important respects. First, it was not intended as a grand narrative, but rather as an account of people's experiences of war. 'Of course the War, all of it and bits of it had been "done" over and over again,' recalled researcher Susan McConachy. 'Ours was to be different. It was to be about people rather than politics, the ordinary soldier rather than the politics or the great commanders.'[26] Second, what the television documentaries of the 1950s had in common with each other, but where *The World at War* was different, was that they relied on major media personalities or historical figures as a hook. The long-running American series *Twentieth Century* (CBS, 1957-65), which for many of its early episodes focused on the war, was introduced by Walter Cronkite, while *The Valiant Years* depended upon Richard Burton reading Churchill's speeches. This represents what Jerome Kuehl refers to as 'magisterial or mandarin history'. 'Their approach,' he suggests, 'is to get a revered figure, or perhaps even a controversial figure, but any rate a *public personality* who tells the audience *what to think*.'[27] *The World at War*, in contrast, did not rely on such devices for audience identification. Most of the interviewees in the series were not well-known historical figures. The majority were lower ranking officers, NCOs and private soldiers rather than senior commanders (Field Marshal Sir Bernard Law Montgomery, for example, declined to be interviewed for the series) and ordinary civilians rather than politicians (with one or two exceptions such as Lord Boothby in the first episode and John Colville in the third). The one concession to 'mandarin history', however, was the use of Sir Laurence Olivier as narrator, which, Isaacs has since admitted, was a decision made 'with international sales in mind'.[28]

Documentary

Although there is an extensive and ever-expanding body of work on documentary film, the television documentary in comparison suffers from a dearth of scholarship.[29] That there is a relationship between film and television documentary is undeniable. *Crusade in Europe*, for example, was produced by Richard De Rochemont using the newsreel techniques of *March of Time*, while *Victory at Sea* has been compared to the celebrated *Why We Fight* series (1942-45) compiled for the US Office of War Information by Frank Capra. More tenuously, perhaps, a lineage could be traced from the British Army Film Unit's *Burma Victory* (1945), released after the end of the Second World War and in nature more of a film record than an outright propaganda piece, through to television documentary series including *The Great War* and *The World at War*, in so far as they are all characterised by a sombre, detached tone that does nothing to glorify or glamourise warfare. And, on a more basic level, the use of Laurence Olivier as narrator for *The World at War* provides a link back to official wartime documentaries for which the distinguished actor provided the commentary, such as *Malta, GC* (1942) and Humphrey Jennings's poetic *Words for Battle* (1941).

These relationships notwithstanding, however, the nature of the television medium is such that television documentary cannot be compared directly with film documentary. *The World at War* could never have been made for exhibition in cinemas due to the sheer length of the project – a total of twenty-six 52-minute episodes, almost twenty-one hours' worth of television. Even the longest documentary released to cinemas, Claude Lanzmann's *Shoah* (1985), an oral history of the Holocaust released in two parts of 274 and 292 minutes, is less than half the length of *The World at War* and, compelling though it is, stretches audience endurance to its limit. The very length of the series attracted comment when it was first shown. 'People go comparatively cheerfully to war because they think it will be over by September,' the television critic of the *Guardian* remarked rather sarcastically after the first episode was broadcast on 31 October 1973. 'The trouble with television is that you know in advance that *The World at War* will still be going strong in May.'[30]

Yet television also imposes limitations on the scope of documentary. Cinema can comfortably accomodate films of different lengths simply by changing the screening times. Broadcast television, however, requires standardised running times in order to allow the planning of schedules. For commercial television, moreover, the necessity of advertising (the amount of which was regulated in Britain by the ITA and then by its successor bodies, the Independent Broadcasting Authority and the Independent Television Commission) imposes strict time restrictions on programmes. So while, on the one hand, *The World at War* enjoyed the luxury of some 21 hours' worth of television, on the other hand it was restricted in that it had to divide that time into 26 self-contained episodes of the same length.

Even at a total length of 21 hours, *The World at War* could not and did not purport to be a comprehensive history of the war. It has repeatedly been claimed, by Jeremy Isaacs and others, that Isaacs consulted Dr Noble Frankland, the Director of the Imperial War Museum who acted as historical adviser to the series, and asked him for the 26 subjects that could not be left out of a popular history of the Second World War, and that a list of topics jotted on the back of a (probably apocryphal) envelope provided the general outline of *The World at War*.[31] The content was also determined to a great extent, of course, by the availability of archive film. A programme on the 'Big Three', for example, was abandoned when access to the Soviet archives was denied and it was discovered there was insufficient film of Stalin in western archives. Jerome Kuehl later indicated that he 'bitterly regretted' leaving out any coverage of events in the neutral countries and how they responded to war.[32] David Elstein believed that 'Thames have run their greatest risk' by omitting certain topics, citing the origins of the war, the decision to withdraw the British Expeditionary Force from Dunkirk, and events in China. 'By calling the series *World at War* [*sic*],' he conceded, 'and by seeming, broadly, to cover all the most important aspects of the war, Thames invited criticism.'[33] There are also some subjects that were not mentioned because they were still secret, especially the role of 'Ultra', the British code-breaking organisation which did not become widespread knowledge until after the series was made.[34]

Quite apart from the general problem of what to leave out of the series as a whole, there were the specific problems of what to include and what not to include in each episode. One of the recurring themes of Kuehl's published writings on the making of television documentaries is the restriction imposed by script length. This is one of the main causes of tension between television documentary makers and professional historians, in that the historian invariably wishes a script to impart more information than a documentary maker considers appropriate. Kuehl estimates that a commentary should take up no more than a quarter to a third of the running time of a programme; any more and it becomes too dense and detailed for audiences to assimilate. Thus, in a 50-minute programme, there would ideally be no more than 15 minutes of commentary. How many historians, Kuehl asks, could condense a 50-minute lecture into a quarter of an hour? To illustrate the point, he uses the example of the first episode of *The World at War*, 'A New Germany', which dealt with the rise to power of Hitler and the Nazis and the events leading up to the outbreak of war:

> [T]he introductory programme, which dealt with domestic events in Germany from 1933 to 1939, was reproached, both in public and in private, for not dealing with events in Germany from 1918 to 1933. It was also reproached for not dealing with international affairs from 1933 to 1939, and for not dealing with international affairs from 1918 to 1933, and for not dealing with British domestic affairs from 1933 to 1939, and even, by one earnest correspondent, for not having examined the United States' government's 1938 contingency plans for the mobilisation of American industrial production in the event of war breaking out in Europe. All this in a programme lasting 50 minutes.
>
> The historian who wonders tartly why we omitted Stanley Baldwin from our account of pre-war Germany should pause to consider what he would have included and what he would have left out, in his own 1500-word comprehensive account of the Third Reich (even if he were not limited by the necessity to confine his exposition to subjects about which film was available).[35]

It is for this reason, Kuehl avers, that most academic criticism of television history is simply inappropriate in that it does not recognise the practical requirements of the medium.

Oddly enough, perhaps, the commentary of *The World at War* actually attracted some criticism for not being brief enough. Clive James complained that it had the effect of 'leaving the reasonably well informed viewer glad that he got the bulk of his information at an earlier date and sorely tempted to run the show as a silent'.[36] 'The commentary left us in no doubt as to what we should think,' Douglas Johnson remarked.[37] In his estimation, therefore, *The World at War* was still very much in the tradition of documentaries which sought to impose a point of view on the audience, something which Kuehl, for one, would deny it set out to do.

One subject which the production team had agreed could not be left out of *The World at War* was the Holocaust. Yet the inclusion of this subject led to complaints from some critics over the use of archive film that was, in their estimation, too harrowing for television. Undoubtedly the episode 'Genocide' contains the most horrific images of the whole series and is difficult to watch even thirty years later when film footage of the Nazi death camps is more familiar to television viewers than it was in the early 1970s. The critics all found the episode disturbing, but they were divided over whether it was appropriate to include the footage in a programme shown on primetime evening television.[38] What these differences illustrate are less the individual tolerances of the critics themselves than the wider question of where the boundaries of restraint are to be drawn by the programme makers. This issue highlights another one of the restrictions which television imposes upon documentary. It is often pointed out that television reaches directly into the home, which makes it a more intrusive medium than, say, the cinema. Whereas the cinema-goer exercises a choice over which films to see and which not to see, the television viewer has no such choice over what is broadcast – the only sanction available is to turn off. The differences of opinion between the critics over the suitability of the 'Genocide' episode for home viewing illustrate that the boundaries of what is and is not acceptable are not fixed and must be carefully negotiated by the makers of television documentaries.

History

Both television documentary makers and professional historians agree in principle that history on television is fundamentally different from scholarly written history and, therefore, that it should not be judged by the same criteria. 'The series is television history,' Kuehl said of *The World at War*; 'in other words, it uses the resources, techniques and style of *television* to inform and entertain mass audiences by saying true things about and showing authentic images of the past.'[39] Arthur Marwick suggests that television historical documentaries, 'at their best, may be regarded as the equivalent of the very highest quality coffee-table history books'.[40] The comparison to 'coffee-table history books' is a useful one: television history is primarily visual (archive film) and provides a basic narrative (the commentary) which is used essentially to tell a story rather than engage in issues of historical controversy. David Elstein explains how television documentary makers have a different approach to the subject matter than professional historians:

> Television history is essentially narrative: it has to tell a story which is clear and to the point. Most historians, on the other hand, present the evidence they have accumulated, weigh it, and reach conclusions based on it. Television history is simply unable to handle material in that way, because the audience cannot be expected to keep several conflicting pieces of evidence in mind while waiting for the programme to reach its conclusion.[41]

Elstein refers to the content of the fourth episode, 'Alone', which told the story of the Battle of Britain, as an illustration of how *The World at War* was unable to engage with different interpretations of the events:

> A typical example of 'filleting' concerns the Luftwaffe's decision to bomb London on September 7, 1940, instead of the RAF fighter bases. Some historians have suggested that the main reason for this change in tactics was that Berlin had been bombed in August, much to Hitler's anger. The scriptwriter and I agreed that a more likely reason was that the Luftwaffe assumed the fighter bases had been put out of action and that, in bombing London, they would either have a clear run, or would force the remaining fighters to defend the capital, and so expose themselves to German gun-power. In the end, we neither mentioned the retaliation idea, nor why we had excluded it: which was poor history in one sense, but 'good' television narrative in another.[42]

Few of the critics were concerned with questions of historical controversy, though Clive James's review of the first episode for the *Observer* did make reference to the programme's 'now standard' line that appeasement of Germany in the 1930s had been misguided and complained that '[y]ou would never have guessed, from the first episode, that a controversy among historians about the war's origins had ever taken place'.[43]

But while television history does not, on the whole, engage with the subtleties of historical interpretation, preferring narrative and exposition to argument and controversy, the television documentary maker is nevertheless bound by some of the same general principles as the professional historian. Just as a professional historian should use primary sources in a critical manner, ascertaining their provenance and assessing the nature of the evidence they provide, television documentarists should in principle exercise the same rigour in dealing with their sources. There are two principal types of source in *The World at War*: archive film and oral testimony. There is every reason to believe that the film researchers were rigorous in ascertaining the authenticity of the archive film they were using. Isaacs impressed upon his production team that 'we are not making "poetic" films with license to use footage where we please. We are making an historic series and should not knowingly use pictures purporting to be what they are not.'[44] Even so, however, there were occasional lapses from the high standards set by the production team. Isaacs later admitted that 'not every shell burst was what we said it was', pointing to the example of the Battle of the River Plate in the second episode, 'Distant War', where the guns shown supposedly firing at the *Admiral Graf Spee* were actually firing off the Scottish coast.[45]

The reliance on oral evidence is rather more problematic, however. The production team were certainly alert to the problem that over a quarter of a century after the events, people's memories may prove fallible.[46] The problem with *The World at War* is not so much that the statements and recollections of interviewees are taken at face value, but rather that there is a tendency for history to be reduced to the level of anecdote. The expressed intention of the production team was to personalise the war through the experiences of 'ordinary people'. 'The main idea was to look at the war from a personal rather than a historical level,' said researcher Susan McConachy, who conducted many of the interviews, unwittingly revealing her view that the personal recollections in the series were not the stuff of history.[47] What they are, it might be argued, is television drama. The anecdotes are, by turns, gripping, humorous, poignant and tragic. Critics commented upon how they made the series compulsive viewing.[48] But it is debatable whether they contribute anything to the sum of historical knowledge. Moreover, it has been suggested that, as most of the interviews were conducted after the archive film had been selected and the draft outline of programme content had been decided, there was a tendency to look for oral testimony that would 'fit' certain pre-conceived ideas. David Elstein explained the procedure thus: 'After the preliminary reading, examination of archives, and talking to "witnesses" has taken place, the draft of the programme is written ... Only then are the "witnesses" interviewed on film, and – certainly as far as my programmes were concerned – they are interviewed to substantiate the conclusions reached in the draft.'[49]

There has often been a tendency for historians to disparage the efforts of television progamme-makers. Even the BBC's series on *The Great War* was not immune. In his introductory address to the seminal conference on 'Film and the Historian' at University College, London, in April 1968, A.J.P. Taylor had declared:

> Any of you seeing 'compilations' made by non-historians will, I am sure, know that few serious standards of scholarship are observed. The overriding interest of the ordinary producer, after all, is to make an effective package and tie things together which may not belong together either in spirit or in time, and I for one sat with great discomfort through such programmes as the BBC's 'First World War' [*sic*]. It was a monstrous use, I thought, of historical material in order to create effects. A very nice thing to do but it is not what we historians want.[50]

Taylor's main point of criticism concerned the way in which historians were used in the production of historical programmes. He complained that 'we are being called in simply as consultants and are used to add prestige to what is basically a non-historical approach'. Instead, Taylor called for historians to be 'the masters and film makers, and the technicians will do what we want'. Ironically, Taylor was one of the few historians who had been his own master, through his series of televised lectures on the BBC over which he had complete control of content because they were unscripted and delivered direct to camera. But his point about the nature of the historian's involvement in historical programmes is a valid one. Taylor's sentiments have been echoed by Arthur Marwick. Marwick has argued that the role of the historian should be proactive ('initiating the work themselves') rather than reactive ('scrutinising work essentially conceived and initiated by the commercial producers').[51] Although *The World at War* credits Noble Frankland as historical adviser, the majority of the episodes were written by members of the production team rather than by professional historians. One notable exception, however, was Angus Calder, author of *The People's War: Britain 1939-45* (1969), who was commissioned to write 'Home Fires', the episode on the British home front.

How did the academic world respond to *The World at War*? Kuehl suggests that those historians who took it seriously were those who already acknowledged the use of filmic evidence in historical teaching and research:

> It's a series which has had a varied career in the academic world. That's not a question of generation but a question of temperament. Historians, professional historians who take *visual evidence* seriously found it valuable; their praise was consistent and of course very flattering. Historians who are word-obsessed cannot see what the point was of making the series and the reason for that is because they feel, I think, that the series has nothing to say to them.[52]

In this respect, it is worth noting that *The World at War* was made at a time when some historians were beginning to take an interest in the use of archive film. The 1968 conference 'Film and the Historian', which brought together historians including J.A.S. Grenville, Nicholas Pronay and A.J.P. Taylor, and film makers and archivists including Thorold Dickinson, Sir Arthur Elton and Ernest Lindgren, is generally held to have been the impetus for the 'film and history' movement in Britain. The conference resulted in the setting up of the University Historians' Film Committee 'with the aim of co-ordinating and promoting activities relating to the use of film (together with still photographs and sound recordings) for historical research and teaching'.[53] The use of archive film in higher education was promoted in the production of teaching programmes by the Inter-University History Film Consortium and by the Open University, by another conference on 'Archive Film in the Study and Teaching of Twentieth Century History' at the Imperial War Museum in 1972, and by the publication of *The Historian and Film*, edited by Paul Smith, in 1976. It is clear that the production team of *The World at War* were keen to keep abreast of developments in the 'film and history' movement. Kuehl, for example, was one of the delegates at the IWM conference in 1972, while both he and Isaacs attended another conference at the University of Delaware in the same year.[54] In its own right, *The World at War* can be seen as a part of the 'film and history' movement. As Penelope Houston observes: 'The programme-makers, and most notably the associate producer, Jerome Kuehl, wanted to persuade professional historians about the value of film as evidence – the old cause, this time taken up not by a pamphlet or an article but by a practical demonstration.'[55]

In so far as this was one of the factors which influenced *The World at War*, then the series needs to be seen within the context of the 'film and history' movement of the 1970s and its commitment to the use of archive film in the teaching of history. There are other ways, too, in which *The World at War* is very much a product of its time. Like any piece of history, popular or scholarly, *The World at War* was influenced to some degree by the attitudes and values that were dominant at the time it was produced. *The World at War* was made at a time when events in various parts of the world had tarnished the image of the military. The American involvement in Vietnam, which saw the carpet bombing of North Vietnam by the US Air Force, the use of napalm against Vietnamese civilians, and incidents such as the My Lai massacre (carried out in March 1968, made public in November 1969), tarnished the image of the American military and caused a wave of anti-war protests. In Britain, the escalation of the 'Troubles' in Northern Ireland led to British troops being stationed in the province and to a series of violent incidents culminating in 'Bloody Sunday' (30 January 1972) when soldiers of the Parachute Regiment shot dead thirteen demonstrators in Londonderry. *The World at War* begins – and ends – with a massacre of civilians: the French village of Oradour-sur-Glane, razed by the Germans in 1944. The incident is held up as one example of the senseless killing and destruction which took place during the war. Arthur Marwick, for one, has argued that the content of the series was pre-determined by the production team having decided upon a particular interpretation:

> [*The World at War*] did in the end follow the old formula of settling first on an interpretation or storyline, then illustrating it with archive film material and 'eye-witness' interviews, rather than working outwards critically from the visual material. The general theme was that all war is dreadful, expressed in the opening sequence of the opening programme where, after the hideous civilian massacre carried out by the Germans at Oradour, the commentator (plummy and sententious Sir Laurence Olivier) remarks that shortly the young German soldiers too will be killed.[56]

The sentiment reiterated throughout *The World at War*, and most noticeable in the last episode, 'Remember', written by Isaacs himself, is that in war there are no victors, only victims. The series reminds us constantly that war is violent, destructive, terrible and horrific. What it never suggests is that war is sometimes necessary and can sometimes be justified – though ironically this was the view of most critics after seeing the 'Genocide' episode. Furthermore, there is testimony from members of the production team that *The World at War* set out with a definite agenda to emphasise the horror and futility of war. 'To me it was a very anti-war series', said Susan McConachy. 'It was looking at the whole pointlessness of ordinary people getting dragged into what, in many ways, was somebody else's argument … and fighting for ideologies which people didn't really understand and hadn't been part of.'[57]

Kuehl, while arguing that 'it's certainly not a pacifist series', suggests that it did nevertheless contain an anti-war message: 'When I finished working on the series, I thought, well the right side won, but Jesus Christ there must be a better way of ordering human affairs. And if that's the lesson which audiences get from it, then it's four years well spent.'[58] The views of its makers, therefore, as well as the tone and the content of the series itself, all point towards the conclusion that *The World at War* was intended as an anti-war text.

I would like to express my appreciation to all those who commented on this paper when it was first presented at the 1999 Leeds IAMHIST Congress *Television and History*, including John Whiteclay Chambers III, David Culbert, Dan Leab, John Ramsden, Peter Rollins and Philip Taylor. A special note of thanks to Jerry Kuehl, who has discussed with me his experience of working on *The World at War* and has kindly loaned me production documents in his possession.

Notes

1   Richard Last, 'Fine Research Inspires "World at War"', *Daily Telegraph*, 29 November 1973; Charles Barr, 'War Record', *Sight and Sound*, 58/4 (Autumn 1989), p. 265.

2   Clive James, 'The way the war was won?', *Observer*, 11 November 1973.

3   James Murray, *Daily Express*, 15 October 1983, p. 21.

4   Donald Watt, 'History on the public screen I', in Paul Smith (ed.), *The Historian and Film* (Cambridge: Cambridge University Press, 1976), p. 171.

5   Arthur Marwick, *The Nature of History*, third edition (London: Macmillan, 1989), p. 315.

6   The critical reception of *The World at War* can be discerned from the press clippings on the British Film Institute microjacket for the series. The first episode was received by some critics with reverence: '... *The World at War* was distinguished not only by its sobriety but by the originality of its historical reporting' (Michael Radcliffe, *The Times*, 1 November 1973); '... the series has been conceived, shaped and executed with impressive professional and imaginative skills' (Peter Black, *Daily Mail*, 1 November 1973). Others, however, were rather less impressed to begin with: '... no overall personality kicking the thing into a dramatic shape' (Elizabeth Cowley, *Evening Standard*, 1 November 1973); '... at this stage I can only express disappointment and hope that the programme as a whole will prove to be better than its first part' (Stewart Lane, *Morning Star*, 3 November 1973). Lane was to be the most equivocal in his attitude towards the series, remarking that it 'continues to fluctuate in its interest as far as I am concerned' (*Morning Star*, 27 February 1974), though, given the political outlook of his newspaper, he was predictably approving of the episode 'Red Star' which focused on the war effort of the Soviet Union: 'A remarkable programme, embellished with eye-witness accounts by ordinary Soviet citizens, and one on which all concerned are to be congratulated' (*Morning Star*, 23 January 1974). When the series ended, however, the majority of critics were united in their admiration: '*The World at War* has been such a distinguished programme that the epilogue demanded more than routine treatment and something beyond plain facts. Jeremy Isaacs, moving spirit of the whole venture, wrote and produced a closing chapter, "Remember", which met the challenge' (Shaun Usher, *Daily Mail*, 9 May 1974); 'This magnificently well-made series has proved itself to the last, the most genuinely educative survey of the 1939-45 period yet produced on television' (*Daily Telegraph*, 9 May 1974); 'There is no superlative that adequately captures the mood of the "World at War" series' (James Murray, *Daily Express*, 9 May 1974).

7   *Daily Telegraph*, 1 March 1995, p. 21.

8   'Jerome Kuehl, Associate Producer' [interviewed by Alan Rosenthal], *Cineaste*, 9/2 (Winter 1978-79), p. 8. Further refereneces to interviews from this source are cited as *Cineaste*.

9   Ibid.

10 Quoted in Barr, 'War Record', p. 265. The documentation in PRO file INF 1/626 'Film History of the War' indicates that two such initiatives were forthcoming in 1941, one from Ian

Dalrymple, the other from Sidney Bernstein, the cinema exhibitor who also acted as honorary adviser to the Films Division. Although the iniatives proved abortive, they did feed into a sustained campaign to preserve and catalogue all the footage taken by official service cameramen. The file contains the minutes of numerous committees where this was discussed, though the paper trail ends in 1946 when the MOI's remaining responsibilities were absorbed into the Central Office of Information.

11 'David Elstein, Director' [interview], *Journal of the Society of Film and Television Art*, 2/9-10 (1974), 'The World at War' issue, p. 10. Further references to interviews from this source are cited as *JSFTA*.

12 Douglas Johnson, 'TV images of war', *New Society*, 31 January 1974, p. 267.

13 Ibid. The same figure was quoted in the *Evening Standard* review of 16 January 1974.

14 'Raye Farr, Film Researcher' [interviewed by Alan Rosenthal], *Cineaste*, p.18.

15 'Jerome Kuehl, Associate Producer', *Cineaste*, p. 8

16 Ibid, pp. 8-9.

17 Quoted in Asa Briggs, *The History of Broadcasting in the United Kingdom. Volume V: Competition* (Oxford: Oxford University Press, 1995), p. 415.

18 Johnson, 'TV images of war', p. 267.

19 'Jerome Kuehl, Associate Producer', *Cineaste*, p. 9.

20 Quoted in Briggs, p. 16. The remark was made by Cecil McGivern, Controller of Television Programmes for the BBC between 1950 and 1957.

21 *Report of the Committee on Broadcasting 1960. Chairman: Sir Henry Pilkington*, Cmnd 1753 (London: HMSO, 1962), p. 67.

22 Andrew Crisell, *An Introductory History of British Broadcasting* (London: Routledge, 1997), p. 113.

23 'Jeremy Isaccs, Producer of "The World at War", defines his objectives', *JSFTA*, p.1.

24 *Guardian*, 13 May 1974.

25 For an account of the production of *Victory at Sea*, setting the series within the context of American Cold War politics, see Peter C. Rollins, '*Victory at Sea*: Cold War Epic', *Journal of Popular Culture* 6 (1973), pp. 463-82. The involvement of the US Navy and Army with the series is considered in Richard C. Bartone, '*Victory at Sea*: a case study in "official" history', *Film and History* 21 (1991), pp. 115-29.

26 Susan McConachy, 'Researching "The World at War", *JSFTA*, p.6.

27 'Jerome Kuehl, Associate Producer', *Cineaste*, p. 10.

28 Sir Jeremy Isaacs, 'Has Television History Come of Age?', lecture given at the 69th Anglo-American Conference of Historians, *War and Peace*, at the Institute of Historical Research, Senate House, London, 7 July 2000. Isaacs's remark was in response to a question from Professor Arthur Marwick.

29 The best history of documentary film in an international context is still Erik Barnouw, *Documentary: A History of the Non-Fiction Film*, 2nd rev. edn (New York: Oxford University Press, 1993). More theoretically oriented studies include Michael Renov (ed.), *Theorizing Documentary* (New York: Routledge, 1993), Dai Vaughan, *For Documentary* (Berkeley: University of California Press, 1999) and Brian Winston, *Claiming the Real: The Griersonian Documentary and its Legitimations* (London: British Film Institute, 1995), while other works focus on case studies of particular films, including John Corner, *The Art of Record: A critical introduction to documentary* (Manchester: Manchester University Press, 1996) and William Rothman, *Documentary Film Classics* (Cambridge: Cambridge University Press, 1997). Studies of television documentary include Richard Kilborn and John Izod, *An Introduction to Television Documentary: Confronting Reality* (Manchester: Manchester University Press, 1997), Charles Montgomery Hammond Jr, *The Image Decade: Television Documentary: 1965-1975* (New York: Hastings House, 1981) and John

E. O'Connor (ed.), *American History/American Television* (New York: Ungar, 1983). The latter two books, especially, focus on American television, whereas British television documentary, in contrast, remains a much under-researched area. This is an odd lacuna given Britain's role in the development of the documentary form.

30 Nancy Banks-Smith, 'World at War', *Guardian*, 1 November 1973.

31 *Daily Telegraph*, 1 March 1995, p. 21; 'Jerome Kuehl, Associate Producer', *Cineaste*, p. 10.

32 'Jerome Kuehl, Associate Producer', *Cineaste*, p. 10.

33 'David Elstein, Director', *JSFTA*, p. 11.

34 Martin Walker, 'War games', *Guardian*, 2 March 1984, p. 12.

35 Jerry Kuehl, 'History on the public screen II', in Smith (ed.), *The Historian and Film*, p.178.

36 James, 'The way the war was won?' *Observer*, 11 November 1973.

37 Johnson, 'TV images of war', p. 267.

38 Nancy Banks-Smith found the content of the episode 'on the borderline of the unbearable'. 'In such a series, the subject had to be done and, produced and directed by Michael Darlow, it was well done, not over-done. And yet I found it, in no narrow sense, wholly obscene and hardly fit to be seen' (*Guardian*, 28 March 1974). The most extreme reaction came from Mary Malone who, unlike Banks-Smith, felt that the episode should not have been shown: 'Helpless, hopeless, heartrending, horrific. Please, now that Episode 20 is over, can we shudder our way back to fiction - and forget?' (*Daily Mirror*, 28 March 1974). Other critics, however, while revulsed by the graphic nature of the footage, recognised both the gravity of the subject and the necessity of showing it: 'The justification for showing "Genocide", which contained the most sickening and harrowing footage I have seen on television, must surely be that it is necessary for us to be reminded, before the events take that neutralising step into the safety of distant history, what a generation still living was capable of' (Peter Lennor, *Sunday Times*, 31 March 1974); 'The compilation was nevertheless abundantly justified. First as showing exactly why the war against Hitler's Germany was necessary and, more importantly, as a warning which needs to be repeated for the benefit of every new generation approaching adulthood' (Sean Day-Lewis, *Daily Telegraph*, 28 March 1974).

39 'Jerome Kuehl, Associate Producer', *JSFTA*, p. 3.

40 Marwick, *The Nature of History*, p. 317.

41 'David Elstein, Director', *JSFTA*, p. 10.

42 Ibid.

43 James, 'The way the war was won?' *Observer*, 11 November 1973.

44 Memorandum from Jeremy Isaacs to 'All Second World War Personnel', headed 'Mistakes' and dated 4 October 1972, from material in possession of Jerry Kuehl.

45 *Daily Telegraph*, 1 March 1995, p. 21.

46 Kuehl cites one particular example: 'We interviewed a woman named Christobel Bielenberg, an Anglo-Irish woman married to a German. Her testimony was invaluable because she was British, but was part of German wartime society. She told a very moving story about the battle for Stalingrad and how the news of it affected the civilian population in Germany. The story wasn't used because she misremembered certain crucial facts. For example, she misremembered the point at which the German civilian population became aware that Stalingrad was not simply an important battle which was not going exactly the way the Germans had intended, but that troops in Stalingrad had been cut off. She mentioned knowing this fact at a particular time when she couldn't possibly have had that information. She had read back into events things which she subsequently knew to be the case. And since I had no wish to discredit her as a witness about other matters, I thought it best to advise the producers not to use that story.' 'Jerome Kuehl, Associate Producer', *Cineaste*, p. 12.

47 'Susan McConachy, Researcher-Interviewer' [intervied by Alan Rosenthal], *Cineaste*, p. 22.

48 'To the end the strength of *The World at War* has been its way of relating great events to

individual experience' (Sean Day-Lewis, *Daily Telegraph*, 9 May 1974); 'As usual, obscure civilians and minor-rank servicemen made the most enlightening talkers. It has been their evidence of the impact of grand-strategy decisions on the humble which has given the series much of its distinction' (Shaun Usher, *Daily Mail*, 9 May 1974).

49   'David Elstein, Director', *JSFTA*, p. 10.

50   *Film and the Historian* (London: British Universities Film Council, 1968), p. 1.

51   Arthur Marwick, 'History in the Modern Media', in Susan Kolbe and Petra Rösgen (eds), *The Culture of European History in the 21st Century* (Berlin: Nicolaische Verlagsbuchhandlung Beuermann, 1999), p. 153.

52   'Jerome Kuehl, Associate Producer', *Cineaste*, p. 12.

53   *Film and the Historian*, p. 44

54   'You should go because of the [US presidential] election, and because there ought to be someone senior at the Conference,' Isaacs wrote to Kuehl. 'I should go for the conference. There ought to be at least two people at the conference because (as you can see from the schedule) one person can't be in two sessions at once.' Undated memorandum in possession of Jerry Kuehl.

55   Penelope Houston, *Keepers of the Frame: The Film Archives* (London: British Film Institute, 1994), p. 121.

56   Marwick, *The Nature of History*, p. 315.

57   'Susan McConachy, Researcher-Interviewer', *Cineaste*, p. 22.

58   'Jerome Kuehl, Associate Producer', *Cineaste*, p. 15.

How the BBC pictured itself

Christine Whittaker

In his introduction to the radio programme, *The BBC Story*, broadcast on the General Overseas Service in October 1958, Robert Mackenzie asked:

> Which public institution reveals most about the life of any nation ?....I think an excellent case can be made for the view that the content and method of broadcasting reveal as much (or more) than any other institution about a particular national community......There is no doubt that the British Broadcasting Corporation is a distinctively British institution, which has no exact counterpart elsewhere, and whose activities reveal a very great deal about life in these islands.

For most of the twentieth century, the BBC ranked alongside the Monarchy and the Church of England as a central part of British life. Like those other two national institutions, the BBC was slow to change and did not often feel it appropriate or indeed necessary to flaunt itself. For most of its life, its qualities were so obvious they remained unquestioned. After all it had been set up to educate, to inform and to entertain, with a public service ethos. Why should anyone doubt that it was performing with the best interests of the audience in mind? There would be the occasional celebration of technical achievement, or a reminder of some of the corporation's most successful programmes on an anniversary. Eventually though, the BBC was forced into more overt self publicising and even self justification, when political and particularly financial circumstances threatened its conservative traditions.

The British Broadcasting Company started daily transmissions on 14 November 1922 two weeks after the introduction of the Broadcasting Licence Fee of 10 shillings. By March 1923 the Post Office had issued 80,000 licences, a figure which did not take long to reach a million. The BBC was to receive 5 shillings from each licence sold, but discussions about the level of the fee were lively even then. Sir Frank Gill and the Broadcasting Committee had pressed for a 15 shilling licence in the days before the BBC was established, 'if this sum is not allotted to the Broadcasting Companies the Committee are afraid the programmes must suffer', but in vain..[1] The system of the licence fee devised to finance the operations of the BBC survives today, but the negotiations over its cost and over the renewal of the BBC Charter, which was inititiated in 1926, have been a regular and often painful feature of the BBC management's working experience ever since.

The first pictures that were seen of the BBC were not created by the corporation itself, but by its colleagues/rivals in the cinema. As the popularity of the wireless grew, so too did the fame of the broadcasting star, and quite soon the BBC's most popular artistes began to feature on the newsreels. Pathé ran a series of musical performances from 1931 onwards. Singers included Leonard Gowings, Trefor Jones and Robert Easton — all 'of BBC Fame' and on 28 July 1932 the cinema audience was treated to Leslie Weston, the BBC's 'Cheery Chatterbox.' Henry Hall's BBC dance orchestra was seen on Movietone early in its lengthy career in 1932 and in March 1934 the BBC made the news on British Paramount with a story called *'Phantom Radio Traced'*. Nineteen-year old Wilfred Barker and his brother were detected as the mystery broadcasters and closed down. The BBC breathed again as it managed to get rid of the first pirate radio station. It was to retain its overall monopoly for another 21 years.

The technology of radio was in itself of great interest to the viewer, but of course the corporation was not able as yet to provide the pictures, and so in 1935 it was the GPO Film Unit, with the cooperation of the engineers of the BBC, who provided that fascinating insight. The producers, John Grierson and Stuart Legg, emphasised the national importance of the BBC with their grandiose title — *BBC, The Voice of Britain*. And a mere eight years after the first radio programmes were broadcast from 2LO, it was indeed a complicated and sophisticated organisation that was shown. The audience were invited to witness an impressionistic and impressive 24 hours at the BBC, starting with early morning at Broadcasting House, the imposing BBC headquarters since 1932. The film included the morning service, a rehearsal of a Shakespeare play, the Oxford-Cambridge boat race, the launch of HMS Queen Mary by the Queen herself and a reading by J.B. Priestly on the English spirit. So the very British nature of the BBC was clearly emphasised and some of the topics chosen were destined to run and run in the BBC's future programmes: God, culture, the Royal Family, some British navel gazing, and a bit of popular music and sport — plus a reminder of Britain's imperial history: G.K. Chesterton talking about the colonies.

The BBC did recognise the need for publicity and good public relations very early on. *The Radio Times* first appeared on 23rd April 1923 and in December 1924 Major Gladstone Murray was appointed Director of Publicity. He canvassed the BBC's case with the public, the government and the press. Reith understood the importance of an effective PR department, particularly at a time when the press were rather hostile to the BBC. In 1923 *The Daily Express* ran a crusade against the company, calling the licence fee into question[2] and in February of that year the press had tried to place an embargo on the free publication of BBC programmes.[3] The Newspaper Proprietors' Association thought the BBC should pay commercial rates for this service. It was then that Reith had the idea of *The Radio Times*. The magazine sold a million copies at Christmas 1927 and by 1939 had a regular weekly circulation of 3 million.[4] Another BBC publication, *The Listener*, was published between 1929 and 1991. Its mission was 'to capture the fugitive word in print'[5] and it contained transcripts of broadcast talks as well as reviews, literary pages and general features. It too aroused hostility from the rest of the press who thought that the BBC should stick to the spoken word and not produce unfair competition for the other weeklies. In the words of *The New Statesman*: 'That the BBC should seek to invade the press with a view to influencing the public through its eyes as well as its ears seems to us to be a wholly intolerable and indefensible proposition.'.[6]

Even in the early days the BBC acknowledged the need for public accountability, publishing its Yearbooks/Handbooks from 1928 onwards. In his introduction to the first *BBC Yearbook*, The Earl of Clarendon, Chairman of the Board of Governors, stated that 'The issue of this handbook is a reminder that Broadcasting is an established and accepted institution, and explained that the *Yearbook* would keep the public properly informed'. *The BBC Yearbook* ceased in 1952, but was reinstated as the BBC Handbook in 1954. Details were given of programme expenditure, viewing figures and progress in the preceding year. The written BBC Annual General Reports continued until it was decided to make a televised version in 1988 – by this time in a very different political climate.

The BBC has frequently invited the public to take part in its birthday celebrations. In fact, the majority of programmes, both radio and television, made by the corporation about the corporation, have been produced at the time of anniversaries. It was assumed at first, presumably correctly, that the radio medium itself was interesting enough to attract an audience. and that the listeners would be happy to hear about the making of programmes and the people who made them. Every year, around 14 November, there would be a BBC birthday programme. These soon became more ambitious. On 14 November 1925, the BBC celebrated its third birthday by broadcasting a light hearted programme about itself, then a programme about the BBC 10 years hence – a comic vision of the future. The following year the birthday programme was *A Fantasy in Red*, specially written and composed by members of the staff. It was explained that 'The idea of the birthday night Fantasy arose from a Programme Board Meeting [yes, they had them then too !] where someone suggested that talks ought to be illustrated more by music, or amplified or pointed in some way'. Representatives from the departments of Music, Talk, Drama, Variety and Engineering were all present, with Peter Eckersley, Chief Engineer, chairing an amusing exchange of ideas. The programme finished with a song, which must be one of the first plugs for the BBC.

> I never dreamt what wireless meant
> Until somebody said to me
> You ought to get a super set
> And listen to the BBC.
> I took advice, got something nice
> A something something supersone.
> An aerial, some valves as well
> And such a dinky pair of phones.
> And when I switch it on
> My loneliness is gone...

The BBC has continued to celebrate major birthdays with anniversary programmes. *The BBC Story*, the 1958 radio programme, describes how 'the BBC has developed over the past 35 years, and how in its present form, it serves the British community.' It provides a brief history of early broadcasting, the formation of the corporation, the birth of television, the External Services department, formerly the BBC's Empire service, and so on. By this time BBC Television was no longer a monopoly, Independent Television having begun three years before and so when – during *The BBC Story* – the Director of Television was asked whether the BBC, as a public service with only one television network, must aim to get as many viewers as possible all of the time, the answer came back: 'No, we don't think of it like that. We are not, you see, concerned with average audiences over a long period in the sense that commercial television has got to be. What we want is big audiences, of course, the bigger the better, but we aim at getting appropriate audiences for each individual programme....' He went on to reassure the listeners of the BBC's independence and complete impartiality.

The importance and significance of BBC values and BBC standards continue to be stressed over the decades as the anniversary programmes kept appearing. The word celebration is often to be found in the billings:

We Are Your Servants: a Gala Programme celebrating 10 years of BBC TV since the re-opening of the service in 1946 after World War Two.

Fifty Years of Music: a programme to celebrate 50 years of broadcasting.

The Lime Grove Story: An A-Z of Light Entertainment – BBC Television presents a celebration programme.

There was a radio programme in November 1943, celebrating twenty-one years of broadcasting. There were programmes celebrating 50 years of the BBC, a programme examining *The Birth of Television*, 40 years after the event in 1976; *Late Night Line Up* remembered 8 years of BBC2, since its inauspicious opening in 1964. The launch was supposed to happen on 20 April 1964, and the BBC had mounted a big publicity campaign to herald its arrival, but unfortunately there was a huge power failure that night, and all the viewers could see were candles. The big night had to be delayed for 24 hours and Michael Peacock, the first Controller of BBC2, was quoted on the anniversary programme: 'We went through the valley of despair last night, but came into the valley of sunshine tonight'.

Late Night Line Up does add that not all the critics were enthusiastic about the first BBC2 programmes, describing some of them as a little slow and stiff jointed (*Line Up* and *Newsroom*) and 'rather amateurish'. However, some of the triumphs of BBC 2 were also remembered by the producers – *The Forsyte Saga*, *The Great War*, *Not Only But Also*, *Master Class*, *Talking to a Stranger*, *The World About Us*, *The Six Wives of Henry VIII*, *One Pair of Eyes*, and as usual selections from the BBC Archives remind viewers how good they really were.

An internal BBC memo in September 1936 warned of a declining interest in the wireless,[7] but later that year the BBC began its television service. It was officially opened on 2 November and on that first night Adele Dixon sang about the wonders of the new medium:

> A mighty maze of mystic magic rays
> Is all about us in the blue,
> And in sight and sound they trace
> Living pictures out of space,
> To bring a new wonder to you...
> One by one they play their part,
> In this latest of the arts
> To bring new enchantment to you.

With 'this latest of the arts' at its disposal, the BBC was able to indulge in a little more self publicising. It had previewed its television service at Radiolympia in August 1936, when Leslie Mitchell introduced a number of programmes transmitted from Alexandra Palace to the exhibition hall. A Television Demonstration Film was made, not only to show viewers the wonders of the new technology, but also to help the television manufacturers to sell their TV sets. The technology was made even more complex by the fact that two systems were being used – Baird and EMI were fighting it out for supremacy. The film shows the Baird apparatus, the transmitting valves and the spotlight scanner. In the experimental studios at Hayes, Emitron cameras are seen being tested on members of staff. Even the cable laying was considered interesting enough to keep the viewers' attention.

The relationship between BBC radio and BBC television has not always been a happy one, but on this occasion their differences were overcome to make a radio programme which was broadcast on Thursday, 29 October 1936, entitled *Television – Looking Ahead: a programme on the Past, Present of Future of Television*. Leslie Mitchell, the television announcer, takes the listener on an imaginary tour of Alexandra Palace. They can hear the noise of the transmitter, the orchestra rehearsing; there is a description of the control room and they hear a producer rehearsing a variety act called 'The Knife Throwing Denvers'. They then go to the film projection room, where the staff are watching *Television Comes to London*, a film which was to be shown several times when the television service opened. Scenes from the film feature in the programme, but as adapted for the radio audience. Jasmine Bligh, one of the announcers, talks about her make-up, and there is a discussion about the difference between stage and television make up techniques. We hear Cecil Lewis at work – he is in charge of the television outside broadcasts. We are informed that he is a tall, fair man, one of the pioneers of sound broadcasting ten years before, and now one of the first men to enter television. The programme narrator ends by informing listeners that from Monday next, the regular service begins on the Baird system for the first week, and then on the EMI and Baird systems each week alternately. Vision has joined sound...

The television service ran for three years. It was shut down in September 1939 for defence reasons, and the technical staff were drafted to work in radio. The Chamberlain government had first declared that there would be no broadcasting during the war,[8] and many of the BBC's employees were called up. When it was decided that radio programmes should continue after all, there was an influx of new personnel who wrought major changes in the output, bringing the BBC closer to the viewers and producing popular and entertaining programmes like *ITMA*, and *Hi, Gang!* with Bebe Daniels and Ben Lyon. However, the workings of the BBC were still considered to be interesting enough to appear in programmes during the war years. There was a series called *BBC Close-Up*, in which listeners were invited to learn, for instance in September, 1943, 'How a Radio Play is Produced.' On the occasion of its 21st birthday, King George VI sent a message to the BBC:

> I send my hearty congratulations to the British Broadcasting Corporation on the 21st anniversary of its foundation. In peace and war alike, it has proved itself a great national institution, rendering high services to the State and to millions of listeners all over the world. I wish the Corporation all success in the future, when broadcasting will play a part of ever-increasing importance in the lives of us all. The BBC had, of course, always been loyal to the crown.

Television returned in 1946, heralded by another Demonstration film – this time called *Television is here again*. Made in the spring of 1946, it was explained that the film was not intended as entertainment for the home viewer, but as an aid for the British radio industry in installing and demonstrating television receivers. 'You radio men who will be seeing it often, will know it by heart and we will modify it occasionally. But we sound a note of caution. Television is home entertainment for the family group audience. If this is not by your own fireside, you enjoy it more in the intimacy of your own home.' The film has a preview of things to come, with a variety of entertainment shows, many dancing girls and a young Petula Clark singing 'Miser Miser'. There were also some sports events eg the Boat Race once again, a studio extract of *School for Scandal*, scenes of the Blackpool funfair and so on – encouraging stuff for audiences who were enduring the austerity of post-war Britain.

Once more the services of BBC radio were called upon to provide some publicity for the reopening of the television service. The billing for the programme read: 'Tomorrow afternoon the BBC Television Service resumes its daily transmission from the Alexandra Palace after an interval of over six years.' The narrator describes the scenes in the studio as Jasmine Bligh prepared to announce that television had returned. The early days of television are remembered, an engineer describes the Emitron camera, and there is even a precursor to the ever popular 'Auntie's Bloomers' as we are reminded of a gaffe made by Freddie Grisewood during the televising of the Lord Mayor's Show. As an agricultural float went by he remarked – 'Oh, look at those little pigs, aren't they grand?' But at that moment the cameras were showing the leading ladies of the Health and Beauty section who were following behind.

In his 1972 film *Looking In*, the documentary film maker, Robert Vas, looked at the Art of Television as part of the BBC's fiftieth anniversary celebrations. In a style fashionable at the time, there was no commentary, but he did include some criticisms of the television medium, using viewers' voices over shots of TV aerials – some of them being very dismissive about the programmes. However, Vas also recognised the power of television when he chose an extract from *Hancock's Half Hour*, in which Tony is desperate that his television should not be taken away, even though it is broken. 'One night without TV is enough to break the strongest of men.' An extract from the 1967 series *Lord Reith Looks Back* has the great leader describing television as 'a potential social menace of the first magnitude'. Vas includes an extract from a debate about television in 1971, in which a participant demands that television must lead and concern itself with the people, and another in which it is stated that there is nothing on television for the working man. In a second extract from *Lord Reith Looks Back*, his interviewer, Malcolm Muggeridge, remarks that the BBC is identified with a certain section of society; that it is an organ of the genteel and respectable elements of society. Reith, true to his beliefs when he founded the BBC, can't see anything wrong with that. Vas's programme includes many memorable clips from the BBC Archives. It is a celebration tempered with a realistic view of current criticisms.

One of the most successful films made about the BBC was *This is the BBC*, which was produced by Richard Cawston in 1959, and transmitted on 29 June 1960 to coincide with the opening of Television Centre – although it only showed the exterior of the new building. The programme went on to win numerous awards, including the BAFTA best specialised film of 1959, and Ed Murrow thought it the best film that he had ever seen 'dealing with an instrument of mass communication'.[9] This was the first film to be made about the BBC for 25 years. When Grierson had made *BBC – The Voice of Britain* the BBC had employed 2000 people; now there were over 16,000. In 1959 the corporation had successfully survived the advent of independent television (known internally as The Competitor) and still had much to brag about.

The format used is similar to that employed by Grierson in 1935, ie an impression of 24 hours in the BBC. On this occasion though, the film starts with night shots of Broadcasting House, rather than showing early morning at the same location. For now the BBC works round the clock and is a more complicated organisation. There is a rehearsal going on an the concert hall; they are setting the studio in Lime Grove, and of course the newsroom at Bush House is busy broadcasting to Russia. Jack De Manio arrives to start the Today Programme. The regions are not forgotten as we visit the BBC office in Northern Ireland. Some things never change - the Morning Service features, as it did in 1935, as does the Boat Race, the Newsroom, the rehearsal of a play – this time Mother Courage, rather than Shakespeare, and of course now it is in a television studio. Radio is not forgotten as we see Desert Island Discs with Beryl Grey, Mrs. Dale's Diary and a discussion among The Archers production team about the rights and wrongs of featuring hornless cattle in a forthcoming episode. Who could fail to be impressed by this panoply of goodies, many of them surviving today? It would be some years before a voice of criticism would be heard on a BBC programme about the BBC.

1997 was a major anniversary year for the BBC and a number of programmes were made to celebrate 75 years of broadcasting. One of the series made was *Auntie: The Inside Story of the BBC* – four programmes produced by Jeremy Bennett, tracing with frankness and humour the days since the formation of the British Broadcasting Company in 1922. In the first programme 'The House that Reith Built', the stuffiness and high minded attitude of the BBC are examined, and we are told how Reith, who ran the BBC with a rod of iron, sent girls home if they weren't wearing stockings, divorcees were not allowed, a staff announcer was dismissed for being homosexual and the highly respected Chief Engineer was sacked for having an affair with a married woman. The BBC's critics accused it of being too patronising, too middle class – even then – and the *Daily Express* published an open letter to the BBC accusing it of stuffed shirtism.

For the first time the producers were given access to the archives of the Oral History Project, which had been started by Frank Gillard in 1973, containing 120 recorded interviews with key BBC personnel, including former Governors, Director-Generals and Heads of the Television and Radio Services, as well as some Producers and Performers. The interviews began as sound only, but under Alasdair Milne's initiative, film and later videotape versions were introduced in 1983. Jeremy Bennett was thus able to draw on personal and intimate memories of the Corporation's early history. We learn that Chamberlain's appeasement policy was treated with deference by the BBC, and that Churchill's views were never reported. Churchill himself never forgot this. In February 1938 the Labout MP Josiah Wedgewood wrote a talk on the dangers of fascism – but the BBC turned it down, and even when Czechoslovakia was invaded the BBC continued the appeasement line. Harold Nicolson's talk about the invasion was vetoed, and the BBC was accused of a conspiracy of silence. However, the corporation managed to emerge from World War II with its image untarnished. Britain was victorious, and the BBC was seen to have contributed to the victory, as Churchill's gift of oratory was heard over the airwaves, public morale was uplifted by *Workers Playtime* and *ITMA* and there were memorable war reports by the great broadcasters like Frank Gillard, Godfrey Talbot and Richard Dimbleby.

The *Auntie* series looks at the beginnings of rebellion under Hugh Carleton-Greene, the Director General who refused to be undermined by Mary Whitehouse's campaign to clean up TV, survived the use of the word 'fuck' by Kenneth Tynan in 1965, and showed influential programmes like *Cathy Come Home*, *Till Death Us Do Part*, and *Culloden*, but along with his Chairman, Lord Normanbrook, decided against transmitting Peter Watkins' controversial next programme *The War Game*. The BBC's relationship with the government was becoming more tense; Harold Wilson felt that he was better served by ITV, which he believed appealed more to his supporters.

The final programme of *Auntie: The Inside Story of the BBC* is subtitled 'When Auntie Met the Iron Lady – Walking the Tightrope, 1970 - 1986.' It is to be noted that the programme does not deal with the Birt years at the BBC – that programme is still to be made. But it does show how open criticism of the BBC became prevalent in the 1970s, and how Margaret Thatcher's campaign to do something about the corporation gained momentum, with enduring consequences.

The level of the licence fee had been the subject of heated negotiation ever since its conception at 10 shillings in 1922. Relationships with the government of the time were always crucial to the BBC's prosperity, and the corporation was subject to numerous investigations and committee reports from early in its history. It survived the Sykes Committee in 1923, the Crawford Committee in 1926, the Beveridge Report in 1951 and came out well from the Pilkington Committee in 1962[10] but in 1969 it published its own report – *Broadcasting in the 1970s* – dealing with internal management. Lord Hill, the new Chairman of the BBC, had brought in McKinseys, the Management Consultants, to examine the BBC's financial and management arrangements. On the eve of the publication of *Broadcasting in the 1970s*, *24 Hours*, the nightly current affairs programme included a long interview with Charles Curran, the Director General, in which he described the extent of the BBC's financial problems and its plans for the future, followed by a studio discussion which included both Labour and Conservative MPs, and a representative from the Musicians' Union. One of the BBC's cost cutting exercises was to get rid of seven of its 12 orchestras, and the union were reacting angrily.

Poor relationships with the trade unions were adding to the BBC's problems. 1969 had seen the first strike by the BBC union, the ABS. Union demands were stretching an already overworked budget. On the screen the corporation continued with its policy of openness about its difficulties throughout the 1970s. In 1972 *Talkback* included a discussion in which Charles Curran, who again faced some heavy criticism from a group of MPs and journalists, some of whom thought the BBC should be broken up. In May 1977 *The Question of Broadcasting* was a special programme on the publication of the Annan Report, the Committee on the Future of Broadcasting, which again included some criticism of the BBC – that it was too large, had too many layers. *On the Record* in 1978 included an interview with Sir Michael Swann, the Chairman of the BBC, discussing the future of the corporation and the steady stream of staff who were leaving to join ITV, which could, of course, offer higher wages. He admitted that he was disappointed about the newly negotiated licence fee which was lower than he had hoped for, making long term plans difficult. The problems of reconciling the public service traditions with the demand for popular programmes were also discussed.

In May 1980 *Man Alive* cotinued the financial debate in *What Price the BBC* – examining the costs of broadcasting in detail, and showing that they could no longer be covered by the licence fee. In the discussion that followed, the BBC's output was compared unfavourably with ITV's. Its critics included eminent broadcasters like Jeremy Isaacs and Michael Grade, whilst Ian Trethowan and Alasdair Milne put the BBC's side.

The BBC had moved into the red in 1976, inflation was rising and drastic methods were called for. One suggestion made by the BBC's Policy Study Group was the possibility of introducing advertising to the corporation - an idea which has been rejected to this day. As well as living beyond its means, the BBC continued to antagonise the establishment. The left accused the BBC of right wing bias, the right of a bias to the left. A major political row had broken out in 1971, when the BBC transmitted *Yesterday's Men*, about the defeated Labour Government of Harold Wilson. There were threats of legal action, and there were more political rows to threaten the BBC's independence and existence in the years to come. The BBC Programme Complaints commission was set up in October 1971 to deal with growing public criticism.

Margaret Thatcher was very suspicious of the BBC which she thought was overmanned and antagonistic towards her government. She wanted to know how it was managed and how it spent the licence fee. The licence fee was set at £46 in 1981, and the BBC began a year-long campaign to have it increased. Meanwhile press and government hostility to the BBC were growing. *The Daily Mail* said the initials BBC stood for (utterly) BIASED: (morally) BANKRUPT and (politically) CORRUPT, and Max Hastings in *The Evening Standard* wrote WHO WILL HALT THE RUNAWAY BEEB?[11] The BBC's coverage of the Falklands War and of Northern Ireland reinforced the Prime Minister's conviction that something had to be done and that the BBC should be privatised. The licence fee was eventually set at £58, well short of the £65 asked for by the BBC. And this was despite the BBC's introduction, for the first time of televised commercials about itself. John Cleese spoke admiringly about the BBC, and Terry Wogan asked 'Is 16p a day really too much to ask?' And part of this increase was to be kept back until another committee of inquiry, the Peacock Committee, reported to Parliament. Its report actually rejected advertising, but it recommended that from 1988 the licence fee was to be pegged to the Retail Price Index, and both the BBC and ITV would have to guarantee that a proportion of ther transmitted programmes would be made by independent producers.

The BBC External Services, always at the mercy of government, made its own publicity film in 1981, *This is London*, in which John Tusa described the history and achievements of the BBC World Service – ending by describing the BBC as the most honest and most accurate of all broadcasters. It spoke in many tongues, but with one voice. The old BBC values had to be maintained, but it was a losing battle.

BBC's management and management structure also changed. The new regime of Chairman Marmaduke Hussey, the Director General, Michael Checkland, and his deputy, John Birt, produced the most overtly public accountability campaign the BBC had ever seen. In 1988 the BBC showed the first *See for Yourself* programme – designed to show the public what it was getting for its money, and hopefully to make the viewers realise that given the marvellous programmes that had been shown in the past year, they were actually getting a bargain. But not only the good things were featured. Sue Lawley described the Government injunction on 3 radio programmes about national security – *Secret Society*. There was a report on the resignation of Alasdair Milne, and even a chance to see how the Programme Review Board worked. A second *See for Yourself* was shown in January 1989. This time viewers were able to see behind the scenes of *Children in Need*, and to witness the studio director losing his cool when things went wrong. A series of BBC meetings was covered; the Radio Planning Group Meeting, the Finance Meeting, the DG's liaison meeting, the Board of Management meeting, the Board of Governors meeting, the Radio Directorate Meeting, and a balance sheet of the licence fee was given to any of the viewers who had managed to stay awake that long. But the highlight of the programme had to be a live phone in to Michael Checkland and Marmaduke Hussey. No wonder that the *See for Yourself* programmes became known to broadcasters as the Mike and Dukey show.[12]

The campaign to give the licence payers the chance to be involved was substantiated by a series of public meetings in which viewers would be able to question the broadcasters: 'It's Your BBC' and even a BBC Listens website at http://www.bbc.co.uk/info/bbclistens.

The BBC felt able to make fun of itself in a drama called *In the Red*, a comedy thriller by Mark Tavener, which was serialized first on Radio 4, and then in a television version in 1998, with screenplay adapted by Malcolm Bradbury. The BBC's Crime Correspondent, George Cragge, is transferred to Policy and Planning Department to deal with listeners' complaints as a punishment for drunken behaviour at the Editor's Summer Party. Stephen Fry, as Controller of Radio 2, and John Bird, as Controller of Radio 4, contemplate the new BBC where 'Nation shall speak ratings unto Nation', and the Director General, a money man, is too busy with licence fee negotiations to speak to his radio chiefs. It is decided that Lord Reith's principles of public service are out of date: 'It's now bums on seats that count: The BBC as we know it today!'

The Broadcasting Act of 1990 confirmed the BBC as 'the cornerstone of British broadcasting' but the changes in the British television industry during the 1990s were huge, and were mirrored by fundamental changes within the BBC itself. Producer's Choice affected everyone in broadcasting, as an internal costing system encouraged producers to use outside resources, and traditional BBC departments subsequently disappeared. In a multi-channel environment, the BBC was competing ever more openly with its rivals in a ratings war, changing its traditional styles of output. Methods of self publicizing have also drastically changed. An independent advertising agency is used to make commercials about the BBC's achievements – which can be enjoyed on *A Perfect Day*. There is a chance for the public to get a closer look at programme making at The BBC Experience. The BBC website is one of the most highly acclaimed and popular sites, and plans not only to survive but to expand in the digital age are optimistically expressed.

For most of its life, the BBC chose not to indulge in a public show of its achievements, but in 1999 its pride in its own past was recognized with the creation of a BBC Heritage department, bringing together a range of BBC history and heritage related projects. Artefacts, internal records, art, disused machinery are being collected, preserved and will eventually be exhibited by a proud BBC. The BBC's past can now be rediscovered on its website and it is not just the British public who appear to be interested. 20,000 visitors attended the BBC Fair in Hankyu Department in Osaka in November 1999, particularly enjoying the collection of vintage radios and televisions.

The history and achievements of the BBC remain unchallenged. In the British Film Institute's list of the top 100 British television programmes published on 5 September 2000, 72 out of 100 were from the BBC, and 8 out of the top 10 chosen were from the BBC's archives. And up till now, like (or perhaps unlike) the Monarchy and the Church of England, the BBC retains the status of a national institution.

Notes

1   A. Briggs *The History of Broadcasting in the United Kingdom. Volume 1*: The Birth of Broadcasting. (Oxford, 1961) p118.

2   '75 Years of the BBC' – lecture by John Birt at the Institute of Engineers Lecture Theatre, Savoy Hill. 21 January 1998.

3   A. Briggs *Vol. 1* p 142.

4   A. Briggs *The History of Broadcasting in the United Kingdom. Volume 2: The Golden Age of Wireless* (Oxford, 1965) p 23.

5   P. Donovan *The Radio Companion* (Harper Collins, 1991) p 161.

6   A. Briggs *Vol 2* p 287

7   Summary of comments by the Vice Chairman, Mrs. Hamilton, on a *Memorandum by the Controller (PR)*. BBC Written Archives Centre.

8   John Birt '75 Years of the BBC'.

9   A. Briggs *History of Broadcasting in the United Kingdom, Volume 5: Competition.* (Oxford, 1995) p 235.

10 J. Cain *The BBC: 70 Years of Broadcasting* (BBC, 1992)

11 C. Horrie and S. Clarke *Fuzzy Monsters: Fear and Loathing at the BBC* (Heinemann, 1994) p.22.

12 ibid. p 150.

French Television looks at the past

Isabelle Veyrat-Masson

The way the past has been and is represented on television is one of the best indicators for us to understand what is the status of historical television. Also, more generally, television representation of the past is an indicator of the status of popular history in our society. From 1950 to 1978 the growth in the number of historical programs increased proportionally more than the rest of television programming. Since then the situation has been less encouraging, at least in France.

Since the beginning of historical television in France we can identify five main periods with their own specific characters. What follows is a general overview of those periods.

The first period was the time of the domination of historical fiction. This period started in 1953 and finished around 1965. In this period, television programmes were broadcast live. Programming was dominated by professional directors. Fiction was their favourite genre. They enjoyed putting into their films the masterpieces of French literature and the main events of French history. So historical dramas engaged French people at that time. The most popular programme was *La Camera explore le temps*, which was a direct copy of an already well-known radio programme *La Tribune de l'histoire*. Director, Stellio Lorenzi, a powerful communist unionist, had been joined by two radio authors to develop a still confrontational television.

Through 47 historical dramas, those three authors from 1956 to 1966 presented a mixture of historical enigmas and anecdotal history and also moments of *grande histoire*. At a time when political discussion was avoided on French television, debates between Danton and Robespierre during the French revolution were particularly appreciated by the audience. When the famous *Camera*, despised by serious historians and hated by the politicians in charge of the French government. Many considered this programme to be a communist vision of our past. The programme was dropped suddenly. The audience reacted strongly and the waves made by this censorship lasted for years and years after.

The second period started around 1965, and was characterised by a desire to open discussion and debates. It is also during this period that the ORTF[1] and the second channel were created. Television film directors initiated at that time a major strike to fight the desire of top management to curb their power. The failure of this strike marked the beginning of their decline.

The second channel gave the opportunity to the humiliated journalists to raise their profile outside of news coverage and to change a certain number of habits created by the directors. They followed two directions, the production of ambitious documentaries and the multiplication of debates. These professionals, until then limited in their initiatives by the monopolistic system of the French television, were finding with history a way to bring political debates on the screen. The most important example in this new trend was the creation in 1967 of *Les Dossiers de l'écran*. Every week an entire evening was devoted to historical programming. A historically based commercial movie was followed by a debate with historians, experts and witnesses, even aficionados. During this debate, the audience could phone and ask the question they want. The journalist's role was usually to handle the conversation on the stage.

Despite this air of freedom the taboo subjects of French History. e.g. the Dreyfus Case and civil conflicts in the French society, war in Algeria and torture for example, and especially the period of French Collaboration with the Nazis and the responsibility of the Government in deportations, even the conflicts and oppositions inside the resistance movement. Before 1975, and with the exception of the war in Algeria, none of those essentials events had been mentioned. The change came only after the end of l'ORTF, and the end of a Gaullist view which had always considered television as one of its personal communications and propaganda medium. In 1975 the new law on media reorganised the competition between the three public channels. The professionals seized an opportunity to treat controversies.

The post-1975 period has been baptised 'the spring of public television'. Stimulated by a soft competition but not enslaved to audience share statistics. In the field of historical programmes complete freedom was given to famous historians like Braudel or Duby to make the programmes they wanted to develop from their own books or current research. Of course some limits still existed, for example the documentary *Le Chagrin et la Pitié* (1973) was still censored. In addition, from 1978, for the first time, the number of historical programmes broadcast slightly diminished in number. The multiplication of poor and cheap so called 'historical series' generated wariness in the audience for the whole genre.

The 'eighties can be seen as a period of contrasts. In 1981, one of the first decisions of the new socialist government was to reform again the broadcasting organisation (and to allow the broadcast *Le chagrin et la pitié*). The monopoly for programming disappeared paving the way to the creation of private channels. *Canal Plus*, and, in 1985, *la Cinq* and *Television 6* were created. The multiplication of the hours of broadcasting and their extension during the night, the installation of a strong competition – reinforced by the privatisation of the first channel, TF1- between six channels instead of two, has changed the nature of the relation between the audience and their programmes.

More and more entertainment programmes were broadcast. The audience lost the feeling that their favourite media had a sort of responsibility in its education - or of its political and cultural identity. 70 per cent of the time dedicated to watching television was for commercial channels. 30 per cent remaining tended to be for programmes that looked more and more alike.

The result at the end of the eighties was:

> – Less historical programmes: none of them on four of the six channels

> – costume dramas instead of docu-dramas

> – programmes broadcast later and later in the evening

In 1992 historical programming on French televison was subject to a number of institutional reactions. The deep transformation of the public service, in particular the striking diminution of the cultural programmes plus the desire of promoting the emerging European community generalised some important reactions from the socialist government. These circumstances produced the return of a weekly historical programme *Les Brûlures de l'histoire*. In addition there was a good deal of space offered to the commemoration of 'D Day' and to the end of the Second World War. The most original decision is the launch of a Hertzien (even Reithian) creation of a public cultural channel – *ARTE* – in 1992. This channel, created by French and German governments gave naturally a prominent position to history. Later, *La Cinquième*, essentially an educational television channel was added to the daytime schedule. This change also gave a significant position to historical television. Recently, two cable channels were created. They are already talking about merging.

Those changes could not hide for long what is, I think, a crisis in historical awareness in France. Pre-war history became a marginal subject whereas very contemporary history invaded the screen. *Arte* does not exceed a 3 per cent audience share on average, and historical documentaries are in the area of 1 per cent. The channel's policy on history does not favour history because audience analysis revealed that those programmes were mostly watched by aged males (admittedly with a superior education). History survives for them – if they stay awake after midnight, if they are at home in the afternoon, and if they can pay to get cable and satellite.

This means that historical programming is no more a must for programme planners. These programmes are now considered as being at best a kind of cultural duty, a civic obligation that private channels will not endorse.

Can we suggest an explanation for this situation? Have the mass media and especially television, through their focus on immediateness not marginalized (increasing the subjective distance) what is not "histoire du temps présent" (history of the present time) ie the period that is more than 50 years ago? Is television an agent and a mirror of this important modification of our perception of time, of a change in our mythic passion for the past?

Are we witnessing an important trend in our culture, the decrease of the traditional interest of French (and possibly all European) people towards the past? If it is the case, are the mass media and especially television, their way of imposing a new relation to time?

Note

1   ORTF, Office de la Radio et de la Télévision Française.

Dillinger is back. Film history and social perceptions of television

Valeria Camporesi

Every once in a while, by means of apparently unexplicable outbursts, visual mass media, under their different historical disguises (film, television, video, computer) are diffusely perceived as precipitating an irreversible anthropological change in our societies.[1] Over the last few years, uncertainty is being sharpened by technological developments which, in some instances, delete what were considered as characteristic dividing lines among the different media and between images and reality.[2] Digital images and interactivity enhance the visual media's ability to simulate reality, and to absorb the viewer/user into their world. The future which we would be facing as a result of these developments, it s said, might imply a loss of control over our lives. The way in which the various media characterize knowledge would be crucial in this progression towards lack of depth and loss of significance. Within this incessantly mobile scenario, the search for steady analytical tools might help to enlarge and stretch out our perspective on the supposed oncoming disaster, so as to possibly think and say something new (or borrowed, maybe, from some peripheral-to-this-centre space and time).

The real and perceived growth of computer-related technologies applied to transmission and manipulation of images is threatening to inflate to a hardly tolerable level the already spectacular importance which audiovisual media acquired in the public and political space in the twentieth century. Its pervasiveness, however, is progressively generating its own counteragents. In different intellectual, artistic[3] and more generally cultural contexts the claim is being made to go back to history to neutralize the growing threat of the future in the present. Far from proposing a monocausal evolutive history of the media,[4] the following pages will nevertheless put forward an itinerary into the past whose goal would be to dig out new hypotheses in our understanding of the media. This proposal is centered in a historical approach to the evolving relationship between cinema and television which takes film history as its framework of reference.[5] Within this approximation, film history is to be read as a reservoir of powerfully operating analytic devices[6] to explore our confused "audiovisual era".[7] But with a precondition: it should be a huge and complex film history as strongly established as possible in its two poles: films, on one side, that is to say materially defined audiovisual documents to be deciphered,[8] and history, on the other, which in this case would basically work as the reconstruction of pattern of intertextualities, in social practices and cultural codes.[9]

Such a huge and ambitious project cannot be pursued here and now. Perhaps, some might add, cannot be pursued at all. Undoubtedly, it entails a long and daring journey amidst all kind of perils. This essay is meant to formulate an hypothesis on a few basic starting points which should work as a methodological compass within the oceanic vastity of film history. The trip is supposed to bring us closer to the social meaning and functioning of the different media, as seen through the cinematographic lenses. But what is really dealt with is the relationship between film and television and its possible implications.

A glance to the past: television in *Dillinger è morto*

Whether left working alone or obsessively watched at, television is more than a simple prop in *Dillinger è morto* (M. Ferreri, 1969).[10] The nameless main character interpreted by Michel Piccoli does not only use it: he accepts it as inevitable. In his claustrophobic world, television works at the forefront or in the background, on or off-screen as a powerful stimulant of human passivity.[11]

Piccoli's casual encounter with Dillinger's story, printed on the pages of an old newspaper or related on the screen in a television documentary, takes place right at the beginning[12] and from that moment an intermittent, minimally described and silent dialogue between Ferreri's main character and the mythical gangster permeates the picture. As for the various appearances of television, they may be summed up with a short description of a sequence which occurs almost halfway along the film.[13] Piccoli is seated eating his slowly elaborated dinner. Then he suddenly stands up, takes the tv trolley, leads it in front of him, at the other end of the table, and switches it on. Then begins a programme on another media myth of the 1940s and 1950s, Fausto Coppi. Shortly thereafter the telephone rings, it is a call for the self-confident and sexually attractive housekeeper, played by Annie Girardot. As she answers the phone she is also watching tv. Her intriguing conversation seems to slowly overcome the presence of the small screen. Piccoli changes channel: a minority programme on a minority filmmaker evokes the unidentifyable identity of television while Girardot is getting more and more desirable. Change of sequence.

This excerpt from *Dillinger è morto* summarizes what television signifies within Ferreri's reconstructed world. As one among the mass media, it contributes to seal up its isolated audiences but, quite differently than in *The Truman Show* (P. Weir, 1998), it does not exert a cold and cruel dictatorship upon otherwise warm and human main characters. What is interesting here is that television is represented as a medium which stands in peaceful harmony within a society which is no better than its myth makers. It does not provoke big disasters itself. It is a piece of an alienated puzzle which material gestures, as long as thoughts, and images are bringing together and which cannot be brought apart.

Dillinger is dead, but he is also alive as an operational image brought to life by the mass media. His presence in the film is crucial as it becomes a metaphor for the desperate artificiality of modern life. It is this fictional Dillinger who inspires the main character's silent, slow, uneventful decision to blow up his silent, slow, uneventful life. Media, and television as one of them, form the all encompassing setting which renders useless the search for non-existent alternatives.[14] Ferreri too is dead, unfortunately. But his sharp pessimism which prevents him from the superficiality of the apocaliptical, has resulted in an analysis of television which has something to tell us. We made it, he is saying, the medium not only is the message: it is also our child. It belongs to a sticky network of intertwined texts produced and endured by a whole society.

As a "calculated combination of moving images and sounds",[15] films often, if not always, provide for interesting information on the society in which they were conceived and produced. As the example of *Dillinger* was supposed to demonstrate, they can drastically redirect our gaze towards unexplored areas of the past. Specific studies on images of television in films where textual analysis on television as a narrative and/or esthetic device is combined with the effort to reconstruct a changing iconography of television[16] might prove a fascinating and fruitful exercise of intertextual analysis which might sharpen our knowledge on changing social perceptions of television.

An attempt at a first generalization: images of television in films

As Michèle Lagny states, any research in intertextuality should be pursued on a twofold level. On one side, it should be carefully built upon specific case studies which should justify "the cultural elements" which "it connects" (a sort of a microhistorical component). But on the other side, intertextual analysis is also in need of a "strong hypothesis," which is "usually derived from a reflection on social representations or ideological functioning of a historical period".[17] But, how to produce an original reflection, specifically generated from film history, which would not simply adopt as an undisputable context a reconstruction of the past based upon other sets of sources? In other words, what can films tell us about television which we do not already know?

Instead of answering this question through the description of a historical investigation, its documents and results, the time has come to discuss a methodology, the object of the enquiry being not to highlight historical developments but the enquiry method itself. The idea would be to describe what questions should be posed to what sources so as to establish a fruitful dialogue, as Ortoleva describes it,[18] between a would be cultural historian and their audiovisual sources.

What can films tell us about television which we do not already know, then?

Various problems, of course, surge as soon as one formulates this question. They all basically refer to the confused, twisted relationship between images and reality, that "most irritating question" which Pierre Sorlin analysed in the pages of the *Historical Journal of Film, Radio and Television*, and which has to do with the relative autonomy of cinematographic representations. As the dwarf who manages to climb to the head of a giant, the tremendous work which historians have done in the last twenty years or so to come to terms with this problem can be assumed without discussing it here again.[19] Sorlin's conclusions may offer therefore a wise starting point. As he says, "although they refer directly to the world, pictures are inserted in representations which compel us to pay more attention to some aspect of their referent. Films borrow their material from reality and offer us a reshaped reality, an interpretation of it".[20]

To define which aspects films orientate our gaze to, within the mobile world of television, is, therefore, the only possible object of a study of images of television in films, and its ultimate outcome shall be a description of "habits of mind", as a *New York Times* critic put it.[21] Films could then tell us something about habits of mind relating to an object, television, which exercise a stronger and stronger influence on widespread practices, while leaving a vague, almost undefinable track on minds and memories. A systematic study of collective representations of televisions such as the ones which films can depict would allow for an in depth, serious, rigurous study of a phenomenon which is generally depicted as frivolous, undetermined, opaque and hardly deserving of any serious investigation.

The first step forward in the direction indicated by Lagny could be to insert a particular film, with its text and contexts, in a wider group where different movies can be classified under a common heading beyond their specificity in time, space, and production circumstances. The aim would be to establish categories of representation, areas of interpretations, and/or iconographic series which, without denying historical specificity and/or auteurial imprints and/or censorship and industrial conditionants, would shed new light on individual productions.

Under this assumption with no pretension of exhaustiveness, it is quite possible to enumerate a list of groups of films where television is utilized rather homogeneously as a narrative device of some importance. It might be interesting to gather under a same heading productions which would comprise, for instance, films representing television produced in the early years of the new medium and which could be analysed to detect social perception of the new medium by contemporaries; films set in the past which use the small screen as an historically defined prop; films where television is portrayed as a synecdoche of society at large and which are built around a more or less superficial, more or less individualistic fault finding perspective on social groups and/or institutions; and films where television is meant to introduce a superior rationality.

As an example of the first group, a case study on images of television in Spanish cinema in the 1960s proves fruitful.[22] The study of the period of the "advent of television",[23] the 10-15 years that in each country accompany the beginning of a regular television service proves, at least in that case, quite interesting. Within that historical context it is possible to explore social perceptions of television in a transition from inmaterial existence to installment, diffusion, and progressive adquisition of a rather definite identity. Within the construction of that cinematographic identity, issues such as the perception of modernity, its identification or lack of identification with the USA might enter in the picture. Besides, the exploration of early years allows for a specific analysis of the peculiar relationship image/reality which can be detected in "late comers", and which is basically due to a chronological lack of synchronization between habits of mind and actual experience. From this standpoint, the dialogue film-television might offer some clues on the weight of the experience of first comers (in television) on the formation of certain collective representations in late or middle comers countries. Under this regard, it would show how the "habits of mind" reflected, for instance, in films, might die hard or have a premature birth in relation with the specific country's actual experience, as it happens in the Spanish case, but concide in time and sign with what is happening, or has happened, elsewhere.

Another set of rather homogeneous questions would arise in relation with the representation of television in films set in the past. In this case, it could be interesting to explore to what extent television is used as a vehicle for a more trustuworthy reconstruction of past ages, as an efficient realistic device by which the spectator can easily recognize specific years, or historical periods. To study what programs, or television personalities, or films screened on television, for instance, were selected as being representative of the time, or especially coherent to the film's purposes, might prove at least as interesting as an investigation on dresses or settings. Amongst the many which could be suggested, the example of how television summarizes social and cultural differences between England and the United States in the early 1950s is to be found in *84 Charing Cross Road* (David Jones, 1984), a US production based upon the letters of Helen Hanff, an American writer living in New York, to an antiquarian bookseller in London between 1949 and 1969.

The third group of representations which may be singled out gather those productions in which television becomes a symbol of the oppression by an established power centre, which can either be the state, society, or private industry. Examples of this interpretation are numerous in films produced all over the world all through the history of television, and utterly different in conception and aim, from *Fahrenheit 451* (Truffaut, 1966), and *The loneliness of the long-distance runner* (Richardson, 1962), to the more recent *Women on the verge of a nervous breakdown* (Almodóvar, 1988), or *Plaesantville* (Ross, 1998) and the already cited *The Truman Show*.

To these, I think one should add at least a fourth group of films portraying television as a culturally creative medium. A recent investigation detected it as a significant trend, for instance, within some authors of the New German Cinema,

Fassbinder being the most notable example, in whose films television is utilised as a metaphor for "rational analytical reasoning".[24] The importance of this phenomenon is not diminished by the fact that it might be a direct result of television's financial support of that movement.

Attempts at a second generalization: cinema and television

Individual films, or groups of films, can therefore be read as symptoms of forgotten or ignored interpretations of reality which should be deciphered. As such, they might add substantially to our knowledge both of film and television, and history. But in an even more ambitious perspective, Lagny's plea for a "strong hypothesis" could be taken to more extreme consequences. If an analytical distinction is introduced within the panorama of sources, between film texts, so far analysed, and cinema, the latter being "the array of activities involved in the production and reception of films". Following this line of reasoning, "the variety of ways in which the film text is intermeshed with a whole set of economic, technological, social, and cultural practices"[25] might also be taken into the picture from the standpoint here assumed of a study on social representations of television.

Recent studies have extensively dealt with the "increasingly close relationship between film and television"[26] in different instances and geographical and historical contexts. The time has come to promote an effort to research upon the history of that relationship in its multifaceted implications, conditions and consecuences within an all-comprehensive approach. To be fully fruitful, such a history should avoid lineal reconstructions in order to explore the problematic meaning of synchronic developments, only later to be inserted in diachronical perspective and generalizations. Among the various lines of enquiry which cinema studies might suggest, the following three seem immediately approachable, from a microhistorical perspective, and crucial from the point of view of the elaboration of a "strong hypothesis" on social representations of television as seen from the standpoint of cinema.

A first strand of questions might arise from an analysis of what could be labelled as language and narrative contamination and/or defence of specificity within the two media,[27] which produces unresolved tensions between a series of audiovisual texts, their creators and their consumers. Differences and similarities might pinpoint crucial elements of the relationship between television and its public. A second group of meaningful interrelationships could be established from a thorough analysis of industrial reactions in public and/or private systems: comparative institutional approaches to the cinema and television industries could reveal a sharper cultural context where television assumes a complex social role.[28] A third area of inquiry could be devoted to reactions to television in the cinematographic world, which would include, on one side, theories and practices of certain crucial filmmakers and movements and, on the other, the published opinion of the specialized press, in its popular or more intellectual version. An effort to analyse and establish conceptual and historical links within the thoughts and experiences of television of, for instance, Roberto Rossellini, Jean Renoir, Orson Welles, Federico Fellini, Rainer W. Fassbinder, Volker Schlöndorff, or Jean Luc Godard, among many others, might sound like a depressingly gigantic endeavour but one which might produce extremely interesting results when approached from a not strictly auteurial perspective. Similarly, a study on how television is portrayed in magazines and periodicals directed to movie fans would add new insights into the changing composition of the audiovisual world.[29]

In conclusion

As Aldo Grasso states, "from the linguistic and behavioural standpoint, the connections between the different communication media are very complex relations".[30] The preceding pages were not meant to investigate that complexity but to claim for it a consequence in historical research on audiovisual media. The idea was to sketch out a tentative framework to force the important work in progress on the history of the interrelationship between cinema and television into a single set of meanings, the drawing up of a map on social perceptions of television. A systematic and committed exploration of that huge and complex landscape in historical perspective might represent an important step forward in our understanding of the functioning of cultural phenomena in the age of mass media. Research on individual cases is basic in this direction. But within that same microhistorical approach, powerful trends emerge which seem to point at a global explanatory context. Its complicated evolution, the difficulties in choosing relevant sources, their opacity and ubiquity should not shut out the view of an overall perspective. That at some point the intertextual game between cinema and television might produce a clear set of images, where complexity and continuous evolution are assumed and described as significant elements of any history of representation.

References

Altman, Rick (1996), "Otra forma de pensar la historia (del cine): un modelo de crisis", *Archivos de la Filmoteca Valenciana*, 22 (February), pp.6-19.

Andrew, Dudley (1998), "Film and History", in J. Hill and P. Church Gibson, *The Oxford Guide to Film Studies*, Oxford/New York, Oxford University Press, pp.176-189.

Benet, Vicente J. (1999), *Un siglo en sombras. Introducción a la historia y la estética del cine*, Valence, Ediciones de la Mirada.

Brunetta, Gian Piero (1991),*Cent'anni di cinema italiano*, Bari, Laterza.

Camporesi, Valeria (1999), "Imágenes de la televisión en el cine español de los Sesenta: fragmentos de una historia de la representación", *Archivos de la Filmoteca Valenciana*, 32 (June), pp. 148-162.

Company, Juan Miguel and José Javier Marzal (1999), *La mirada cautiva. Formas de ver en el cine contemporáneo*, Valencia, Generalitat.

Di Giammatteo, Fernaldo (1994), *Lo sguardo inquieto. Storia del cinema italiano (1940-1990)*, Florence, La Nuova Italia.

Fullerton, John and Astrid Söderbergh Widding, eds. (2000), *Moving Images: From Edison to the Webcam*, Sidney, John Libbey.

Gonzo, Cosetta (1996), "Effetto *Immedia*", in L. Quaresima, ed., *Il cinema e le sue arti*, Venice, Biennale di Venezia/Marsilio, pp. 413-420.

Grasso, Aldo (1996), "Cinema e televisione. Il frammento, l'archeologia, la domesticità", in L. Quaresima, ed., *Il cinema e le sue arti*, Venice, Biennale di Venezia/Marsilio, pp. 145-150.

Hill, John (1998a), "Film and television", in J. Hill and P. Church Gibson, *The Oxford Guide to Film Studies*, Oxford/New York, Oxford University Press, pp.605-611.

Hill, John (1998b), "General Introduction", in J. Hill and P. Church Gibson, *The Oxford Guide to Film Studies*, Oxford/New York, Oxford University Press, pp. Xix-xxii.

Hill, John and Martin McLoone, eds. (1996), *Big picture. Small screen. The relations between film and television*, Luton, John Libbey/University of Luton.

Lagny, Michèle (1992), *De l'histoire du cinéma. Méthode historique et histoire du cinéma*, Paris, Armand Colin.

Ortoleva, Peppino (1991), *Cinema e storia. Scene dal passato*, Turín, Loescher.

Ortoleva, Peppino (1999), "Cinema e televisione", in G.P. Brunetta, *Storia del cinema mondiale*, Vol. I "L'Europa. 1. Miti, luoghi, divi", Turin, Einaudi, pp. 993-1012.

Palacio, Manuel and Santos Zunzunegui (1995), *El cine en la era del audiovisual*, Madrid, Cátedra; Historia general del cine vol. XII.

Sjöholm, Charlotte (1998), "Television Scenes in the New German Cinema", unpubl. paper, Stockholm, Technologies of the Moving Image Conference.

Sorlin, Pierre (1999), *L'immagine e l'evento. L'uso storico delle fonti audiovisive*, Turin, Paravia.

Sorlin, Pierre, "That Most Irritating Question: images and reality", *Historical Journal of Film, Radio and Television*, 16, 2 (June 1996), pp.263-266.

Stam, Robert; Robert Burgoyne; and Sandy Flitterman-Lewis (1992), *New Vocabularies in Film Semiotics*, Londres, Routledge.

Taiuti, Lorenzo (1996), *Arte e media. Avanguardie e comunicazione di massa*, Milano, Costa & Nolan.

Tranche, Rafael R (1989), "Las nuevas tecnologías y el relato electrónico", en E. Jiménez Losantos and V. Sánchez Biosca, *El relato electrónico*, Valencia, Filmoteca de la Generalitat Valenciana, 1989, pp.235-242.

Wyver, John (1989), *The moving image. An international history of film, television and video*, London(New York, Basil Blackwell.

Zagarrio, Vito (1996), "Incroci mediologici nella New Hollywood", in L. Quaresima, ed., *Il cinema e le sue arti*, Venice, Biennale di Venezia/Marsilio, pp. 403-410.

Zunzunegui, Santos (1996), *La mirada cercana. Microanálisis fílmico*, Barcelona, Paidós.

Notes

1   For the recurrent character of diffused worries related to different visual media see, for instance, Ortoleva (1999), where "the fact that many fears associated with cinema in a certain historical period appeared again, the following generation, associated with television in almost identical terms" is remarked and explained (p. 1001).

2   Examples of this media panic in cinema will be referred to below. As for its literary counterpart, the list and history would be too long to be told here. What can be said is that television is a recurrent presence in quite a few contemporary novels. See, for instance, Jean-Philippe Toussaint's *La télévision* (Paris, 1997), an example of a delicate description of a television age where the small screen, although not threatening, is nevertheless quite perverse in its promotion of passivity.

3   "Art processes which worked in the direction of creating models, patterns and links with mass instruments and languages share an extraordinary fragility, and a technical difficulty in the tasks of documentation, archive building and consulting. While in the past this precariousness was part of an overtly stated status of artistic processes which consumed their essence through self-destruction (happenings), a necessity to redefine and preserve is rightly aiming at rescuing them to show their operational wedge and historical usefulness in our new sociocultural contexts". Taiuti (1996), p. 202.

4   See Benet (1999), pp.51-55. Benet refers explicitly to Altman (1996).

5   Ortoleva (1999) represents here a crucial point of reference, in its effort to draw up "a solid history of the institutional *and* cultural-expressive *and* professional relationships between the two medias" (p. 994).

6   See Sorlin (1999).

7   As it is described in the last volume of the "Historia general del cine" recently published in Spain: see Palacio and Zunzunegui (1995). For a sketchy reference to the idea of the "hybridization" between cinema and television in the "audiovisual age", see Company-Marzal (1999), p.16.

8   This methodology has been effectively described by Spanish film historian, Jenaro Talens, as follows: "Films are not looked at as 'monuments', but as 'documents'; documents which do not represent a truth certificate but where a place is being shown where ways of seeing, thinking and living the world which surrounds us are inscribed". Jenaro Talens, "Presentación" in Zunzunegui (1996), p. 11.

9   See Stam, Burgoyne, Flitterman-Lewis (1992), chap. 5.

10 As Brunetta explains, in this film "characters ... do not communicate, but all around them the media presence is growing in an abnormal and obsessive way, media that steal, guide and organize people's time". Brunetta (1991), p. 514.

11 Indeed, Ferreri's description would fit perfectly Ortoleva's interpretation of the peculiarity of television: "while films occupy the whole field of vision and (possibly) of sound, television ... only dwells upon a part of it, so it can be used as a mere 'image-and-soundtrack' of life. Television presents itself as a *domestic* medium, even if this does not at all imply that it would reproduce and respect passively the traditional order of family life" (Ortoleva, 1999, p. 996).

12 It is Sequence 7 (15 to 17 ms.).

13 It is Sequence 14 (35 to 41 ms.).

14 "The last image ... shows a symbolic suicide ... A human being got lost. Nothing might help him ... We have witnessed a grotesque suicide" (Di Giammatteo, 1994, p. 344). Companys and Marzal propose a similar reading of *Short Cuts* (Altman, 1993). See Companys and Marzal (1999), p. 94.

15 Sorlin (1999).

16 For a problematic definition of cinema-television intertextuality, see Grasso (1996), p. 146.

17 Lagny (1992), p. 227.

18 Ortoleva (1991), pp. 99-108.

19 For a recent assessment, see Andrews (1998).

20 Sorlin (1996), p. 265.

21 See Wiliam McDonald, "Memo to Hollywood, Re TV: It's Not That Bad", *New York Times*, March 28, 1999, p. 32.

22 See Camporesi (1999). An English version of the article was published in Fullerton and Söderbergh Widding, eds. (2000), pp.149-158.

23 Whose "facts" were reconstructed from a multi-media perspective in Wyver (1989), chs. 4 and 13.

24 Sjöholm, 1998. This would contradict the "violently anti-television attitude of the 'new cinemas'" in Europe, as described in Ortoleva (1999), p. 1007.

25 Hill (1998b), p. xix. Also preceding quotation.

26 Hill and McLoone, eds. (1996), p. 1. See also Hill (1998a).

27 For an interesting contribution on the subject, see Peter Kramer "The Lure of the Big Picture: Film, Television and Hollywood", in Hill and McLoone, eds. (1996). pp. 9-46. For an example of the fruitfulness of the comparative approach see Gonzo (1996).

28 See John Hill's penetrating essay on the British case, "British Television and Film: The Making of a Relationship", in Hill and McLoone, eds. (1996), pp. 151-176.

29 These three aproaches are strictly intertwined and can profitably be evoked in film analysis, as in Zagarrio (1996).

30 Grasso (1996), p. 146.

Television and the future historian

Philip M. Taylor

The 'goggle box' which usually sits in the corner of an average household's living room is about to change considerably. The TV set is about to get wider, flatter and interactive. Having already migrated into bedrooms and kitchens, it may even possibly change its location from the floor to the wall. The digital revolution signals the end of an era for analogue technology, including television as we have known it (both in terms of its production and its delivery) and it is difficult to ignore the prospect of an equally significant change for the role of the medium in everyday life.

All the signs are already present – from rising internet access in developed nations, growing numbers of pay-per-view channels, new TV sets attached to telephone lines, and a new generation of mobile phones that can access the internet. Size of screen is no longer a matter. Some years ago, when there was much talk of convergence between the TV screen and the computer screen, sceptics argued that people read words from a distance of around eighteen inches but that they would always view images from a distance of eight foot or so. Besides, they said, teletext services already existed on most broadcasting systems and people didn't sit down for an evening to scroll through pages of text. The old cathode ray tube needed to deliver three-dimensional audio-visual broadcasting as distinct from the front projection of cinema-type images began to converge with the invention of the Liquid Crystal Display (LCD). The arrival since then of DVD, ever improved video streaming, the M-PEG compression formats and other ways of accessing images and sounds as 'zeros and ones' has meant that even the concept of 'broadcasting' now has to be rethought. Casio now produce affordable wristwatch devices capable of not only playing MP3 recordings via earphones but also with built in digital photographic cameras. We are not that far away from moving picture equivalents, at the dawn of the broadband revolution. On Virgin Atlantic, for example we do indeed watch movies, selected from a choice of six or more, on 10 X 6 inch screens located eighteen inches before our eyes on the rear of the seat in front of us.

From the point of view of major corporate investment in the new technologies of delivery, a major breakthrough occurred in 1997 when, for the first time, home computers in the United States outsold television sets. The process of production was already undergoing significant change. Whereas once – and not so long ago, after all – we could expect a major terrestrial broadcaster to provide a broad prime time package of programmes in an evening, starting with the news, followed perhaps by a game show, a soap opera instalment, a documentary, a drama or film followed by news and weather and perhaps a current affairs programme, now there are separate channels for all of these genres. The arrival more recently of channels like *Sky Sports (Interactive)* means that viewers no longer have to wait until the broadcasters decide when to show an action replay of a goal; the viewers can do it themselves. This shift from broadcasting to narrow-casting, from passive viewing to interactivity, has meant that programmers have struggled to attract new audiences, which is why we are seeing innovative and controversial programming on the mainstream channels like *Who Wants to be a Millionaire*, *Big Brother* or even *Survivor*.

Creative programme-makers will always insist that, regardless of the technology, there is no substitute for 'quality' output based upon good ideas. In other words that 'content is king.' Perhaps so, but given the sheer number of channels now broadcasting on a twenty-four hour schedule, there is also a need for quantity *and* variety of service. The tensions which result from this clash of financial and creative imperatives in the contemporary broadcasting landscape are plain for all to see. Cultural commentators queue up to argue that 'more means worse'. Such value judgments are often based upon individual opinions and prejudices rather than a genuine understanding of what the audience actually wants. Television has to compete with a range of other entertainment options now available to traditional audiences, such as video games and video film rentals. It needs to be more than a simple provider of programmes. What analysts are left with is simply 'more' – and that presents them with considerable quantitative problems. How, for example, could the future historian cope with the sheer quantity of broadcast output that would need to be seen before making any sensible judgments about the role and significance of television at any given moment in time?

In the ratings war to keep audiences from straying into alternative sources of entertainment and information, it would seem that programme-making broadcasters have already conceded defeat in the areas of news and current affairs via traditional television. This is not just reflected in the row in the UK over when to schedule the late evening news. The BBC has invested massively in its website *BBC Online* – now the most visited in Europe – and even *CNN.com* appears to be an admission that such people – now a global audience across all the different time zones – who want to access the latest news are happier to do so when it suits them rather than the broadcasters. Meanwhile, in traditional television terms, the broadcasters, especially in public service television, are accused of 'dumbing down' the news. The major American networks cover less and less foreign policy news – always an expensive option – and instead leave it to others, like CNN, Visnews or Associated Press – to supply them with pictures when there is a foreign story deemed to be worthy of mention by them. We can also see the rise in what

Nick Gowing has termed 'the tyranny of real time'. This phrase summarises the process by which news editors increasingly rely upon live broadcasting to make the news more exciting. Accordingly, a reporter on the spot will have to 'go live' at a predetermined moment in time to report on events, even though nothing may be actually happening at the precise moment when the highly expensive satellite air time has been pre-booked. Consequently, we see reporters summarising what has already happened earlier in the day or speculating as to what may happen later, thereby changing the nature of what we have traditionally understood to be 'news'. The arrival of ENG (Electronic News Gathering) in the 1980s may have encouraged the arrival of 24-hour news channels like CNN, Sky News and BBC World but the technology has also altered the nature of traditional regular evening news bulletins as well. The fusion of news and views which results makes television news more like an audio-visual version of newspapers, encapsulated by the phrases 'infotainment' and 'tabloid television'.

In a highly competitive, commercialised and deregulated broadcasting environment, only those programmes which can attract high audiences, and hence high advertising revenue, are deemed worthy of value, finally laying to rest the paternalistic values of Lord Reith and his belief that broadcasting was too serious a business to be left to the panderings of the audience. The pace of technological innovation can, however, seem as bewildering as it is daunting to many viewers, especially when in a multi-channel universe it can often take longer to find and select a programme than to actually view one. The 'digital revolution' allows the audience not just a greater choice of programming, old and new, but it also allows greater choice of timing of when to watch.

How much of this is, in fact, new or different does need to be placed in some kind of perspective. From the 1930s, when there were 15 cinemas to choose from even in a medium sized town in England, to the breaking of the BBC's 'brute force of monopoly' and the arrival of alternative radio and television channels, from the arrival of the domestic video tape recorder which allowed viewers to 'time shift' programming to suit their own timetables to even the remote control 'zapper' which enabled viewers to quickly and easily change programmes that were not sustaining their interest, the history of broadcasting has always been about improving choice. Broadcasters have not always been happy about innovation – from the switch from film to videotape or, more recently, from conventional to wide-screen cameras – but the conservatism of the actual programme makers tends to be rooted in qualitative rather than in the kind of quantitative issues that their producers and managers have been forced to address. How much time it will take for the current changes to become acceptable as normal, both on the part of broadcasters and indeed of audiences, may itself now have become and outmoded concept. The digital revolution, indeed, offers the prospect of perpetual change as we see the shift from a bi-media environment to a tri-media or multi-media environment where change itself is, paradoxically, a constant.

Under such circumstances, it will surely not be long before historians begin to talk of a 'golden age of television' – by which they will mean the analogue era in which choice of programming was simple because it was limited and in which programmers could be reasonably sure that their output was being watched by a sizeable chunk of the population at the same time, providing a point of common reference and subsequent social interaction. Perhaps, like the O.J. Simpson trial in the USA or the funeral of Princess Diana in the UK, there will always be individual events that feed a sense of national and even international cohesion (the assassinations of the Kennedy's, the Moon Landing, Olympic Games, even the Gulf War) but the idea that television, as a medium which enjoys near universal social penetration, can unite a nation is in decline. The likelihood of an affirmative answer to the question 'did you see on TV last night?' has diminished in less than a generation.

We tend to rely upon sociologists, especially of the empirical variety, to gather data about these trends. Audience research, however, especially of the large scale variety, is expensive for academics and there has been a tendency to deride the commercially motivated raw data gathered by the large Market Research organisations, such as NOP or BARB. As a result, much media studies audience research is either small scale (sample) or theoretical. If that has been the case for the age of analogue television, we can only expect even more difficulties in our new multimedia universe. This is a universe where it will be increasingly impossible to talk about 'mass' communications except in highly generalised terms and where the study of 'niche' channels for 'niche' audiences may be our only hope in evaluating the impact and influence of any given programming at any given moment in time. It is a depressing prospect for the empirical sociologist and future historian alike. It will return us to the early days of film research when scholars were able to talk about individual films and the production processes involved in their making rather than their impact upon audiences, about which little was known in the age prior to public opinion or market research.

Whatever can be said for the future of television, its past has not been served well by historians. Despite being the prevalent medium for information and entertainment in most advanced countries since the 1960s, there remain remarkably few serious works of history that embrace television as a primary source of information for those years. In diplomatic history, this is perhaps less surprising since, until the arrival of DBS (Direct Broadcasting by Satellite) in the 1980s, television was largely a domestic medium. In Europe, of course, signals would frequently spill over into neighbouring countries – from West Berlin, for example, into East Germany – but television producers largely thought of domestic programmes for domestic audiences. For social historians, however, the oversight is more serious.

Part of the problem is access to such a rich source. Television companies, especially in the commercial sector but also, to a large extent, public service companies like the BBC as well, never saw themselves as archivers of the material they created – unless the material could be rebroadcast or sold to other companies. This in itself provides a clue as to one of the major obstacles we face as historians. Even the creators of programmes saw their work as having a limited life cycle. TV was about now, not then. As such, however, television programming can tell us a great deal about the prevailing social mores of a given period in time, much in the same way that films can.

Historians themselves were sceptical at first as to the likely value of television. From the late 1950s onwards, when television was maturing as a medium, especially in areas like news and current affairs and in television drama, many historians – like many academics generally – did not even possess a TV set, regarding it as unworthy of their attention. When it came therefore to television's interest in history, many senior historians wanted nothing to do with it. A.J.P. Taylor's now legendary television lectures in the early 1960s merely served to confirm Taylor as a rogue and, because of their traditional academic lecture format, television's inability to approach history creatively. It took the BBC's series *The Great War* to bring out the tensions between traditional history and television's creative needs, with rows between the historians and programme makers about the integrity of film footage usage. Copyright problems have prevented the series from being repeated to this day – despite good evidence that a whole generation of Great War scholars was first encouraged to become professional historians by watching the series as young people.

The Great War was the first milestone of television history, *Victory at Sea* notwithstanding. It was an important learning ground and helped to pave the way for its Second World War counterpart produced by a commercial company, Thames, a decade later. *The World at War* has been repeated many times and is near universally recognised as a model for how television can treat history seriously and with integrity. In turn, it inspired Ted Turner of CNN to produce *The Cold War*, using many of the same programme makers. The existence of The History Channel on satellite and cable services would suggest a coming of age for the past is so far as the medium is concerned. For many professional historians, however, the medium remains far from mature. They complain about the medium's predisposition to 'take liberties' with spatial compression, its preoccupation with events and personalities rather than issues (a sort of 'human interest history') and – especially for the massive period of history without film 'evidence' – its recreation of the past through the values of the present.

Historians can admittedly still be very precious about their discipline. They regard themselves as custodians of a past which does, in fact, belong to everyone. When outsiders like television programme makers commandeer some of their self proclaimed custodial functions, they are never going to be happy with the end results. This is especially so when television history is consumed by more people in a half hour than the number who will ever read a history book on the same subject in a historian's lifetime. But, of course, this is what makes television history so important. Its capacity to shape the contemporary popular perception of the past – including the creation and perpetuation of myths, stereotypes and simplifications – is what places enormous responsibilities on the programme makers. Historians who see television as being irresponsible – and perhaps Bruce Cummings is the most outspoken of these[1] – perhaps misunderstand the programme making process which prevents the medium from ever being able to quite replicate historical research in a manner that would satisfy them completely. The best history programmes involve good research and extensive consultancy. But the deeper the research, the more programme makers realise that there is no 'universal view' amongst professional historians. With that realisation, television history becomes the art of the possible within a climate of majority interpretation and consensus. More recently, historians like Simon Schama have been given freer reign to present the history of Britain through their own individual 'label'. Thus, it is not so much television's history of Britain but 'Simon Schama's'.

This development has the potential to reduce television history to a form of journalism. It may be well-informed journalism but it is a reminder that journalists and historians are more like cousins than is often appreciated. Both are ultimately in search of the same thing: 'the truth'. Of course, traditionally, the work of historians is dependent upon surviving archives but rarely will they have a comprehensive archive that answers all questions. They have also enjoyed the luxury of greater time on which to form judgements and opinions which are judged by their peers. Journalists in particular no longer enjoy the same degree of time on which to base their judgments about what is happening here and now. In a technologically driven profession being increasingly driven by ever shorter deadlines, journalism is being forced increasingly to make snap judgments without the luxuries of verification and cross verification they once enjoyed. As the writers of 'the first drafts of history', journalists are finding that their drafts are becoming increasingly rough. Accordingly, their familial ties with the historians may be becoming more remote.

It is not just the quality of the media as historical evidence which future historians will need to be wary of. The sheer quantity of material will also be highly intimidating. Historians of more recent times have always had to come to terms with the fact that there is much more evidence available than for earlier periods. But with the explosion of information in recent years, the problem is compounded. A further problem is the transient nature of much of our contemporary information, such as emails or webpages which have a relatively short life and are often discarded when read. Unless they are printed out and stored in some archive, they will be lost to the future. There is, however, a danger that the same situation will pertain to television output since there is no television station anywhere in the world where the entirety of its broadcast output has survived. Some historians, backed up by many archivists, will argue that not everything needs to survive to serve the needs of future history. After all, the Public Record Office contains only the tip of an iceberg since the vast majority of government records are actually discarded and destroyed each year as they are released for public scrutiny under the Thirty Year Rule. The problem with this approach is that we cannot be convinced that the selection process serves the future better than the present.

For all the methodological problems, difficulties of access and cost for researching surviving broadcast output, it is surely no longer feasible for any historian of the new millennium to either ignore or simply dismiss as a trivial sideshow the role of television in society, first on a largely national basis and, latterly, internationally. Like newspapers, cinema and radio before it, television as the dominant medium for news and information provides a unique and rich source of information about the way we were, or at least how broadcasters reflected their belief of what we wanted. Much television is of the moment, relevant only to the time in which it was originally transmitted. But some of it can legitimately fall into the category of art that wasn't appreciated as such at the time but can still command audiences today. Perhaps the most obvious genre that falls into this category is British situation comedy, since many programmes from the 1960s and 1970s – *Till Death Do Us Part*, *Dad's Army*, *Monty Python's Flying Circus*, *The Good Life*, *Porridge*, *Fawlty Towers*, *Blackadder* – can still attract appreciative audiences when they are repeated many years later. More recently, American situation comedy – *M★A★S★H★*, *The Golden Girls*, *Friends* – have attracted sizeable television audiences all over the world. This cultural element to the process of globalisation is an important topic for the future, if it is not already.

Once again, how will the future historian cope? Even now, I am struck by the piecemeal nature of historical research into television. Most concentrates upon sampled material – of genres or events – rather than treating the output as a whole. Some work concentrates on the production process without actually viewing or listening to the media under discussion. Others approach the topic the other way round, deconstructing the imagery without reference to the production process. The best work avoids both of these pitfalls. Until there is more of the best, other scholars are unlikely to take seriously media research into television. But first they need to take television itself more seriously.

Note

1   In his *War on Television* (1990), Cummings raged against the makers of the series on the Korean War for which he was historical adviser for their distortion of the past for the needs of their programmes.

Index